EARTH and WORD

D1637351

EARTH
and WORD

Classic
Sermons
on
Saving
the
Planet

Edited by David Rhoads

continuum

NEW YORK • LONDON

2007

The Continuum International Publishing Group Inc
80 Maiden Lane, New York, NY 10038

The Continuum International Publishing Group Ltd
The Tower Building, 11 York Road, London SE1 7NX

www.continuumbooks.com

Printed in the United States of America

Library of Congress Cataloging-in-Publication Data
Earth and Word : classic sermons on saving the planet / [edited by] David Rhoads.
     p. cm.
   Includes bibliographical references and index.
   ISBN-13: 978-0-8264-2827-1 (hardcover : alk. paper)
   ISBN-10: 0-8264-2827-4 (hardcover : alk. paper)
   ISBN-13: 978-0-8264-2828-8 (pbk. : alk. paper)
   ISBN-10: 0-8264-2828-2 (pbk. : alk. paper)
   1. Human ecology—Religious aspects—Christianity—Sermons. 2. Sermons, American—21st cen-
tury. I. Rhoads, David M. II. Title.

BT695.5.E25 2007
261.8'8—dc22

                                        2007006461

Acknowledgments will be found on page xii, which constitutes an extension of the copyright page.

green
press
INITIATIVE

Continuum Publishing is committed to preserving ancient forests and natural resources. We
have elected to print this title on 50% postconsumer waste recycled paper. As a result, this book
has saved:
1 ton of wood
524 lbs of solid waste
4,082 gallons of water
8 million BTUs of total energy
983 pounds of greenhouse gases
Continuum is a member of Green Press Initiative, a nonprofit program dedicated to supporting
publishers in their efforts to reduce their use of fiber obtained from endangered forests. For
more information, go to www.greenpressinitiative.org.

For Joseph Sittler,
PIONEER AND MENTOR

CONTENTS

Contents

Contents

ACKNOWLEDGMENTS

"To Live as People of Dust and Spirit" from SISTERS OF DUST, SISTERS OF SPIRIT by Karen Baker-Fletcher, copyright © 1998 by Karen Baker-Fletcher. Used by permission of Augsburg Fortress Publishers.

WE ARE . . . By Ysaye M. Barwell, © 1993, Barnwell's Notes Publishing. All rights Reserved. Used by Permission.

"Moments of Grace" from THE GREAT WORD by Thomas Berry, copyright © 1999 by Thomas Berry. Used by permission of Bell Tower, a division of Random House, Inc.

"Christianity and the Survival of Creation" from SEX, ECONOMY, FREEDOM, AND COMMUNITY by Wendell Berry, copyright © 1992, 1993 by Wendell Berry. Used by permission of Pantheon Books, a division of Random House, Inc.

"A Passion for the Possible: A Message to US Churches" from *A Passion for the Possible.* © 1993 William Sloane Coffin. Used by permission of Westminster John Knox Press.

"Whose Earth Is It Anyway?" From *Risks of Faith* by James H. Cone. Copyright © 1999 by James H. Cone. Reprinted by permission of Beacon Press, Boston.

"The Care of the Earth" from *The Care of the Earth and Other University Sermons* by Joseph Sittler, originally printed in *The Care of the Earth and Other University Sermons*, Fortress Press, 1964. Used by permission of Franklin H. Littell.

Excerpt from "Advice to a Prophet" from ADVICE TO A PROPHET AND OTHER POEMS by Richard Wilber, copyright © 2004 by Richard Wilbur. Published by Harvest Books, a division of Harcourt, Inc.

"Creation as Kin: An American Indian View" by George E. Tinker from *After Nature's Revolt* by Dieter T. Hessel, copyright © 1991 by Dieter T. Hessel. Used by permission of Augsburg Fortress Publishers.

INTRODUCTION

DAVID RHOADS

EVERY DAY WE HEAR NEWS about the deterioration of the natural world: global warming, extreme weather patterns, droughts, holes in the ozone layer, the destruction of forests, fires out of control, the erosion of arable land, problems of waste, loss of species, threats to clean air and clean water, the population explosion, and on and on. Occasionally we hear good news about some new effort being made to address one or more of these issues. But generally the news is overwhelming and deeply discouraging.

How are we to cope with these phenomena? How do we find the resources to keep going? Denial is not an option; the problem will not go away. Minimizing the problem will not do either, for unless we look squarely at the size of the problem, we will not find solutions adequate to address it. Rather, we must act, because we *can* make a difference. We can take actions in our homes, in our places of work, and in our communities, such as our congregations. We can also advocate for legislation and policy changes that provide far-reaching solutions to environmental degradation. We should be embracing these actions and advocacies wholeheartedly. We should be pursuing changes in our lifestyles and changes in our society that alter the behavior and the structures of our world.

It is a long, arduous journey that humanity is embarking on to address these issues. The degradation of nature is not a problem with a short-term solution. We need to be prepared to be in this endeavor for the long haul. If we are to attain a level of human activity that is ecologically sustainable, we will need spiritual strength and sustenance. We need to engage in a process that will transform us and our society in an enduring way. We need to hear words that lift us and challenge us. We need to clarify our values in ways that give us a solid center of commitment to the whole natural world. We need to understand the ways in which our ordinary daily activities can have a positive impact on the intricately woven web of creation. We need to have compassion for the vulnerable people who are most profoundly affected by our destructive treatment of creation. And we need to respect the whole earth, with all its flora and fauna. In short, we need to give our daily attention to the care of the earth as a spiritual discipline.

At its most profound level, the ecological crisis is a spiritual crisis. It comes as a result of our alienation from nature, our estrangement from the very ground from which human life, indeed all of life, has emerged. Our civilization has built so many barriers against an attachment to the rest of nature: to the soil, to the incredible diversity of plants and animals, to the rocks, to the seas, and to the geological formations that comprise our landscapes. Most of us no longer have a sense of belonging to the earth, an experience of solidarity with plants and animals, such that we deeply desire for all forms of life to thrive along with us.

Instead, we have reduced nature to things. We treat nature as a commodity. We are interested in nature primarily in terms of the ways we can use it to make *our* life better. And we seem to believe that we can exploit the earth without much regard to the ways it affects the natural world. We do not see the sacredness of life, the presence of the glory of God in all reality. We have lost the experience of the livingness of all things and the sanctity of all life. We need to recover a sense of reverence for life that will lead us to treat all creatures with love and respect and thereby to walk lightly on the earth.

In addition, we have lost our sense of appropriate human limitations in the presence of nature and in relation to the divine. We seem to believe that we are unlimited in potential. We believe our world should know no boundaries. We believe there is no end to earth's bounty. Our economy is based on the hypothesis of unlimited resources and unlimited growth. We take for granted that we can discard unlimited amounts of trash in a use-and-throw-away society. We assume that we can put unlimited amounts of pollutants in the air and water. We are guilty as a whole society of unbelievable hubris and arrogance, because we have no sense of boundaries. We think that if we are *able* to do something, that power in itself gives us the *right* to do it. And we do all of this with no real sense of the consequences of our lifestyle on the poor, on people with less power, and on the rest of nature. We need to recover a sense of humility that will put limits on our activity—limits that will respect the rest of life and give space for all to thrive.

One of the signs of our hubris is that we want technological solutions to fix the earth's problems without any sacrifice on our part. We want to believe we can come up with scientific solutions to the environmental crises that will require no negative effect on our economy or our lifestyle. With American ingenuity, we think, surely we will come up with an answer that will enable us to maintain or even expand our standard of living. Surely we will not personally have to cut back on energy use, or pay more for green products, or drive smaller cars, or travel less. We really do not want to adapt to a simpler lifestyle that will lead us to have less and force us to slow down and to take each step on the earth lightly. We want an easy fix.

Yet even when we try to adopt a simpler, more limited lifestyle, we are confronted with the unbelievably fast pace of our modern world and its corollary—efficiency. We have come to expect that there will be ways to make everything we do more efficient—that is, easier and quicker—than ever before. We fail to see that the resulting products and processes of efficiency so far are among the most devastating to the earth. How can we slow down? How can we stop living at such a breakneck pace? How can we find a center out of which we will attend, slowly and carefully, to the world around us and the people around us with fresh regard and thoughtfulness? It is not easy.

It is not easy partly because all of the messages we get from our capitalist society tell us that our hunger for meaning and satisfaction will be filled by the *acquisition* of things. If only we could have this car or those clothes, this cell phone or that gadget, this convenience or that luxury, then we would be all right. We need to rethink our values and priorities and begin to live an alternative lifestyle, one that finds meaning and satisfaction from the very source of life itself in a relationship that can restore us to solidarity with nature and bring us new life.

A spirituality rooted in creation would be a way forward; it would mean a relationship with God that honors God's creation and that would orient us to fresh values, to an alternative lifestyle, and to a centering of ourselves for kindness and thoughtfulness toward all of life. Our delight in nature will be the right basis for our use of nature. We will be less likely to exploit that in which we delight. Or to put it another way: We will not save what we do not love. A spirituality that encompasses our relationship with nature will help us to make the needed changes.

For two decades now, I have struggled with this effort to reorient myself to care for the earth with integrity. When I first became interested in the environment, the church was not taking much of a role at all. In preparation for a lecture at my seminary in 1989, I read about twenty books on the ecological state of the world. What a disheartening picture of the future these books gave! And they were written by scientists and social scientists who knew what they were talking about. I became deeply depressed. I had to decide what would sustain me in this commitment to care for creation. Would it be fear of what lay before us? Would it be guilt for my own part in this ongoing degradation of creation? Would I be motivated by shame over the direction our society is taking? Or would I act out of grief over the loss of life on earth? Would I be driven by anger, indeed outrage, at the wanton greed of corporations and the willful neglect by our government toward these problems? What would be an adequate source of energy for this work? In some sense, all of these emotions might contribute to action. But in the end, none of these emotions seemed sustaining and nourishing. How could this work be life giving and not life depleting?

In my struggle, I have been helped by a relationship with God. I could not have found the resources in myself. Rather, I have sought to be sustained by the vast reservoir of God's graces and what Gerard Manley Hopkins depicts as "the dearest freshness deep down things." Only by seeking to be fed by God's grace—the same love of God that is *in* all things and the same delight that God has *for* all things—will we be able to face, with some measure of equanimity, the threat of being overwhelmed. Only in this way will we have joy and energy for the task.

And so I began a journey at my work and in my home and in myself to find a different way. The seminary where I teach became a "green zone," as a group of us tried to figure out what it would mean for our community and our space to be earth friendly in the worship life of the seminary, the educational program, the care for the property, the personal commitments of the members of our seminary community, and our responsibility to bring this concern before the wider public. I have learned so much from so many. Nevertheless, even now, I feel that I am only beginning the journey of transformation necessary to express the care for the earth and the love for the earth that will be needed for the work ahead—which brings me to the purpose of this volume.

For the last ten years, I have directed a Web site, Web of Creation (http://www.webofcreation.org), which provides resources for faith communities around issues of ecology and faith. From this project has sprung the Green Congregation Program, which seeks to incorporate care for creation into all aspects of the life and mission of congregations. In my efforts to provide resources, I discovered one gaping hole in these programs—namely, inspiring meditations and sermons on the celebration of the earth and the care for creation. So with the help of a colleague at the Web of Creation, George Zachariah, I embarked several years ago on an effort to provide such a collection for people to read and ponder, a collection that might also serve as a source for preaching and teaching on care for the earth. There is a fine collection of sermons already available by evangelicals—*The Best Preaching on Earth: Sermons on Caring for Creation*, edited by Stan Lequire (Judson Press, 1996). This new collection is an effort to expand the range and diversity of voices. Encouragement from Henry Carrigan, former editor at Continuum Publishing Group, moved the project forward.

George and I began this project by collecting published sermons and sermonlike essays on the environment. We invited people who had published or preached on the environment to contribute a sermon or meditation—not so much an academic essay or a lecture, but an expression of their faith and their appeal to the faith of others. We were thrilled by the eagerness of people to share in this project. Some pieces had been printed previously, most were preached on some occasion by the contributor, and some were written for this collection. Each contribution has a brief statement at the beginning explaining its context. At the end of each is some biographical information about the contributor.

There is significant variety here. Many denominations, faith traditions, and ethnic communities are represented. Each contributor chose a biblical passage as a starting point, and the choices brought great diversity to the collection. Most are sermons focusing completely on issues of care for creation—calling us to account, challenging our attitudes, witnessing to the writer's own conversion to care for creation, proclaiming grace. In some offerings the issues of earth are not the focus, but they nevertheless contribute significantly to the themes developed. These latter sermons offer a variety of models for how to incorporate ecological concerns into any and every sermon. Also, the contributions represent a variety of occasions and contexts: a marriage ceremony, a commencement liturgy, a college chapel service, a ritual for the blessing of animals, Thanksgiving Day, and a children's sermon, among others.

I hope this collection of sermons and meditations serves several purposes. The offerings may be used as devotional literature for you to read as part of your daily meditation. Perhaps they will change your mind, or deepen your convictions, or impel you to action. In addition, these pieces can assist in theological reflection as you seek to relate your faith to the concrete realities of the world and your sense of justice toward your companion humans and all other forms of life. Everywhere I speak these days, people are eager to relate their concern for the environment with their faith. Perhaps this collection will provide nourishment for the journey.

These reflections may also assist pastors in the preparation of sermons, either by providing material to use in preaching or as a model for how to go about developing one's own approach to preaching on care of the earth. Preachers may be glad to know that there are two Internet sites that provide "green" reflections on the lessons for each Sunday in the three-year cycle of the common lectionary. The first, the Christian Ecology Link, is from a multi-denominational organization in the United Kingdom for people concerned about the environment. They provide "Ecological Notes on the Common Worship Lectionary" at http://www.christian-ecology. org.uk/econotes-index.htm#index. The second, the Environmental Stewardship Commission of the Episcopal Diocese of Minnesota (MEESC), has collected environmental and earth-centered reflections, sermons, and commentaries on the lectionary readings. These notes can be found at http://www.env-steward.com/lectnry.htm. Also, there is an extensive bibliography on reading the Bible from the perspective of the earth on the Earth Bible page, located on the Web of Creation Web site.

It will also be helpful to seek further transformation through worship. For congregations that wish to locate resources on liturgy, there are several very helpful sites. There is now an international effort to offer an alternative season in the church year—the Season of Creation, a four-week season to be celebrated in a month during

Pentecost season (September is recommended)—that celebrates God the creator, the wonders of the created world, and the human relationship with creation. The materials include alternative lessons for the three-year cycle, full liturgies, and suggestions for earth ministry (http://www.seasonofcreation.com). In the worship section at the Web of Creation site are prayers of petition related to creation that follow the three-year lectionary. Also, each year the National Council of Churches offers extensive resources for the celebration of Earth Sunday, the Sunday nearest to Earth Day on April 22 (http://www.nccecojustice.org). The Earth Ministry Web site (http://www.earthministry.org) has many resources for worship.

For those who want to bring care for creation into the life and mission of their congregation, there are several options. Earth Ministry has a wonderful guidebook and many resources to "green" your congregation. A comprehensive set of materials is available from the Green Sanctuary Program of the Unitarian Universalist Fellowship, designed to enable congregations to be certified as Green Sanctuary fellowships (http://www.uuministryforearth.org). Our Web of Creation site offers a Green Congregation Program that provides resources for almost every aspect of congregational life, with a training manual and an extensive guide for the buildings and grounds. Also on the Web of Creation you will find a comprehensive list of annotated links to other informative faith-based sites.

We are entering an age in which environmental events and concerns will be dominant issues of the day. As Father Thomas Berry says, developing a sustainable life on earth in the face of ecological challenges is the "great work" of our time. It is a great work that everyone can be part of at some level. It is work that will involve transformation of people and structures. It is work that will require vision and sacrifice. It is also work to be done with joy and grace. It is my hope that the reflections by the contributors to this volume may in some way empower you to participate actively in this great work of our time.

THE RIGHT TO LOVE THE LAND

NEDDY ASTUDILLO

THIS SERMON WAS PREACHED in the rural town of Marengo, Illinois, to an Anglo Presbyterian congregation that had just recently begun the process of opening its doors to the Latino people in its community. The goal of the sermon was to lead the people to see their commonalities and to demonstrate for them the divine purpose in the experience of being a migrant and in the experience of working with migrants.

> These are the words of the letter that the prophet Jeremiah sent from Jerusalem to the remaining elders among the exiles, and to the priests, the prophets, and all the people, whom Nebuchadnezzar had taken into exile from Jerusalem to Babylon. This was after King Jeconiah, and the queen mother, the court officials, the leaders of Judah and Jerusalem, the artisans, and the smiths had departed from Jerusalem. The letter was sent by the hand of Elasah son of Shaphan and Gemariah son of Hilkiah, whom King Zedekiah of Judah sent to Babylon to King Nebuchadnezzar of Babylon. It said:

Thus says the LORD of hosts, the God of Israel, to all the exiles whom I have sent into exile from Jerusalem to Babylon: Build houses and live in them; plant gardens and eat what they produce. Take wives and have sons and daughters; take wives for your sons, and give your daughters in marriage, that they may bear sons and daughters; multiply there, and do not decrease. But seek the welfare of the city where I have sent you into exile, and pray to the LORD on its behalf, for in its welfare you will find your welfare. (Jer 29:1–7)

◈

During my first years in seminary, I read a book called *Becoming Native to This Place.* Being a migrant myself and struggling to find my identity in a new land, it had not dawned on me until then that you could live in a place and still be disconnected from it. After reading that book, I realized that the struggle to live in intentional relationship with a new place that feeds you and gives you identity is as universal as it is local.

It was also in those first years in seminary that I heard the theologian Jay McDaniel say that justice (a very passionate issue for those of us who are minorities) meant "faithfulness to relationships." I went to seminary seeking to understand the concept of ecological justice. As I tried to translate this concept among Latinos in general and church people in particular, I realized that I needed to embrace the tension between our environmental responsibility and the social structures that move us away from that same environment.

As I tried to work for eco-justice in a new land (I am a native of Venezuela), I realized that I needed to open my heart to the ecology and the souls of this place. As I reflected upon my need to be in a relationship of justice with this new environment, I realized how my heart was still tied to the natural landscape of my homeland—to the point of not allowing me to be present in full to the new land and to my responsibility in it. In this journey to become native to a new place—all the while keeping my foreign branches—I have met many other migrants who, in spite of their settled life in the United

States, still mourn their disconnection from the land. They experience this distance as an inevitable and overpowering by-product of a life in exile, especially when legal issues shadow their sense of identity and belonging.

As the church seeks to minister to and from the experience of the migrant, and as the church seeks to create relationships of justice with its natural environment, the issues of belonging and the right to love the land need to be addressed as well. I recently heard the Latin American theologian Gustavo Gutierrez say that "to do theology is to find the good news—the gospel—in any human situation."

What is the good news that is found in the experience of exile and migration today? We have thousands of migrant farmers coming inside the US borders each year who never touch the soil again. We have a land that mourns mistreatment, species in danger due to increasing population, and a consumerist lifestyle that threatens the future of the planet. What then is the good news? What then is our calling?

To reflect upon our reality at hand, let us look into the life of Jeremiah and the Israelites in exile. The passage in Jeremiah sprouts from the life of a community needing to feel native to a place, and it points to a loving God who seeks to restore the life of the people in exile.

> Build houses and live in them; plant gardens and eat what they produce. Take wives and have sons and daughters. . . . But seek the welfare of the city where I have sent you into exile, and pray to the LORD on its behalf, for in its welfare you will find your welfare. (Jer 29:5–7)

Jeremiah is speaking to the Israelites now living in Babylon, who had been sent into exile by God and who had been taken away at the hands of the Babylonian king Nebuchadnezzar. This group of exiles, as described in the passage, was represented by the middle and upper classes of Israel. The poor of the land, the farmers, the lame, and the sick had stayed behind, very probably now working for the new landowners. Hence, the message to build houses and to plant gardens seems to have been given to a group of elite people, now in Babylon, who perhaps had never before had to build houses or plant gardens for themselves, who perhaps had had someone else do these things for them. Jeremiah sends a pastoral message to these new landless Israelites, these migrants in a foreign land.

I believe that in Jeremiah's instruction God was calling God's people back to the land—not the geographical land of their parents but the homeland of their hearts—and to the most basic vocation and relationship that identified them as keepers and tillers of the land. In Jeremiah's instructions, we hear echoes of the most basic and primary aspect of Israelite faith, namely, to "be fruitful and multiply" and "to till [the land] and keep it" (Gen 1:28; 2:15). These instructions had been given not only for Israelites but for all humanity and all creatures from the beginning of time. The experience of migration or exile, then, forces people to find again that which is universal in their faith. It challenges us to translate our identity beyond that which is finite and local (such as the attachment to the land). Ultimately, it challenges us to open our hearts to a new place and to its people.

Those who plant gardens or trees in their homes know the relationship that comes to birth with every seed that is put into the ground, with every effort given to water the plant, and with the patience to await the firstfruits. When we care and pray for the land, we begin to feel it as our own, we begin to love it and to suffer its pains, and we seek to create relationships of justice with its inhabitants.

In God's instructions through the prophet Jeremiah, God gives these migrant people the opportunity to go back to the garden of Eden. God invites them to live as if they are in the kingdom of God. God renews their calling to represent God's ways among the other nations, seeking the shalom of the land. If exile was the will of God for Israel, it is clear to me that "feeling" like an exile, or living like one, was not God's ultimate plan for Israel.

Can today's migrants be convinced of the same calling? Can Jeremiah's message be translated to our experience of migration and to our disconnection from the land? I certainly hope so.

As in the past, we need to find today's good news behind the experience of migration and the experience of our disconnection from the land. I cannot say why there are so many migrants in the world today (according to the United Nations, 32 million migrants live in the United States alone), but I can say that in our faith we have enough tools and instructions to know what to do about it and how to understand it in God's terms. In God's terms, it becomes a right and a responsibility to create loving relationships with the land that feeds and covers us.

For migrants, this calling has a redeeming and healing effect: "I can now begin to love again! I can now relate and live my spirituality in this place!"

For the land itself and all its living creatures, this calling holds the promise that new lovers will arrive and that new opportunities to be cared for may develop.

For the people of the land, this calling brings an opportunity to give back a part of what has been received, an opportunity to be generous, and a chance to stay related with the larger world. It can also be an opportunity to nurture old and new ways of living that are more sustainable and that are sensitive to other cultures and future generations.

If we look at Jesus' life from a migrant perspective, we realize that good things come with being a migrant. Christ himself chose to live as a migrant when he came from heaven to live among us. Christ chose to become a migrant when he lived as the Son of Man: "Foxes have holes, and birds of the air have nests; but the Son of Man has nowhere to lay his head" (Matt 8:20). And Jesus called his disciples to leave everything they had in order to follow him. Jesus called his disciples to put their hearts in the things of the kingdom—that which could be carried in a small bag and in their hearts.

In the Old Testament, God says to the Hebrews before they enter the promised land: "The land shall not be sold in perpetuity, for the land is mine; with me you are but aliens and tenants" (Lev 25:23). Like Israel before us, we too have the weakness of putting too much of our trust in our nationalities, our languages, our ownership of the land, or our memories of our native landscapes.

Behind these passages, there is a real calling to place our trust and identity in God. Finding ourselves as migrants in this way, finding ourselves as landless people with an ancient purpose, can become a very good thing. Being a spiritual sojourner, or a moral migrant in a world that is not Christ's world, can only enable us to understand what it means to follow Jesus.

When we seek the realm of God, we realize that we are not home yet. When the earth needs healing and our bodies ache, we realize that we are not home yet. When we lose our sense of security, we realize that we are not home yet. When we struggle to restore our *imago Dei* and our vocation, we realize that we are not home yet. When there is no peace in the world, we as children of God know that we are not home yet.

When we follow Jesus' steps in a world that has not reached God's ultimate shalom, we become migrants. When we embark on a journey with Abraham to an unknown land filled with people from different nations, we become migrants. When we find that on the road we can also find Jesus, we live the experience of the migrants. When we accept the risk of hosting the millions of Marys and Josephs that cross borders each day to protect their children, we become migrants ourselves.

When we follow Christ, we journey with his disciples. We journey with the pilgrims who came to this country to seek freedom to worship. We journey with the Native Americans who found their communal lands sealed off by private spirits. We journey with the buffalo, the bears, the wolves, the eagles, and other endangered species that have seen their numbers fall with the arrival of humankind.

In the commitment to our neighbors and to the land, we not only become native to a place, but we also embark on a divine journey that ends only in the kingdom of God. When we love and pray for the shalom of the land that feeds us, we allow for God's grace to be poured out throughout the world—healing and bringing abundant life, redeeming our sorrows, and filling our lives with ancient purpose.

The right to love the land and all its creatures, the right to give thanks and partake of the fruits of the harvest, was given by God to all the people and creatures of the earth. May God bless, then, our "rooted migration."

Neddy Astudillo graduated from McCormick Theological Seminary with a master of divinity degree focused on eco-justice ministry. She is an ordained minister of the Presbyterian Church (USA) and has been living and working in Northern Illinois for the past fifteen years, linking environmental issues to the role of the church in the world.

TO LIVE AS PEOPLE
OF DUST AND SPIRIT

KAREN BAKER-FLETCHER

THIS REFLECTION CULTIVATES the earthy expression of black womanism. It seeks to recover the strong historic ties of black people to the land and thereby to evoke an experience of God in nature. In so doing, it leads readers to grow closer to the earth and to God.

> Then the LORD God formed man from the dust of the ground, and breathed into his nostrils the breath of life; and the man became a living being. **(Gen 2:7)**

⬧

> Let [all things in creation] praise the name of the LORD. **(Ps 148:13)**

⬧

> Truly I tell you, just as you did it to one of the least of these . . . , you did it to me. **(Matt 25:40)**

⬧

For each child that's born,
a morning star rises
and sings to the universe
who we are. . . .
We are our grandmothers' prayers
We are our grandfathers' dreamings
We are the breath of the ancestors
We are the spirit of God.
("We Are," lyrics by Ysaye M. Barnwell)

My maternal grandmother loved poetry and literature. She could recite poems, and she herself wrote poetry and short stories. She had a beautiful soprano voice and sang songs about beauty, nature, and children. She was the poet laureate of her church and of the local YWCA. Her mother also liked to write stories, and she preserved family history orally as well as on paper. Love for literature and music and the practice of writing are some of my maternal grandmother's dreams and prayers that continue to live on in me. My paternal grandmother loved color, fabric, sewing, cooking, wallpapering, and gardening. While my parents and I never kept a garden at our house, I carry on my paternal grandmother's tradition as an adult at my own home, where I plant strawberries, tomatoes, and herbs. From her I learned to sew, an activity I rarely have time for anymore but which I continue to appreciate by being particular about fabrics, texture, and color. Some of her dreams and prayers continue in me. We continue our ancestors' dreams and prayers, often unaware that we are doing so.

Growing up, I was very fond of both my grandmothers and liked to spend time with them learning all that they knew about the mysteries of life, whether they were sewing, planting, praying, or writing. The song "We Are" by Ysaye M. Barnwell encourages us to remember who we are in the vastness of the universe and in the spirit of God. It encourages us to remember our history and that we are the dreams and prayers of our grandmothers. In other words, each child, each human being, has the potential to fulfill some of the best dreams of our ancestors.

The lines from "We Are" quoted above are of blessing. They point not to our familiar failures, whether ancestral or contemporary, but to the prayers and promises of who we can become and what we can fulfill. The song continues to name several different ways in which we may express who we are in God:

> We are Mothers of courage, Fathers of time
> Daughters of dust, the Sons of great visions,
> Sisters of mercy, Brothers of love,
> Lovers of life, Builders of nations.

While we may choose to do far less, we are called to bring new life to the universe, to participate in God's spirit of renewal and revival as people of dust, courage, mercy, love, life, and wisdom. The song reminds us of who we are in our depths. We are the spirit of God, breath of the ancestors, daughters (and sons) of dust. We need to be reminded and blessed by these words again and again, because we all too easily forget who we are. We are people of dust and spirit. The problem is that we too easily disconnect ourselves from the land and the Spirit. We too easily disconnect our children from the land and the Spirit when we forget our integrated relationship with both. Such disremembering leads to callous relationships with the earth and one another.

When we separate ourselves from the earth by ignoring it, by not growing plants, fruits, herbs, vegetables, we lose touch with something deep in our own spirits and the spirit of God. There is something healing about planting in whatever piece of soil one can find. The healing connection that takes place is not just physical or earthy; it is spiritual. To give up the tradition of connecting dust with spirit, of planting with praying, decreases the abundance of life promised by Jesus Christ for all people. There is something about planting in earth—whether in a flowerpot, a roof garden, or a backyard patch of ground—that symbolizes the ability to survive in and revitalize desert places. Such revitalization is necessary for the well-being and survival of all peoples and life-forms that make up our planet. Yet we cannot romanticize traditional acts like gardening during an era in which the soil available for planting is often contaminated. To continue traditions of connectedness to the land in an abundant way requires not only revitalizing traditions but revitalizing the environment.

Active, concrete commitment to God, who is the strength of life (Ps 27) as empowering spirit, makes revitalization possible. The strength and endurance of all that lives, the way it survives best when its inner power is respected as sacred along with the rest of creation, remind us what it means to be created in the likeness of God. Jesus, who is God as dust and spirit, is the exemplar of God as incarnate, embodied Spirit who loves both the earthy bodily-ness of creation and the Spirit that God has breathed into all life. To love ourselves, body and soul, to the fullest requires loving God, who is revealed in the earth and in our own dusty, earthy bodies. By loving one another, indeed by loving every sentient being, we love God. This also means we are called to resist the poisoning of peoples and earth.

We humans have choices about how we treat the natural environment and one another. We can be apathetic to destruction, or we can take a step of genuine faith by awakening from spiritual torpor and fighting for the lives of one another and the planet we depend on. Churches, educators, communities, and health professionals have choices about taking a proactive interest in the well-being of all of us who are affected by the environmental crisis. If we are to live into the new creation of a new heaven and a new earth, we must do so by working in harmony with God as the spiritual empowerment of creation. To work in harmony with God's intention for the well-being of the planet means that we must work toward the salvation, redemption, and freedom of entire environments. We must look to free both people and the planet that sustains us from a variety of health hazards.

As a Christian, I understand Jesus Christ as embodying spirit in creation. As an African-American who appreciates traditional African cosmologies, I see Jesus as a great ancestor. And because I believe that God has been present in every region of the globe throughout time, I think it is possible that there have been embodiments of God in other religions. Christ as fully human and fully God is a manifestation of spirit in creation working in harmony with itself. For Jesus Christ, to be fully human is to be fully dust, because according to Genesis we humans are created from dust. Dust is a metaphor for our bodily and elemental connection to the earth. Dust includes within it water, sun, and air, which enhance the vitality of its bodiliness and the vitality of its ability to increase life abundantly. So "dustiness" refers to human connectedness with the rest of creation. Jesus as dust represents God, who is spirit, fully embodied in creation. Jesus fully represents such connection, while we strive not to forget it.

For Jesus Christ, to be fully God is to be fully spirit. Just as we humans, according to Genesis, are empowered by the breath or spirit of God, so also is Jesus empowered by spirit. The Nicene Creed states that Jesus is fully God and fully human. We might say then that since God is spirit and humans are dust, *Jesus is fully spirit and fully dust. Jesus as God incarnate is spirit embodied in dust. Jesus is God as dust. God as dust is Immanuel, God who is with us in our joy, our suffering, our bodiliness, our spiritual growth and struggles.* Jesus reminds us of God's intimate love of creation, which is so deep that God, who is spirit, chooses to be one with creation, transcending it yet permeating it even as it moves out and beyond into all that is unknown to human beings. God as spirit is the lovingness in creation that empowers life and that aims for balance or justice. In *Daughters of the Dust*, a film by Julie Dash, the Gullah matriarch Nana Peazant insists that she will not "be watching from heaven while there's soil still here for [her] for planting." She does not separate heaven from earth, dust from spirit. To be spiritual is to be deeply, intimately connected with the earth.

If Jesus was dust and spirit, like us, then the rest of us humans are likewise called to embrace a holistic relationship with the planet. I have come to see God's embodiment in Jesus as significant, not only because God is embodied in a human but also because God is embodied *in a creature* and, by extension, *in all creation*. God, embodied in Jesus, joins with the dust of the earth, reconciling the broken relationships with God and with creation in which we humans have involved ourselves. Jesus realized harmony of creation and spirit in the actions associated with his life and work. As Rosemary Radford Ruether astutely observes, Jesus' prayer—which we know as the Lord's Prayer—contains remnants of the Jewish Jubilee tradition, connecting heaven with the renewal of earth and its peoples: "Thy kingdom come. Thy will be done on earth as it is in heaven." Over time, she explains, we have lost the traditions that underlie the full meaning of Scripture, which spans more than simply humans in its covenant. We ought to practice Christianity in such a way that we reclaim our need for spiritual and physical healing and wholeness both for the earth and for humanity.

If Jesus is on the side of "the least of these," as Matthew 25 suggests, then the least of these includes the earth that we as embodied spirits depend on for life. To follow Jesus entails a love for the very soil, air, and water of the earth, as well as for God, who is spirit. To embody God well requires healthy bodies, which in turn are dependent on a healthy planet. Our beauty, like the beauty of Jesus, is our earthiness and our spiritualness. The entire earth cries out with humankind for justice. The Psalms make several references to the entire earth singing praises to God (e.g., Ps 148). Jesus builds on First Testament Scripture, observing that "even the rocks will cry out" for righteousness (Luke 19:40). In Genesis, the earth is described as fallen because of humankind's corruption. So the earth too is in need of the salvific power in the universe "to make the wounded whole." Restoration of right relationship with God includes restoration of right relationship with one another as well as with the earth. Restoration of right relationship with the earth requires restoration of right relationship between peoples across class lines, so that a healthy environment becomes a right of all instead of a privilege of the wealthy. Such restoration is redemptive, because we move toward God's intention of harmonious interrelatedness of the whole creation.

Jesus, who is God as dust and spirit, is organic to creation's physical and spiritual sustenance. Women and men are called to participate in such embodiment of spirit. Finally, if Jesus is God as dust and spirit, what does this say about Jesus' empathy with people of the land and the earth? If we, like Jesus, are called to embody God, who is spirit, what does that say about God's feeling with us and for us? Jesus, as Immanuel, feels with us. Jesus not only sustains us but Jesus also teaches us to feel anew the interconnectedness of life. Feeling such interconnectedness moves people out of the prisons of individualism to relearn compassion, to understand experientially that injustice anywhere is a threat to justice everywhere, that when one suffers all suffer, and that when one rejoices all rejoice. Such interconnectedness moves believers to act for justice.

Out of this interconnectedness we are called into a vision of new creation, a moment by moment, day by day, generation by generation process of earthly and spiritual renewal. Creation of a new heaven and a new earth requires that the sisters and brothers of dust more fully embody spirit with our earthly, lovely, and beloved selves. Spirit is the dusty fleshiness of our bodies as well as the invisible breath of life. To love spirit, we must then more fully love one another and the environment that sustains us. That is not an otherworldly, abstract activity of self-gratification. Rather, it involves dealing both with the generating dust of the earth that produces food and with the dust that threatens to bury the poor, the hungry, the homeless, the ill, the dying, and the weeping—dust that needs to be removed. By the Spirit, we are called to realize the apocalyptic vision of a new heaven and a new earth by being wise stewards of body, dust, and spirit engaged in the task of healing all.

Karen Baker-Fletcher is associate professor of systematic theology at the Perkins School of Theology at Southern Methodist University. Her books include *Sisters of Dust, Sisters of Spirit: Womanist Wordings on God and Creation* and *Dancing with God: The Trinity from a Womanist Perspective.* She is in wide demand as a conference speaker and workshop leader.

LANDSCAPE OF GRACE

Home, Commons, Sanctuary

PETER BAKKEN

IN PREACHING THIS GUEST SERMON on Earth Day at Wesley United Methodist Church in Kenosha, Wisconsin, my strategy was to engage those who might not identify themselves as environmentalists by appealing to the more primal, personal, and universal experience of "place"—highlighting the biophysical dimensions of place but not reducing the meaning of place to those dimensions alone. While the particular geographical references are essential to the sermon, the general method and overall structure can be adapted to any location.

> Bless the Lord, O my soul.
> > O Lord my God, you are very great.
> You are clothed with honor and majesty,
> > wrapped in light as with a garment.
> You stretch out the heavens like a tent,
> > you set the beams of your chambers on the waters,
> You make the clouds your chariot,
> > you ride on the wings of the wind,

You make the winds your messengers,
　　fire and flame your ministers.

You set the earth on its foundations,
　　so that it shall never be shaken.
You cover it with the deep as with a garment;
　　the waters stood above the mountains.
At your rebuke they flee;
　　at the sound of your thunder they take to flight.
They rose up to the mountains, ran down to the valleys
　　to the place that you appointed for them.
You set a boundary that they may not pass,
　　so that they might not again cover the earth.

You make springs gush forth in the valleys;
　　they flow between the hills,
giving drink to every wild animal;
　　the wild asses quench their thirst.
By the streams the birds of the air have their habitation;
　　they sing among the branches. (Ps 104:1–12)

◈

I consider that the sufferings of this present time are not worth comparing with the glory about to be revealed to us. For the creation waits with eager longing for the revealing of the children of God; for the creation was subjected to futility, not of its own will but by the will of the one who subjected it, in hope that the creation itself will be set free from its bondage to decay and will obtain the freedom of the glory of the children of God. We know that the whole creation has been groaning in labor pains until now; and not only the creation, but we ourselves, who have the first fruits of the Spirit, groan inwardly while we wait for adoption, the redemption of our bodies. For in hope we were saved. Now hope that is seen is not hope. For who hopes for what is seen? But if we hope for what we do not see, we wait for it with patience. (Rom 8:18–25)

◈

In the beginning was the Word, and the Word was with God, and the Word was God. He was in the beginning with God. All things came into being through him, and without him not one thing came into being. What has come into being in him was life, and the life was the light of all people. The light shines in the darkness, and the darkness did not overcome it. . . . And the Word became flesh and lived among us, and we have seen his glory, the glory as of a father's only son, full of grace and truth. **(John 1:1–5, 14)**

◈

Celebrating Earth Day in Sunday morning worship is both commendable and appropriate. The earth is God's wonderfully intricate, awesomely beautiful, and life-sustaining creation. How could we *not* celebrate it in our churches?

But I wonder if in some ways it's too big of an idea to really get our minds around—a whole planet, with all of its problems of air and water pollution, violence, species extinction, poverty, deforestation, injustice, and all the rest. These problems seem so overwhelming that it is hard not to get discouraged. No wonder so many of us feel powerless and throw up our hands and try not to think about it. But a bit of practical wisdom we all use in our everyday lives may help: A big task becomes a lot more manageable if you can break it down into smaller, more doable and digestible pieces.

Perhaps we can apply this to "the Earth and its distress," a phrase suggested by ethicist Larry Rasmussen. If we start out by focusing on a *piece* of the earth—namely, our own home place or region—we can get a handle on what it means truly to love this earth as God's creation. Caring for creation in our own regions and communities is not as dramatic a project as "saving the earth." As we come to know how our own places work and what makes them healthy or unhealthy, whole or broken, we will open a window into understanding and learning how to care for the wider world. And with each community doing its part, the pieces will add up to a much larger whole.

HOME PLACES

What images and memories come to your mind when you think of your home place? Are they images and memories of the house and neighborhood and city where you live, the part of the country you grew up in and where your parents and grandparents lived? Are they images of the special places you love and return to from time to time—whether in memory or reality: a corner of your yard or a nearby park, a favorite vacation spot, a place where you love to walk or camp or hunt or fish or swim? Are they visions of the city, or the country, or something in between? Are they thoughts of places of quiet and solitude, or of bustling crowds and happy conversation?

I am sure if we all got together and compared notes, we would come up with an amazing mosaic of known and loved and remembered places, each different but with common features and joined by common threads of meaning and remembrance and affection. Some would be places of obvious beauty and wide appeal; others may have to be known deeply in order to be loved.

What I want to suggest is that the particular places in which we dwell and through which we journey are gifts of God, signs and channels of God's grace to us and to all creatures, and that, as recipients of such gifts, we are called to respond in certain ways.

LAKE MICHIGAN AND ITS LANDSCAPE

Being with you here in Kenosha today, I cannot help but think that one geographical feature we all have in common in some way is that vast body of freshwater just a few miles to the east—namely, Lake Michigan—and the land that surrounds it. From the sand dunes and steel mills of the south shore to the sprawling metropolitan areas of Chicago and Milwaukee, up past Sheboygan and Manitowoc to Door County and the paper mills and harbors of Green Bay, past the islands clustered at the northern end of the lake, across the long suspension bridge over the Straits of Mackinac, and back down the eastern side, the shoreline of Lake Michigan runs the gamut from inner city to north woods wilderness, from heavy industry to "vacationland."

Radiating out from the lake in all directions are the many rivers that feed into it and that define the Lake Michigan watershed. And in that basin, too, is a patchwork of human and natural landscapes: cities and farms, small towns and state parks, lakes and prairies, and woods and wetlands. It is a landscape rich in natural beauty, fertile soils, and human enterprise.

What would it mean to see Lake Michigan and the surrounding landscape as a place and a mosaic of places in which we daily encounter God's grace—whether we recognize it or not? Let me suggest three ways of looking at this or any other place as a divine gift: as a home, as a commons, and as a sanctuary.

Home

For some of us, the Lake Michigan landscape is our native home. I was born and raised in Fargo, North Dakota—a long way from here and a very different environment. But my wife was born in Milwaukee and grew up in Kenosha and Waukegan before her family moved to Madison, and her grandparents lived in the Sheboygan area. Her grandmother worked as a lifeguard, and Martha learned to swim and ride the waves in the sometimes very cold waters of Lake Michigan. One of her most vivid childhood memories is of the sound and smell of the wind in the pine trees along the shore.

But we contemporary Americans are a nomadic people, and not many of us stay in one place for long. I lived for several years in Chicago as a graduate student at the University of Chicago Divinity School. It was a way station to an extent, but it helped to set my future course, for it was where I developed my interest in the interface between ecology and theology and also where I met my wife. There was much I enjoyed about the city, but I remember how refreshing it was to travel down to the Indiana Dunes National Lakeshore and to realize there how much I missed the experience of being surrounded by the color green.

Whether we dwell in a place for a few years or a lifetime, it becomes part of our story, part of our identity. Through the places we call home, God gives us the gifts not only of shelter and sustenance but of selfhood as well. The places of our life story are part of what makes us who we are. It is no accident that when we want to get to know a person, we ask, "Where are you from?"

Commons

As a home, a place has this sort of a private side, full of individual and personal significance. But home places also have a public side, because there is no place that is not part of a larger history or that is completely disconnected from other places. Each is a piece of the mosaic, a thread in the tapestry of our common world, a crossroads of many individual paths. It is never *our* home alone; we share it with other people, as family or neighbors. A shared home place connects us to one another through a common history, and through complex linkages of economics and politics and ecology.

History gives a place its character. Lake Michigan itself is a product of history on a geological scale; it is a one-time gift of the glaciers that reshaped the landscape of Wisconsin, Michigan, Illinois, and Indiana, and that left behind the Great Lakes—which now hold 18 percent of the world's surface freshwater.

The Native Americans who first lived here are part of this region's history, as are the European-Americans, African-Americans, and Asian-Americans who settled here. That history leaves its own legacy of challenges—and of promises—as we confront issues of racial and cultural diversity, justice, and peaceful coexistence. In my own experience, Chicago, with its extremes of wealth and poverty, culture and deprivation, was a dramatic contrast to the moderately sized Midwestern community I had grown up in. Chicago enlarged my horizons and deepened my sensitivities to the complex issues of racial and social justice.

The history of a place is also the history of how we have lived on and from the land and its waters, and how our livelihoods and ways of life have affected ourselves and the other creatures around us. My nine-year-old daughter Mara loves the *Little House on the Prairie* series—not only the original stories about Laura Ingalls Wilder but also the series that have spun off from them about Laura's daughter, mother, grandmother, and even great-grandmother. Laura's mother, Caroline, grew up in Brookfield and Concord and went to school in Milwaukee. These series chronicle the struggles and successes of the people who settled here, such as the farmers who cleared the land and the sailors who brought goods and people across the water (Caroline's father perished in Lake Michigan when his schooner sank). To these figures we can add the loggers who harvested the northern woods to build Chicago and other cities, and later those who worked in the steel mills, paper mills, and automobile factories.

The benefits of these enterprises for our prosperity and well-being have been immense. But they have not always been fairly distributed, and they have come at a high price—to the rest of creation and even to our own health and well-being. One of my wife's memories of Kenosha is of finding a sick, helpless bird and trying to help it to fly again just after her neighborhood had been sprayed with DDT.

The horrendous wildfires that swept through cutover timberlands and devastated the town of Peshtigo; the sewage that sucked the oxygen out of the lake water and fed huge, smelly algae blooms; the invasion of exotic species like alewives and zebra mussels; the soup of toxic chemicals like PCBs—nobody *wanted* these things to happen. Yet, however we want to argue about where to place the blame, or how to weigh the costs and benefits, or which consequences were avoidable and which were not, these events have taught us some important truths. They have taught us that life on earth must be a matter of giving as well as taking. They have taught us that we have to learn to live *with* as well as *from* the land and waters.

When we understand the Lake Michigan landscape as a commons—as a place of shared space and shared resources where the lives of all are bound together in a shared past, present, and future—we can recognize in it God's gift of community with others, both human and nonhuman. The gift of community is the gift of relationships, of caring and being cared for, of giving and receiving, of working side by side on the task of leaving a better place for those who follow after us.

Sanctuary

Finally, I want to suggest that the landscape in which we live can become for us a sanctuary—holy ground—where we recognize and respond to God's presence among the things of this world.

Before going to graduate school, I read an article in *National Geographic* that described Chicago as "a city bounded on one side by infinity." It sounded like a good place to study theology! And indeed, walking from campus out to "The Point," a small promontory that juts out into the lake, you encounter the vast expanse of water and the waves that crash against the massive stone blocks laid down to protect the shore from erosion. The lake is indeed an apt symbol for the power and majesty and mystery of God.

The writer of Psalm 104 saw that power and majesty and mystery in the light, the clouds, the winds, and the lightning. The psalmist saw how God could take the awesome, destructive power of water and make it serve the needs of life: the springs that give drink to the wild animals, the streams that water the trees in which the birds sing.

God meets us among the things of this world. In the prologue to his Gospel, John the Evangelist emphasizes how the Word, through whom all things were made, became flesh and dwelt among us. A more literal translation might be "pitched his tent among us."

Christ dwells with us and among us even now. Christ shapes our identities as Christians in our church communities, in our places of worship and of service. Christ calls us to love our neighbors and to do the works of justice and peacemaking, and Christ offers us forgiveness and redemption for our broken relationships. The incarnate Christ, the Word made flesh, shows us how God's holiness shines in and through the creation. All the natural gifts of our earthly home places are restored and elevated, given new power and depth through God's gift of Christ.

But how do we respond to the gifts of God's grace in the places and encounters of our everyday life, in the natural as well as in the human world? The proper response to grace is gratitude. Gratitude is a matter of being attentive, appreciative, caring, and gentle. Gratitude is not a matter of taking gifts for granted or of judging them simply according to how useful they are. Gratitude is a matter of treating them with care and respect.

Too often we have treated the gifts of the Lake Michigan landscape ungratefully, even disgracefully. Thirty years ago, Lutheran theologian Joseph Sittler, who taught in Chicago, recalled Paul's words about creation waiting with eager longing for the revealing of the children of God:

> Does this not suggest that the Creation, in its suppliant and open way, waits for such human operation by [people] of faith as shall challenge them to be what they [as people of God] are called to be—[children] of God—and not simply operators within the resources of the world? One is not falling into words only in sentiment or poetic fancy but extrapolating from a clear theological position when [one] makes the affirmation that *Christianly* [speaking] Lake Michigan must be regarded as "groaning in travail, waiting to be set free from its bondage of decay."[1]

How can we begin to deal more gratefully and graciously with the gifts God has given us in this magnificent lake and landscape? Consider these four guidelines: First, know your place. Know its human and natural history, its blessings and its problems, how it functions, and how it relates to the wider world. Do not just read about it, but explore and experience it firsthand. Second, take responsibility. Pay attention to how your own actions have consequences, for better or worse, for the people and creatures around you. What are the local impacts of the energy you use, the car you drive, the way you care for your lawn, or the food and other products you buy? Third, get involved. There are many groups and initiatives in this region that are working to make it a better place for people and other creatures, whether by caring for hungry and homeless people or by protecting and restoring wildlife habitats. Find out what legislative issues at the state or federal level will affect the quality of life in your community. Finally, say grace. By recognizing and naming the everyday things that sustain and enrich us as forms of grace, we deepen and strengthen our connection to the One who is "the giver of every good and perfect gift" and to the Christ whom poet Gerard Manly Hopkins said "plays in ten thousand places."

For the gifts of home, community, and sanctuary that come to us in this magnificent, vulnerable lake and landscape, thanks be to God!

Peter Bakken is public policy coordinator for the Wisconsin Council of Churches, and he previously served as coordinator of outreach for the Au Sable Institute of Environmental Studies. He has contributed to *Evocations of Grace: Writings on Ecology, Theology, and Ethics*, *Ethics for a Small Planet: A Communications Handbook on the Ethical and Theological Reasons for Protecting Biodiversity*, and *Finding the Center of the World*.

Note

1. Joseph Sittler, "Ecological Commitment as Theological Responsibility," in *Evocations of Grace: Writings on Ecology, Theology, and Ethics* (Grand Rapids: Eerdmans, 2000), 84.

EXPANDING OUR CIRCLE
OF COMPASSION

TANYA MARCOVNA BARNETT

THIS SERMON WAS PREACHED during the first Tuesday of Holy Week during weekly chapel at Seattle Pacific University (Free Methodist). It uses Scripture and a poem by Rabbi Abraham Isaac Kook ("Four-Fold Song") to expand notions of compassion to encompass all of creation. The sermon serves as an example to others seeking to incorporate creation-honoring themes into Lenten and Easter services.

> Praise the LORD!
> Praise the LORD from the heavens;
>   praise him in the heights!
> Praise him, all his angels;
>   praise him, all his host!
> Praise him, sun and moon;
>   praise him, all you shining stars!
> Praise him, you highest heavens,
>   and you waters above the heavens!

Let them praise the name of the LORD,
for he commanded and they were created.
He established them for ever and ever;
he fixed their bounds, which cannot be passed.

Praise the LORD from the earth,
you sea monsters and all deeps,
fire and hail, snow and frost,
stormy wind fulfilling his command!

Mountains and all hills,
fruit trees and all cedars!
Wild animals and all cattle,
creeping things and all flying birds!

Kings of the earth and all peoples,
princes and all rulers of the earth!
Young men and women alike,
old and young together!

Let them praise the name of the LORD,
for his name alone is exalted;
his glory is above earth and heaven.
He has raised up a horn for his people,
praise for all his faithful,
for the people of Israel who are close to him.
Praise the LORD! **(Ps 148)**

As they went out, they came upon a man from Cyrene named Simon; they compelled this man to carry his cross. **(Matt 27:32)**

Like many of you, I am just returning from spring break. It was actually my husband's spring break—he is the student in our family—and I blissfully piggybacked onto it. We decided to take a road trip, and so we went to visit his father in Colorado. We brought our dog,

Kani, along with plenty of water, food, and clean socks, and we left watches, calendars, work, and even maps at home. We just traveled— through mountains and deserts, through canyons filled with breath- taking spires of the reddest rocks. We camped, hiked, ate, played, and slept. Time became very liquid, so liquid that I would describe it as liminal. The word *liminal* literally means "at the threshold." Our break was a place and a time at the threshold between two realities. This liminal journey represented the shedding of many distractions and a reentry into our relationships with one another, with friends and family, with God, and with rhythms of the sun, moon, and land. It was a time like no other. It was a time in between time.

In the seasons of our Christian faith, this "holy" week is like no other. It is also an in-between time. We are living and moving within Holy Week, within "Passion Week." This is a time when we place our distractions off to the side and reenter the heart of our relationship with God through the passion of our beloved Christ. Passion, from the word *pati* in Latin, means "to suffer." When we reenter Christ's passion, we journey into his suffering with all that lives, moves, and has being. And by entering into his suffering, we begin to experience what it might feel like actually to transform the world's suffering from the inside out. This journey with Christ is the core of our Christian faith. This is no ordinary week.

For a brief moment, let us journey with Jesus into his passion as Simon of Cyrene did. Simon, as you may remember, was seized by Jesus' captors and made to carry the cross. This stranger from Africa labored to navigate the road with Jesus into the depths of suffering, literally shouldering a portion of Jesus' burden along the way. Simon embodied *compassion*, a word that means "to suffer with." If you were Simon, burdened by the heaviness of the cross, what urges would you feel? No matter how or when compassion seizes us, it is by its very nature accompanied by an urge to help alleviate suffering. Once we experience deep brokenness from the inside, compassion compels us to transform it. Compassion, writes author and pastor Frederick Buechner, "is that sometimes fatal capacity for feeling what it is like to live inside another's skin, knowing that there can never really be peace and joy for any until there is peace and joy finally for all."[1] "'Apathy,'" writes theologian Larry Rasmussen, "contrasts with compassion—it is the denial of the senses and of our inherent connectedness to all things."[2] Simon could have rightly said that Jesus' suffering was not his own, that he had no connection to it—why should he share Jesus' passion? And Jesus could have said that the world's suffering was not his own—why should he share it? Why should he drink from that most bitter cup of suffering? These are examples of apathy, the sense that the suffering of others has absolutely nothing to do with me and my well-being. Each one of us has the freedom to deny our connections with others and to shrink our circle of compassion down to the bare minimum—a bubble just big enough to safeguard my own well-being.

Abraham Isaac Kook, the first Ashkenazi chief rabbi in Palestine, writes in his beautiful poem "Four-fold Song" that every person's life is ultimately a song that they sing. He suggests that there are at least four different songs, and each song sings of the degree to which we see our life and our well-being intertwined with that of others. Each is a song of compassion.

First, Rabbi Kook writes about those who sing the song of the individual self alone. This is the song that our culture has helped many of us to sing very well. It is the song of individualism, the song of the smallest circle of compassion. To be clear, individualism has made many contributions to the world. For example, individualism is partly responsible for lifting up the intrinsic worth of every human being. This recognition has given rise to the acknowledgment of human rights, which supports countless people and communities who suffer under the weight of life-threatening oppression. Individualism also values our unique, God-given blessedness and gifts. This part of the first song can be truly beautiful to hear. What individualism cannot fully recognize is that all of us are profoundly relational beings; in reality, a person who is not in relationship with others can hardly be said to exist. Individualism also exaggerates our sense of self-importance to the point that we are cut off from the knowledge that *everything* that God creates, sustains, and redeems is sacred.

Next, Rabbi Kook writes about those who sing the song of their own people. These singers have expanded their circle of compassion to include those who typically look, think, believe, and/or act like themselves. This is the beautiful song that family members sing when they gather together and rejoice in the fullness of their relationships. It is also the song of communities, cultures, and nations that celebrate their full stories: their places of brokenness, transformation, and blessedness. But if the circle of compassion stops widening at this level of relationships, this song can be heard accompanying excessive patriotism and jingoism, classism, sexism, racism, and a host of other life-crushing "isms."

Rabbi Kook's third song is the song of all humanity. Thankfully, many faith communities sing this glorifying song very well. They go beyond their own bounds both to empathize with and to transform the suffering of all of God's children. You can hear this song in mission work, interfaith dialogue, CROP walks, Habitat for Humanity projects, in shelters for the homeless, and in other acts and places of justice and compassion. You can hear this song through the work of the Truth and Reconciliation Commission in South Africa, through the work of Doctors without Borders, and so many others. Yet even with the truly expansive nature of this third song of compassion, Rabbi Kook has yet another song for us—the song that sings of the suffering, transformation, and beauty of everything.

This is the fourfold song, the song of all creation. In this fourfold song, "the song of the self, the song of the people, the song of [humankind], the song of the world all merge . . . at all times, in every hour."[3] The fourth song sings of the most expansive circle of compassion. It is found in places like Psalm 148 in which the psalmist goes on and on exhorting, "You heavens; you angels and hosts; you sun, moon, and shining stars; sea monsters and all deeps; fire and hail, snow and frost, stormy wind; you mountains and hills; you fruit trees and all cedars over there; wild animals and all cattle, creeping things and flying birds; all peoples, young men and women alike, old and young—all of you together, join in this ecstatic chorus of praise to our Creator!" In this song, we move beyond another life-crushing "ism," namely, anthropocentrism. Anthropocentrism is an "ism" that says this: if other people, creatures, and habitats have no value to us, then our subjugation or even destruction of them poses no moral dilemmas for us. Nevertheless, our hearts see through this "ism" when we glimpse Christ's heart in whom "all things hold together . . . [;] all things, whether on earth or in heaven" (Col 1:17–20).

In his article "Nature's Praise of God in the Psalms," theologian Terence Fretheim writes, "It is only as all creatures of God join together in the chorus of praise that the elements of the natural order or human beings witness to God as they ought." This insight calls human beings "to relate to the natural order in such a way that nature's praise might show forth with greater clarity."[4] Consider a choir with only sopranos who can sing within a three-note range. The tune might be intriguing at first, but ultimately, woefully limited. In a similar vein, Fretheim might suggest that a hymn of praise that includes only human beings—and that therefore excludes creeping things, sun and stars, trees, or any other part of creation— would create a monochromatic musical picture and a substantially less glorifying one. The contrition of St. Basil the Great laments this sad picture:

> O God, enlarge within us the sense of fellowship with all living things, our brothers the animals [and all creatures] to whom thou gavest the earth as their home in common with us. We remember with shame that in the past we have exercised the high dominion of humans with ruthless cruelty; so that the voice of the earth, which should have gone up to Thee in song, has been a groan of travail. May we realize that all creatures live not for us alone but for themselves and for Thee, and that they love the sweetness of life.

Basil prayed these words in the fourth century. But how much more powerful and relevant they are today when, as reported by the Worldwatch Institute, 11 percent of the world's bird species, 25 percent of mammal species, and 34 percent of all fish species face immediate danger of extinction as a result of human-created habitat loss, pollution, and global warming.[5] And in the words of the World Wildlife Fund, "Every species loss diminishes the diversity of life on Earth with untold consequences for the web of life. Yet, at present rates of extinction, as much as a third of the world's [plant and animal] species could be gone in the next twenty years."[6] And the most fragile part of this web of life surely includes the poorest of humanity—those people whose well-being is immediately and directly connected to the well-being of creation. This is the heartbreaking news: Humankind is, knowingly and unknowingly, muting the "voice of the earth," a voice that should go up to our God in a song of praise rather than in a groan of travail.

Our individual life song is also part of this groan of travail. With such groaning, not only does God miss out on the opportunity to be glorified by all of creation, but we also miss out on hearing the unique expressions of what God is doing throughout creation. Paul expresses it well: "Ever since the creation of the world [God's] eternal power and divine nature, invisible though they are, have been understood and seen through the things [God] has made" (Rom 1:20). Or consider these powerful words from D. H. Lawrence:

> Oh, what a catastrophe for man when he cut himself off from the rhythm of the year, from his unison with the sun and the earth. Oh, what a catastrophe, what a maiming of love when it was made a personal, merely personal feeling, taken away from the rising and setting of the sun, and cut off from the connection with the solstice and equinox. This is what is wrong with us. We are bleeding at the roots.[7]

What song is your life singing? What if we stretched our circles of compassion? What if we stretched our hearts as wide as they could possibly go? Yes, as Fredrick Buechner suggested, this can feel extremely painful and "sometimes fatal," but also consider the transformative, powerful joy of Easter that rushes into this wide-open space. It is a joy that stops the bleeding at our roots and at the roots of all creation. Consider the joy of John 3:16, in which the heart of God stretches so wide that it encompasses not only you and me, not only our nation, not only humankind, but literally (as we read in the Greek) the entire cosmos. "For God so loved the cosmos . . ." This is indeed the song of Passion Week—the most expansive, fourfold song of compassion. In this week, let us be like Simon of Cyrene. Let us be seized by the profound suffering and deepest, transforming joy of Christ's full compassion.

Tanya Marcovna Barnett graduated from Valparaiso University and Vanderbilt Divinity School. She has worked with migrant and urban farm workers and has served as an agro-forestry extension volunteer with the Peace Corps in Niger. She formerly served as program director with Earth Ministry, where she coordinated congregational organizers and developed and wrote the *Greening Congregations Handbook* and other publications. She currently is associate director for the United Methodist Foundation of the Northwest and helps to lead the "Whole-Life" stewardship program for United Methodist churches in that region.

Notes

1. Frederick Buechner, *A Room Called Remember: Uncollected Pieces* (New York: HarperCollins, 1992), 152.

2. Larry Rasmussen, *Earth Community, Earth Ethics* (Maryknoll, NY: Orbis, 1996), 285.

3. Abraham Isaac Kook, "Four-Fold Song," in *Lights of Holiness*, vol. 2 (New York: Paulist Press, 1972), 445.

4. Terence E. Fretheim. "Nature's Praise of God in the Psalms," *Ex Auditu* 3 (1987): 29.

5. http://www.worldwatch.org/node/1605.

6. http://www.worldwildlife.org.

7. D. H. Lawrence, *Lady Chatterley's Lover and A Propos of 'Lady Chatterley's Lover'*, ed. Michael Squires (Cambridge: Cambridge University Press, 1993).

A NEW UNDERSTANDING
OF OUR PLACE IN CREATION

DIANNE BERGANT

THIS SERMON CHALLENGES the anthropocentric perspective that values the natural world only to the extent that it serves human goals. It shows that humankind is a part of and not the primary focus of creation.

> I have uttered what I did not understand. **(Job 42:3)**

◈

We are probably all acquainted with the expression "the patience of Job." However, if this is all we know about Job, we have not grasped the essence of his eponymous book's exceptional message. Some of us may maintain that the story is an account of an innocent man who valiantly endured multiple setbacks and who, because of his enduring loyalty, was ultimately abundantly rewarded by God. This point of view also misses an important dimension of the story. However, if we allow Job's own words to suggest the heart of the message, we find his last response to God provocative: "I uttered what I did not understand." Just what were the things that Job did not understand?

Job is described as a righteous man. In fact, he was an extraordinarily righteous man. God refers to him as "my servant Job" and says, "There is no one like him on the earth, a blameless and upright man who fears God and turns away from evil" (1:8). It would be very difficult to get a better endorsement than that! Despite his righteousness—actually, it was because of it—a bargain was struck between God and "the Satan," a mysterious figure who had access to the court of heaven. However, despite the familiarity of the name, the Satan was not the devil as we have come to know that evil force. What was the bargain? To test Job to the limits of human endurance in order to see whether or not his righteousness was authentic. God believed that Job would prove to be loyal even in the face of suffering, while the Satan maintained that Job was upright only because God protected him from the difficulties of life that most other people have to face.

As the story unfolds, with disaster after disaster, Job loses everything—property, flocks, servants, and even his children. In the face of it all, he remains loyal to God: "Naked I came forth from my mother's womb, and naked shall I return there. The LORD gave, and the LORD has taken away; blessed be the name of the LORD" (1:21).

The Satan is not satisfied. Job himself has been spared. "Touch his bone and his flesh," the Satan says to God, "and he will curse you to your face" (2:5). Once again, God agrees to an assault on Job, this time on his very person. Stricken with loathsome boils, Job remains steadfast: "Shall we receive the good at the hand of God, and not receive the bad?" (2:10). This is the picture that has earned Job the reputation of being a patient man. But we must notice that such patience is only found in the first two chapters of this forty-two-chapter book.

In the rest of the book, we find a very different man. Job rails against the hardships that have crashed down upon him. He curses the day of his birth (3:3), and he accuses God of capricious behavior (9:15–18). Job is guilty of no offense that could merit such tribulations (16:12). And as far as agreeing with those who have come to offer him solace, he finds neither comfort nor wisdom in their words: "Miserable comforters are you all! Have windy words no limit?" (16:2–3). Out of affection for their friend, again and again Job's visitors encourage him to admit his guilt and to ask for God's forgiveness so that his tribulations might end, his lost possessions be replaced, and his position in society be reestablished. Job will hear none of it. As often and as strongly as they make their plea, just as often and strongly does he declare his innocence. He ends his defense on a note that might appear to be brash and foolhardy: "Oh, that I had one to hear me! (Here is my signature! let the Almighty answer me!)" (31:35). Such an argument would invite divine reprisal in the case of one who was guilty. But Job asserts his innocence, and so this final claim is a bold challenge to God. How will God respond? Will God chastise Job for his audacity? Will God relent and vindicate Job's righteousness? Job waits, as if suspended in air. But so do we who are taken in by the force of the story.

At this point especially, the book provides profound irony. God does respond, but with questions rather than answers. And the questions address the design and operation of the natural world, not the specifics of Job's afflictions. As we marvel at the vistas of creation painted by God's questions, we should not overlook their distinctive form. These are not requests that seek information. They are questions filled with irony. They serve to correct Job's short-sighted perception of his ability to grasp some of the mysteries of creation. God asks such questions as: "Where were you when I laid the foundation of the earth?" "Have you commanded the morning since your days began, and caused the dawn to know its place?" "Do you know when the mountain goats give birth?" "Do you give the horse its might? Do you clothe its neck with mane?" (38:4, 12; 39:1, 19). God's response is curious. Why does God not address Job's concerns? How are questions about creation related to the plight of an innocent sufferer?

God's questions are meant to lead Job to a depth of understanding far greater than any level of knowledge mere answers would provide.

The marvel of God's questions is seen in their ability to bring Job to real wisdom despite, or perhaps because of, their indirectness. We may not see the connection between Job's questions and God's response, but Job certainly does. His own response to God indicates this. If we look closely we will see that God asks questions about the broad scope of nature, and Job gains insight into the narrow scope of human nature. Like Job, we want answers about innocent suffering. However, if, like Job, we are going to ask such questions of God, we will have to learn the answers in the same way that Job did—by listening to what God has to say. But just what is God saying?

Job's obvious struggle may cause us to overlook how powerful the revelatory role of nature is in this book. It is not nature in itself that is so important, but the fact that the awesome God shines forth through the natural world. In other words, the artistry of God can be seen in the splendor of the universe; God's wisdom is evident in its delicate balance; God's imagination spills over in the variety of nature's diverse manifestations; God's providence is enjoyed in its inherent fruitfulness. The natural world was not only born of the creativity of God; it actually bears the features of this creativity. Everything in creation mirrors something of the Creator. It is not enough to say that creation is the medium through which God is revealed. In a very real sense, the medium (creation) is itself the revelation.

The wonders of creation that are paraded before Job were not unknown to him before this extraordinary experience. By and large, they made up his everyday world. However, God's questions show Job that he has not really understood this world. Though it was the ordinary world within which he lived, he seems to have taken this world for granted. Job's breathtaking, even mystical, experience of creation catapults him out of his narrow view of human concerns into the vast expanses of the mystery of creation. It makes him realize that *human history unfolds within the broader context of the natural world, and not the other way around.* Job comes to see that *the natural world does not merely serve the ends of human history.* His encounter with the ineffable Creator God leads him to this new insight. It is an insight that transforms him from a self-pitying victim of circumstances into a human being who has endured the struggles of human limitation and has emerged chastened, yet nonetheless a mystic.

In his last response to God, Job admits that he has been converted to God's point of view, even without comprehending it: "I understood what I did not understand" (42:3). What is it that Job did not understand? Is it God? Yes—the God whom he previously knew and to whom he had been faithful was a God of righteousness, one who recognized Job's integrity and apparently rewarded him for it. The God whom Job now knows is the mysterious power who brought forth the world, as a man begets or as a woman gives birth, and who is somehow revealed in and through that wondrous world. This is a God who can provide for the entire resplendent universe without being distracted from the specific needs of fragile human beings. God can do this, because God's designs are grander than, yet still include, human history.

Is it human life that Job does not understand? Yes—it seems that God has taken human suffering, the most pressing concern of human life, and has situated it within a broader context. That context is material creation in its entirety. God's questions have brought Job to see that, in the midst of measureless natural grandeur, the ambiguity of human life can be confronted. But to do so demands honesty and humility, an honesty and humility that can admit to and accept one's own limited capacity to comprehend. Creation itself has expanded Job's vision and has called him to a deepening of faith that goes beyond understanding.

Is it the entire scheme of creation that Job does not understand? Yes—the book of Job demonstrates the profound human struggle between human-centered interests and cosmos-centered realities or, understood theoretically, between anthropology and cosmology. It pits the search for understanding against the enormity of the universe in such a way that the human spirit is enraptured yet not broken. The commonplace yet strangely unfamiliar natural world awakens amazement at its wonders and leaves the humbled gazer aghast. Having called on God to put things right in his particular life, Job was led beyond himself by the magnitude of creation, there to see that he could not fathom the laws by which God governs. In the end, cosmology does not defeat anthropology; rather, it opens its arms to welcome back its prodigal child.

Our journey into an understanding of the book of Job began on the note of the man's patience in the midst of tribulation. We soon moved from there to the question of innocent suffering. Finally, we discovered that the resolution of Job's struggles takes place within the natural world itself. There patience ceases to be the issue, and human suffering itself seems to recede into the background. The immensity of the universe and the intricacy of its working led Job to see that there is so much that he will never grasp. He now realizes that just as the entire natural world is in the hands of the Creator God, so all of human life is held in those same hands.

The implications of Job's transformed attitude are profound as well as wide reaching. The shift from an anthropocentric to a cosmo-centric worldview requires not only a new way of understanding the universe itself but also a reexamination of how we understand humankind within that universe. We are natural creatures, and everything about us is a part of the natural world or mediated to us through it. We are not independent of it; we are dependent on it. Technology has often led us to believe that we can step outside of our environment to examine it and control it. However, it is important to remember that we do not merely live within our environment as we live within a building. We may be a unique dimension of the natural world, but we are not separate from it. We are part of it, and it is part of us. Humankind is embedded in nature, in the very creative matrix that has given life and continues to give life.

Nature is also embedded in human beings. We are truly chil-dren of the universe, made of the same stuff as the mountains and the rain, the sand and the stars. We are governed by the laws of life and growth and death, as are the birds and the fish and the grass of the field. We thrive in the warmth of and through the agency of the sun, as does every other living thing. We come from the earth as from a mother, and we are nourished from this same source of life.

It should be easy to see that the intrinsic integrity of all creation is basic to everything about us.

Job's new realization of his place in the broader creation made demands on him. He was challenged to accept his new understanding of human limitation and to trust that, despite his hardships, his life was in the hands of God.

We too are faced with the profound implications of this understanding of our place in creation. Our struggles may not be the same as Job's, but we, too, must fashion a new way of understanding our place in creation. We will have to deal with challenging ideas such as frugality and sufficiency in our use of natural resources. Our concern for the viability of human life and the earth's ability to sustain it will play indispensable roles in our thinking, and it will require our readiness to make hard decisions. We will come to see that human self-centeredness is irresponsible and impertinent. We must replace it with respect for the rest of natural creation and with responsible stewardship. We must cease using natural resources simply as disposable commodities to satisfy our selfish whims. Instead, we are called to enter into an aesthetic contemplation of nature's beauty, a contemplation not unlike that of Job: "I had heard of you by the hearing of the ear, but now my eye sees you" (42:5).

Dianne Bergant, Congregation of Saint Agnes, is professor of biblical studies at Catholic Theological Union, Chicago. She writes the weekly column "The Word" for *America,* and her publications include *Israel's Wisdom Literature: A Liberation-Critical Reading* and *The Earth Is the Lord's: The Bible, Ecology, and Worship.*

MOMENTS OF GRACE

THOMAS BERRY

THIS REFLECTION SEEKS TO PLACE OUR TIME within the larger story of the universe as a critical moment of grace, the beginning of a new "Ecozoic Era" in which humans have an opportunity to be a determining force in the present transformation that the earth is experiencing. Creating a new, mutually enhancing human presence on earth among all creatures is the great work of our time.

> Let [creation] praise the name of the LORD. **(Ps 148:13)**

◈

> The time is fulfilled, and the kingdom of God has come near.
> **(Mark 1:15)**

◈

As we enter the twenty-first century, we are experiencing a moment of grace. Such moments are privileged moments. The great transformations of the universe occur at such times. The future is defined in some enduring pattern of its functioning.

There are cosmological and historical moments of grace as well as religious moments of grace. The present is one of those moments of transformation that can be considered as all three. Such a moment occurred when the star out of which our solar system was born collapsed in enormous heat, scattering itself as fragments in the vast realms of space. In the center of this star, the elements had been forming through a vast period of time until in the final heat of this explosion the hundred-some elements were present. Only then could the sun, our star, give shape to itself by gathering these fragments together with gravitational power and then leaving some nine spherical shapes sailing in elliptical paths around itself as planetary forms. At this moment the earth took shape, life was evoked, and intelligence in its human form became possible.

This supernova event of a first or second generation star could be considered a cosmological moment of grace, a moment that determined the future possibilities of the solar system, the earth, and of every form of life that would ever appear on the earth.

For the more evolved multicellular organic forms of life to appear, there then had to appear the first living cell, a procaryotic cell capable—by the energy of the sun, the carbon of the atmosphere, and the hydrogen of the sea—of a metabolic process never known previously. This original moment of transition from the nonliving to the living world was fostered by the fierce lightning of these early times. Then, at a critical moment in the evolution of the original cell, another cell capable of using the oxygen of the atmosphere with its immense energies appeared. Photosynthesis was completed by respiration.

At this moment the living world as we know it began to flourish until it shaped the earth anew. Daisies in the meadows, the song of the mockingbird, the graceful movement of dolphins through the sea all became possible at this moment. We ourselves became possible. New modes of music, poetry, and painting all came into being in new forms against the background of the music and poetry and painting of the celestial forms circling through the heavens.

In human history there have also been such moments of grace. Such was the occasion in northeast Africa some 2.5 million years ago when the first humans stood erect and a cascade of consequences was begun that eventuated in our present mode of being. Whatever talent exists in the human order, whatever genius, whatever capacity for ecstatic joy, whatever physical strength or skill, all this has come to us through these earlier peoples. It was a determining moment.

There were other moments in the cultural-historical order when the future was determined in some comprehensive and beneficial manner. Such a moment was experienced when humans first were able to control fire, when spoken language was invented, when the first gardens were cultivated, when weaving and the shaping and firing of pottery were practiced, when writing and the alphabet were invented. Then there were the moments when the great visionaries were born who gave to the peoples of the world their unique sense of the sacred, when the great revelations occurred. So, too, there were the times when the great storytellers appeared—Homer and Valmiki and others who gave to the world its great epic tales. There was also the time of the great historians: Ssu-ma Ch'ien in China, Thucydides in Greece, Ibn Khaldun in the Arab world.

So now in this transition period into the twenty-first century, we are experiencing a moment of grace, but a moment in its significance that is different from any previous moment. For the first time the planet is being disturbed by humans in its geological structure and its biological functioning in a manner like the great cosmic forces that alter the geological and biological structures of the planet or like the glaciations.

We are also altering the great classical civilizations as well as the indigenous tribal cultures that have dominated the spiritual and intellectual development of vast numbers of persons throughout these past five thousand years. These civilizations and cultures that have governed our sense of the sacred and established our basic norms of reality and value and that have designed the life disciplines of the peoples of earth are terminating a major phase of their historical mission. The teaching and the energy they communicate are unequal to the task of guiding and inspiring the future. They cannot guide the great work that is before us. We will never be able to function without these traditions. But these older traditions alone cannot fulfill the needs of the moment. That they have been unable to prevent and have not yet properly critiqued the present situation is evident. Something new is happening. A new vision and a new energy are coming into being.

After some four centuries of empirical observation and experiment, we are having a new experience of the deepest mysteries of the universe. We see the universe both as a developmental sequence of irreversible transformations and as an ever renewing sequence of seasonal cycles. We find ourselves living both as cosmos and as cosmogenesis. In this context we ourselves have become something of a cosmic force. If formerly we lived in a thoroughly understood, ever renewing sequence of seasonal change, we now see ourselves both as the consequence of a long series of irreversible transformations and as a determining force in the present transformation that the earth is experiencing.

As happened at the moment when the amount of free oxygen in the atmosphere threatened to rise beyond its proper proportion and so destroy all living beings, so now awesome forces are let loose over the earth. This time, however, the cause is from an industrial economy that is disturbing the geological structure and life-systems of the planet in a manner and to an extent that the earth has never known previously. Many of the most elaborate expressions of life and grandeur and beauty that the planet has known are now threatened. All this is a consequence of human activity.

So severe and so irreversible is this deterioration that we might well believe those who tell us that we have only a brief period in which to reverse the devastation that is settling over the earth. Only recently has the deep pathos of the earth's situation begun to sink into our consciousness. While we might exult in our scientific and technological achievements, we must also experience some foreboding, lest through our industrial uses of these same scientific and technological processes we reduce the wonder and beauty as well as the nourishing capacities of the earth. We might lose the finest experiences that come to us through all those wondrous forms of life expression as well as the sources of the food, clothing, and shelter that we depend on for our survival.

It is tragic to see all those entrancing forms of life expressions imperiled so wantonly, forms that came into being during the past sixty-five million years, the lyric moment of the earth's development. Yet as so often occurred in the past, the catastrophic moments are also creative moments. We come to appreciate the gifts that the earth has given us.

Such is the context in which we must view this transition period into the twenty-first century as a moment of grace. A unique opportunity has arisen, for if the challenge is so absolute, the possibilities are equally comprehensive. We have identified the difficulties but also the opportunities of what is before us. A comprehensive change of consciousness is coming over the human community, especially in the industrial nations of the world. For the first time since the industrial age began we have a profound critique of its devastation, a certain withdrawal in dismay at what is happening, along with an enticing view of the possibilities before us.

Much of this is new. Yet all during the last few decades of the twentieth century, studies gave us precise information on what we must do. A long list of persons, projects, institutions, research programs, and publications indicated that something vital was happening. A younger generation is growing up with greater awareness of the need for a mutually enhancing mode of human presence to the earth. We have even been told that concern for the environment must become "the central organizing principle of civilization."[1]

The story of the universe is now being told by scientists as the epic story of evolution. We begin to understand our human identity with all the other modes of existence that constitute with us the single, universal community. The one story includes us all. We are cousins to one another. Every being is intimately present to and immediately influences every other being.

We see quite clearly that what happens to the nonhuman happens to the human. What happens to the outer world happens to the inner world. If the outer world is diminished in its grandeur, then the emotional, imaginative, intellectual, and spiritual life of the human is diminished or extinguished. Without the soaring birds, the great forests, the sounds and coloration of the insects, the free-flowing streams, the flowering fields, the sight of the clouds by day and the stars by night, we become impoverished in all that makes us human.

There is now developing a profound mystique of the natural world. Beyond the technical comprehension of what is happening and the directions in which we need to change, we now experience the deep mysteries of existence through the wonders of the world about us. This experience has been considerably advanced through the writings of natural-history essayists who have presented with the literary skill and interpretative depth appropriate to the subject our full entrancement with various natural phenomena. This is true especially in the writings of Loren Eiseley, who has recovered for us in this century the full wonder of the natural world about us. He has continued the vision of the universe as presented in the nineteenth century by Ralph Waldo Emerson, Henry David Thoreau, Emily Dickinson, and John Muir.

We are now experiencing a moment of significance far beyond what any of us can imagine. What can be said is that the foundations of a new historical period, the Ecozoic Era, have been established in every realm of human affairs. The mythic vision has been set into place. The distorted dream of an industrial technological paradise is being replaced by the more viable dream of a mutually enhancing human presence within an ever renewing, organic-based earth community. The dream drives the action. In the larger cultural context the dream becomes the myth that both guides and drives the action.

But even as we make our transition into this new century we must note that moments of grace are transient. The transformation must take place within a brief period, otherwise it is gone forever. In the immense story of the universe, that so many of these dangerous moments have been navigated successfully is some indication that the universe is for us rather than against us. We need only summon these forces to our support in order to succeed. Although the human challenge to these purposes must never be underestimated, it is difficult to believe that the larger purposes of the universe or of the planet Earth will ultimately be thwarted.

Thomas Berry, a Passionist priest, is a cultural historian who directed the graduate program at Fordham University from 1966 to 1979 and founded and directed the Riverdale Center of Religious Research. His published works include *The Dream of the Earth, The Universe Story*, with Brian Schwimme, *Befriending the Earth, The Great Work: Our Way into the Future*, and *Evening Thoughts: Reflecting on Earth as Sacred Community*.

Note

1. Al Gore, *Earth in the Balance* (Boston: Houghton Mifflin, 1992), 269.

CHRISTIANITY AND THE SURVIVAL OF CREATION

WENDELL BERRY

THIS ESSAY WAS DELIVERED AS A LECTURE at the Southern Baptist
Theological Seminary in Louisville, Kentucky, in 1992.

> And of Joseph he said:
> Blessed of the LORD be his land,
> for the precious things of heaven, for the dew,
> and for the deep that coucheth beneath,
> and for the precious fruits brought forth by the sun,
> and for the precious things put forth by the moon,
> and for the chief things of the ancient mountains,
> and for the precious things of the lasting hills,
> and for the precious things of the earth and fulness thereof,
> and for the good will of him that dwelt in the bush. **(Deut 33:13–16)**[1]

◈

> The earth is the LORD's, and the fulness thereof; the world and they
> that dwell therein. **(Ps 24:1)**

◈

I

I confess that I have not invariably been comfortable in front of a pulpit; I have never been comfortable behind one. To be behind a pulpit is always a forcible reminder to me that I am an essayist and, in many ways, a dissenter. An essayist is a writer who attempts to tell the truth. Preachers must resign themselves to being either right or wrong; an essayist, when proved wrong, may claim to have been "just practicing." An essayist is privileged to speak without institutional authorization. A dissenter, of course, must speak without privilege.

I want to begin with a problem, namely, that the culpability of Christianity in the destruction of the natural world and the uselessness of Christianity in any effort to correct that destruction are now established clichés of the conservation movement. This is a problem for two reasons.

First, the indictment of Christianity by the anti-Christian conservationists is, in many respects, just. For instance, the complicity of Christian priests, preachers, and missionaries in the cultural destruction and the economic exploitation of the primary peoples of the Western Hemisphere, as of traditional cultures around the world, is notorious. Throughout the five hundred years since Columbus's first landfall in the Bahamas, the evangelist has walked beside the conqueror and the merchant, too often blandly assuming that their causes were the same. Christian organizations to this day remain largely indifferent to the rape and plunder of the world and of its traditional cultures. It is hardly too much to say that most Christian organizations are as happily indifferent to the ecological, cultural, and religious implications of industrial economics as are most industrial organizations. The certified Christian seems just as likely as anyone else to join the military-industrial conspiracy to murder creation.

The conservationist indictment of Christianity is a problem, second, because, however just it may be, it does not come from an adequate understanding of the Bible and the cultural traditions that descend from the Bible. The anti-Christian conservationists characteristically deal with the Bible by waving it off. And this dismissal conceals an ignorance that invalidates it. The Bible is an inspired book written by human hands; as such, it is certainly subject to criticism. Our predicament now, I believe, requires us to learn to read and understand the Bible in the light of the present fact of creation. I have attempted to read the Bible with these issues in mind, and I see some virtually catastrophic discrepancies between biblical instruction and Christian behavior. I do not mean disreputable Christian behavior either. The discrepancies I see are between biblical instruction and the allegedly respectable Christian behavior of those peoples supposed to have been biblically instructed.

If because of these discrepancies Christianity were dismissible, there would, of course, be no problem. We could simply dismiss it, along with the twenty centuries of unsatisfactory history attached to it, and start setting things aright. The problem emerges only when we ask, Where then would we turn for instruction? We might, let us suppose, turn to another religion—a recourse that is sometimes suggested by the anti-Christian conservationists. Buddhism, for example, is certainly a religion that could guide us toward a right respect for the natural world, our fellow humans, and our fellow creatures. I owe a considerable debt myself to Buddhism and Buddhists. But there are an enormous number of people—and I am one of them— whose native religion, for better or worse, is Christianity. We were born to it; we began to learn about it before we became conscious; it is, whatever we think of it, an intimate part of our being; it informs our consciousness, our language, and our dreams. We can turn away from it or against it, but a better possibility is that this, our native religion, should survive and renew itself so that it may become as largely and truly instructive as we need it to be. On such a survival and renewal of the Christian religion may depend the survival of the creation that is its subject.

II

If we read the Bible, keeping in mind the desirability of the survival both of Christianity and the creation, we are apt to discover several things about which modern Christian organizations have kept remarkably quiet or to which they have paid little attention.

We will discover that we humans do not own the world or any part of it: "The earth is the LORD's, and the fulness thereof; the world and they that dwell therein." There is in our human law, undeniably, the concept and right of land ownership. But this, I think, is merely an expedient to safeguard the mutual belonging of people and places without which there can be no lasting and conserving human communities. This right of human ownership is limited by mortality and by natural constraints on human attention and responsibility; it quickly becomes abusive when used to justify large accumulations of "real estate," and perhaps for that reason such large accumulations are forbidden in the twenty-fifth chapter of Leviticus. In biblical terms, the "landowner" is the guest and steward of God: "The land is mine; for ye are strangers and sojourners with me" (Lev 25:23).

We will discover that God made not only the parts of creation that we humans understand and approve but all of it: "All things were made by him; and without him was not any thing made that was made" (John 1:3). And so we must credit God with the making of biting and stinging insects, poisonous serpents, weeds, poisonous weeds, dangerous beasts, and disease-causing microorganisms. That we may disapprove of these things does not mean that God is in error or that he ceded some of the work of creation to Satan; it means that we are deficient in wholeness, harmony, and understanding— that is, we are "fallen."

We will discover that God found the world, as he made it, to be good, that he made it for his pleasure, and that he continues to love it and to find it worthy, despite its reduction and corruption by us. People who quote John 3:16 as an easy formula for getting to heaven neglect to see the great difficulty implied in the statement that the advent of Christ was made possible by God's love for the world—not God's love for heaven or for the world as it might be but for the world as it was and is. Belief in Christ is thus dependent on prior belief in the inherent goodness—the lovability—of the world.

We will discover that the creation is not in any sense independent of the Creator, the result of a primal creative act long over and done with, but is the continuous, constant participation of all creatures in the being of God. Elihu says to Job that if God "gather unto himself his spirit and his breath; all flesh shall perish together" (Job 34:14–15). And Psalm 104 says, "Thou sendest forth thy spirit, they are created" (Ps 104:30). Creation is thus God's presence in creatures. Greek Orthodox theologian Philip Sherrard has written that "Creation is nothing less than the manifestation of God's hidden Being."[2] This means that we and all other creatures live by a sanctity that is inexpressibly intimate, for to every creature the gift of life is a portion of the breath and spirit of God. As the poet George Herbert put it:

Thou art in small things great, not small in any.

For thou art infinite in one and all.[3]

We will discover that, for these reasons, our destruction of nature is not just bad stewardship, or stupid economics, or a betrayal of family responsibility; it is the most horrid blasphemy. It is flinging God's gifts into his face, as if they were of no worth beyond that assigned to them by our destruction of them. To Dante, "despising Nature and her goodness" was violence against God.[4] We have no entitlement from the Bible to exterminate or permanently destroy or hold in contempt anything on the earth or in the heavens above it or in the waters beneath it. We have the right to use the gifts of nature but not to ruin or waste them. We have the right to use what we need but no more, which is why the Bible forbids usury and great accumulations of property. The usurer, Dante said, "condemns Nature . . . for he puts his hope elsewhere."[5]

William Blake was biblically correct, then, when he said that "everything that lives is holy." And Blake's great commentator Kathleen Raine was correct both biblically and historically when she said that "the sense of the holiness of life is the human norm."[6]

The Bible leaves no doubt at all about the sanctity of the act of world making, or of the world that was made, or of creaturely or bodily life in this world. We are holy creatures living among other holy creatures in a world that is holy. Some people know this, and some do not. Nobody, of course, knows it all the time. But what keeps it from being far better known than it is? Why is it apparently unknown to millions of professed students of the Bible? How can modern Christianity have so solemnly folded its hands while so much of the work of God was and is being destroyed?

III

Obviously, "the sense of the holiness of life" is not compatible with an exploitive economy. You cannot know that life is holy if you are content to live from economic practices that daily destroy life and diminish its possibility. And many if not most Christian organizations now appear to be perfectly at peace with the military-industrial economy and its "scientific" destruction of life. Surely, if we are to remain free and if we are to remain true to our religious inheritance, we must maintain a separation between church and state. But if we are to maintain any sense of coherence or meaning in our lives, we cannot tolerate the present utter disconnection between religion and economy. By "economy" I do not mean "economics," which is the study of moneymaking, but rather the ways of human house-keeping, the ways by which the human household is situated and maintained within the household of nature. To be uninterested in economy is to be uninterested in the practice of religion; it is to be uninterested in culture and in character.

Probably the most urgent question now faced by people who would adhere to the Bible is this: What sort of economy would be responsible to the holiness of life? What, for Christians, would be the economy, the practices and the restraints, of "right livelihood"? I do not believe that organized Christianity now has any idea. I think its idea of a Christian economy is no more or less than the industrial economy, which is an economy firmly founded on the seven deadly sins and the breaking of all ten of the Ten Commandments. Obviously, if Christianity is going to survive as more than a respecter and comforter of profitable iniquities, then Christians, regardless of their organizations, are going to have to interest themselves in economy—which is to say, in nature and in work. They are going to have to give workable answers to those who say we cannot live without this economy that is destroying us and our world, who see the murder of creation as the only way of life.

The holiness of life is obscured to modern Christians also by the idea that the only holy place is the built church. This idea may be more taken for granted than taught; nevertheless, Christians are encouraged from childhood to think of the church building as "God's house," and most of them could think of their houses or farms or shops or factories as holy places only with great effort and embarrassment. It is understandably difficult for modern Americans to think of their dwellings and workplaces as holy, because most of these are, in fact, places of desecration that are deeply involved in the ruin of creation.

The idea of the exclusive holiness of church buildings is, of course, wildly incompatible with the idea, which the churches also teach, that God is present in all places to hear prayers. It is incompatible with Scripture. The idea that a human artifact could contain or confine God was explicitly repudiated by Solomon in his prayer at the dedication of the temple: "Behold, the heaven and heaven of heavens cannot contain thee; how much less this house that I have builded?" (1 Kgs 8:27). And these words of Solomon were remembered a thousand years later by Paul, preaching at Athens: "God that made the world and all things therein, seeing that he is Lord of heaven and earth, dwelleth not in temples made with hands. . . . For in him we live, and move, and have our being" (Acts 17:24, 28).

Idolatry always reduces to the worship of something "made with hands," something confined within the terms of human work and human comprehension. Thus, Solomon and Paul both insisted on the largeness and the at-largeness of God, setting him free, so to speak, from *ideas* about him. He is not to be fenced in, under human control, like some domestic creature; he is the wildest being in existence. The presence of his spirit in us is our wildness, our oneness with the wilderness of creation. That is why subduing the things of nature to human purposes is so dangerous and why it so often results in evil, separation, and desecration. It is why the poets of our tradition so often have given nature the role not only of mother or grandmother but of the highest earthly teacher and judge, a figure of mystery and great power. Jesus' own specifications for his church have nothing at all to do with masonry and carpentry but only with people; his church is "where two or three are gathered together in my name" (Matt 18:20).

The Bible gives exhaustive (and sometimes exhausting) attention to the organization of religion: the building and rebuilding of the temple; its furnishings; the orders, duties, and paraphernalia of the priesthood; the orders of rituals and ceremonies. But that does not disguise the fact that the most significant religious events recounted in the Bible do not occur in "temples made with hands." The most important religion in that book is unorganized and is sometimes profoundly disruptive of organization. From Abraham to Jesus, the most important people are not priests but shepherds, soldiers, property owners, workers, housewives, queens and kings, manservants and maidservants, fishermen, prisoners, whores, even bureaucrats. The great visionary encounters do not take place in temples but in sheep pastures, in the desert, in the wilderness, on mountains, on the shores of rivers and seas, in the middle of the sea, in prisons. And however strenuously the divine voice prescribed rites and observances, it just as strenuously repudiated them when they were taken to be religion:

> Your new moons and your appointed feasts my soul hateth: they are a trouble unto me; I am weary to bear them.
>
> And when ye spread forth your hands, I will hide mine eyes from you; yea, when ye make many prayers, I will not hear: your hands are full of blood.

Wash ye, make you clean; put away the evil of your doings from before mine eyes; cease to do evil;

learn to do well; seek judgment, relieve the oppressed, judge the fatherless, plead for the widow. (Isa 1:14–17)

Religion, according to this view, is less to be celebrated in rituals than practiced in the world.

I do not think it is enough appreciated how much an outdoor book the Bible is. It is a "hypaethral book," such as Thoreau talked about—a book open to the sky. It is best read and understood outdoors, and the farther outdoors the better. At least, that has been my experience of it. Passages that within walls seem improbable or incredible, outdoors seem merely natural. This is because outdoors we are everywhere confronted with wonders; we see that the miraculous is not extraordinary, but the common mode of existence. It is our daily bread. Whoever really has considered the lilies of the field or the birds of the air and pondered the improbability of their existence in this warm world within the cold and empty stellar distances will hardly balk at the turning of water into wine—which was, after all, a very small miracle. We forget the greater and still continuing miracle by which water (with soil and sunlight) is turned into grapes.

It is clearly impossible to assign holiness exclusively to the built church without denying holiness to the rest of creation, which is then said to be "secular." The world, which God looked at and found entirely good, we find none too good to pollute entirely and destroy piecemeal. The church, then, becomes a kind of preserve of "holiness," from which certified lovers of God assault and plunder the "secular" earth.

Not only does this repudiate God's approval of his work; it refuses also to honor the Bible's explicit instruction to regard the works of the creation as God's revelation of himself. The assignation of holiness exclusively to the built church is therefore logically accompanied by the assignation of revelation exclusively to the Bible. But Psalm 19 begins, "The heavens declare the glory of God;

and the firmament showeth his handiwork" (Ps 19:1). The word of God has been revealed in facts from the moment of the third verse of the first chapter of Genesis: "Let there be light: and there was light" (Gen 1:3). And Paul states the rule: "The invisible things of him from the creation of the world are clearly seen, being understood by the things that are made" (Rom 1:20). Yet from this free, generous, and sensible view of things, we come to the idolatry of the book: the idea that nothing is true that cannot be (and has not been already) written. The misuse of the Bible thus logically accompanies the abuse of nature: if you are going to destroy creatures without respect, you will want to reduce them to "materiality"; you will want to deny that there is spirit or truth in them, just as you will want to believe that the only holy creatures, the only creatures with souls, are humans—or even only Christian humans.

By denying spirit and truth to the nonhuman creation, modern proponents of religion have legitimized a form of blasphemy without which the nature- and culture-destroying machinery of the industrial economy could not have been built—that is, they have legitimized bad work. Good human work honors God's work. Good work uses no thing without respect, both for what it is in itself and for its origin. It uses neither tool nor material that it does not respect and that it does not love. It honors nature as a great mystery and power, as an indispensable teacher, and as the inescapable judge of all work of human hands. It does not dissociate life and work, or pleasure and work, or love and work, or usefulness and beauty. To work without pleasure or affection, to make a product that is not both useful and beautiful, is to dishonor God, nature, the thing that is made, and whomever it is made for. This is blasphemy: to make shoddy work of the work of God. But such blasphemy is not possible when the entire creation is understood as holy and when the works of God are understood as embodying and thus revealing his spirit.

In the Bible we find none of the industrialist's contempt or hatred for nature. We find, instead, a poetry of awe and reverence and profound cherishing, as in these verses from Moses' valedictory blessing of the twelve tribes:

And of Joseph he said,
Blessed of the LORD be his land,
for the precious things of heaven, for the dew,
and for the deep that coucheth beneath,
and for the precious fruits brought forth by the sun,
and for the precious things put forth by the moon,
and for the chief things of the ancient mountains,
and for the precious things of the lasting hills,
and for the precious things of the earth and fulness thereof,
and for the good will of him that dwelt in the bush.
(Deut 33:13-16)

IV

I have been talking about a dualism that manifests itself in several ways—that is, as a cleavage, a radical discontinuity, between Creator and creature, spirit and matter, religion and nature, religion and economy, worship and work, and so on. This dualism, I think, is the most destructive disease that afflicts us. In its best known, its most dangerous, and perhaps its fundamental version, it is the dualism of body and soul. This is an issue as difficult as it is important.

The crucial test of a dualism of body and soul is probably Genesis 2:7, which gives the process by which Adam was created: "The LORD God formed man of the dust of the ground, and breathed into his nostrils the breath of life; and man became a living soul." My mind, like the minds of most people, has been deeply influenced by dualism, and I can see how dualistic minds deal with this verse. They conclude that the formula for man-making is man = body + soul. But that conclusion cannot be derived, except by violence, from Genesis 2:7, which is not dualistic. The formula given here is not man = body + soul; the formula here is soul = dust + breath. According to this verse, God did not make a body and put a soul into it, like a letter into an envelope. He formed man of dust, and then by breathing his breath into it, he made the dust live. The dust, formed as man and made to live, did not *embody* a soul; it *became* a soul. "Soul" here refers to the whole creature. Humanity is thus presented to us, in Adam, not as a creature of two discrete parts temporarily glued together, but as a single mystery.

We can see how easy it is to fall into the dualism of body and soul when talking about the inescapable worldly dualities of good and evil or time and eternity. And we can see how easy it is, when Jesus asks, "For what is a man profited, if he shall gain the whole world, and lose his own soul?" (Matt 16:26), to assume that he is condemning the world and appreciating the disembodied soul. But if we give to "soul" here the sense that it has in Genesis 2:7, we see that he is doing no such thing. He is warning that in pursuit of so-called material possessions, we can lose our understanding of ourselves as "living souls"—that is, as creatures of God, members of the holy community of creation. We can lose the possibility of the atonement of that membership. For we are free, if we choose, to make a duality of our one living soul by disowning the breath of God that is our fundamental bond with one another and with other creatures.

But we can make the same duality by disowning the dust. The breath of God is only one of the divine gifts that make us living souls; the other is the dust. Most of our modern troubles come from misunderstanding and misvaluation of this dust. Forgetting that dust, too, is a creature of the Creator, made by the sending forth of his spirit, we have presumed to decide that the dust is "low." We have presumed to say that we are made of two parts: a body and a soul, the body being "low" because it is made of dust, and the soul "high." By thus valuing these supposed-to-be parts, we inevitably throw them into competition with each other, like two corporations. The "spiritual" view, of course, has been that the body, in Yeats's phrase, "must be bruised to pleasure soul." The "secular" version of the same dualism has been that the body, along with the rest of the material world, must give way for the advance of the human mind. For a long time, the dominant religious view has been that the body is a kind of scrip issued by the Great Company Store in the Sky, which can be cashed in to redeem the soul but is otherwise worthless. And the predictable result has been a human creature able to appreciate or tolerate only the "spiritual" (or mental) part of creation and full of semiconscious hatred of the "physical" or "natural" part, which it is ready and willing to destroy for "salvation," for profit, for "victory," or for fun. This madness constitutes the norm of modern humanity and of modern Christianity.

But to despise the body or mistreat it for the sake of the "soul" is not just to burn one's house for the insurance, nor is it just self-hatred of the most deep and dangerous sort. It is yet another blasphemy. It is to make nothing—and worse than nothing—of the great Something in which we live and move and have our being. When we hate and abuse the body and its earthly life and joy for heaven's sake, what do we expect? That out of this life that we have presumed to despise and this world that we have presumed to destroy we would somehow salvage a soul capable of eternal bliss? And what do we expect when with equal and opposite ingratitude we try to make of the finite body an infinite reservoir of dispirited and meaningless pleasures?

V

Despite its protests to the contrary, modern Christianity has become willy-nilly the religion of the state and the economic status quo. Because it has been so exclusively dedicated to incanting anemic souls into heaven, it has been made the tool of much earthly villainy. It has, for the most part, stood silently by while a predatory economy has ravaged the world, destroyed its natural beauty and health, divided and plundered its human communities and households. It has flown the flag and chanted the slogans of empire. It has assumed with the economists that "economic forces" automatically work for good and has assumed with the industrialists and militarists that technology determines history. It has assumed with almost everybody that "progress" is good, that it is good to be modern and up with the times. It has admired Caesar and comforted him in his depredations and defaults. But in its de facto alliance with Caesar, Christianity connives directly in the murder of creation. For in these days, Caesar is no longer a mere destroyer of armies, cities, and nations. He is a contradictor of the fundamental miracle of life. A part of the normal practice of his power is his willingness to destroy the world. He prays, he says, and churches everywhere compliantly pray with him. But he is praying to a God whose works he is prepared at any moment to destroy. What could be more wicked than that, or more mad?

The religion of the Bible, on the contrary, is a religion of the state and the status quo only in brief moments. In practice, it is a religion for the correction equally of people and of kings. And Christ's life, from the manger to the cross, was an affront to the established powers of his time, just as it is to the established powers of our time. Much is made in churches of the "good news" of the Gospels. Less is said of the Gospels' bad news, which is that Jesus would have been horrified by just about every "Christian" government the world has ever seen. He would be horrified by our government and its works, and it would be horrified by him. Surely no sane and thoughtful person can imagine any government of our time sitting comfortably at the feet of Jesus while he is saying, "Love your enemies, bless them that curse you, do good to them that hate you, and pray for them which despitefully use you, and persecute you" (Matt 5:44).

In fact, we know that one of the businesses of governments, "Christian" or not, has been to reenact the crucifixion. It has happened again and again and again. In *A Time for Trumpets*, his history of the Battle of the Bulge, Charles B. MacDonald tells how SS colonel Joachim Peiper was forced to withdraw from a bombarded château near the town of La Gleize, leaving behind a number of severely wounded soldiers of both armies. "Also left behind," MacDonald wrote, "on a whitewashed wall of one of the rooms in the basement was a charcoal drawing of Christ, thorns on his head, tears on his cheeks—whether drawn by a German or an American nobody would ever know."[7] This is not an image that belongs to history but rather one that judges it.

Wendell Berry taught in New York and California before returning to his native Kentucky, where for several decades he has lived and worked on his one hundred and twenty-five acre farm. He is the recipient of numerous fellowships and awards. He has authored many books of fiction, poetry, and social commentary, including *What Are People For?*, *The Unsettling of America: Culture and Agriculture*, *Sex, Economy, Freedom, and Community*, and *A Place on Earth: A Novel*.

Notes

1. Scripture quotations in this essay are from the King James Version.
2. Philip Sherrard, *Human Image: World Image* (Ipswich, England: Golgonooza Press, 1992), 152.
3. George Herbert, "Providence," in *The Poems of George Herbert*, ed. Helen Gardner (London: Oxford University Press, 1961), 54.
4. Dante Alighieri, *Inferno*, trans. Charles S. Singleton (Princeton, NJ: Princeton University Press, 1970) , canto 11, lines 46–48.
5. Ibid., lines 109–11.
6. Kathleen Raine, Golgonooza: City of Imagination (Ipswich, Suffolk, England: Golgonooza Press, 1991), 28.
7. Charles B. MacDonald, *A Time for Trumpets* (New York: Bantam, 1984), 458.

JESUS VISITS THE ZOO
A Sermon for Children and Adults

ELIZABETH BETTENHAUSEN

THE PURPOSE OF THIS SERMON is to make us wonder how we humans, children and adults alike, might live humbly and justly with all of God's creation.

> All who exalt themselves will be humbled, and those who humble themselves will be exalted. **(Luke 14:11)**

◇

Very early one morning, when the summer sun was just coming up, Jesus got out of bed and walked to the zoo. The animals were waking up, too. The peacocks were fluffing their blue and green and purple feathers. "Hi, peacocks!" said Jesus. "How are you?"

"Hi, Jesus!" said the peacocks. "We're fine." Their beautiful tails opened wide.

Jesus smiled a wide smile and said, "Let's walk together."

So they walked and talked, and soon they came to beautiful rolling stripes of black and white lying on the grass. "Who is looking so good?" called the peacocks.

The zebras opened their eyes and laughed. "We heard you coming, peacocks. Hi, Jesus!"

Jesus said, "Hi, zebras! How are you this morning?"

"Frisky!" said the zebras. "May we come along?"

"Sure!" replied Jesus and the peacocks. The zebras started a flowing, bouncing black and white dance right ahead of them.

"We can do that," said the peacocks. They joined the zebra dance. Jesus did, too.

Soon they came to the huge rocks where the lions lived. "O lions, would you dance with us?" called the zebras.

"Great invitation!" roared the lions. "Hi, Jesus!"

Jesus said, "Hi, lions! How are you this morning?"

"Flexible and full," said the lions. They strode to join the zebras and peacocks and Jesus in the flowing, bouncing dance.

The boa constrictor heard them, yawned, and crawled out onto a big tree branch to watch them dance along. "Hi, big boa!" roared the lions. "Would you like to ride along in our dance?"

"An expansive idea," said the boa. "Hi, Jesus!"

Jesus said, "Hi, boa! How are you this morning?"

"Fluid," said the boa and smiled happily as it crawled down the tree and up on the lion's back. The boa and the lions and the zebras and the peacocks and Jesus danced along in a flowing, bouncing dance.

Soon they came to the gorillas' trees and rocks. "Uh oh," said the boa, looking from high on the lion's head. The gorillas were talking together in a very serious way.

Jesus called to them. "Hi, gorillas! How are you this morning?"

The gorillas looked up. "Hi, Jesus. We are fervent this morning!"

"Hmm," said Jesus slowly. "Do fervent gorillas dance?"

"Of course gorillas dance, Jesus," said the gorillas, "but not this morning."

"Why not?" asked the boa.

"The dancing is flowing, bouncing pleasure," called the lions.

"We are glad you are enjoying it," said the gorillas. "But we are not in the mood."

"Did you have a bad night's sleep?" asked the zebras.

"Was it full of crickets' loud clicking?" asked the peacocks.

"No," said the gorillas. "We had a deep sleep and are full of energy this morning. That is why we are talking today."

"Talking about what?" the peacocks cried, getting a bit impatient.

"Leaving!" called the gorillas, and they pounded their fists on their chests.

"Leaving your cage?" the boa asked.

"Leaving the whole zoo!" said the gorillas, very, very seriously. "That is what we have always planned to do. And today is the day."

"That's like flying over the farthest, highest fence," a peacock whispered dreamily.

The zebras and lions started stretching their leg muscles. Jesus looked into the eyes of all the animals. Then he said, "Behind some bushes and trees the metal fence has a large hole."

"Let's go!" cried the gorillas.

"Yes!" the dancers all said, except for one peacock.

"What about the children?" the peacock asked. "They will come to visit, and we won't be here." Everyone grew still and thoughtful.

Then Jesus said, "I will write a note in the smooth sand at the playground." And he did. When the animals read the note they smiled and followed Jesus. They danced a flowing, bouncing, joyful dance to the hole in the fence and out of the zoo.

When the zoo opened that day, some children ran to the playground first. They saw the note Jesus had written in the smooth sand. What do you think happened then?

Living in California, Elizabeth Bettenhausen volunteers in the Grammar School, watches gray and humpback whales and western snowy plovers, and engages in the politics of a community of humans hollering for too much water. She used to teach Christian ethics, work for the Lutheran Church in America, and watch whales in the Atlantic.

IF NOT US, THEN WHO?

SALLY G. BINGHAM

THIS SERMON WAS FIRST PREACHED on Earth Sunday 2003. The message is a strong call to recognize that the two Great Commandments are the best mandate we have in Scripture for environmental stewardship. While there are many other biblical mandates, this one is the simplest and easiest to explain. People seem to get the idea that if you love your neighbor, you will not pollute his air or water. Furthermore, love for God and neighbor clearly belongs to people of faith.

> One of the scribes came near and heard them disputing with one another, and seeing that [Jesus] answered them well, he asked him, "Which commandment is the first of all?" Jesus answered, "The first is, 'Hear, O Israel: the Lord our God, the Lord is one; you shall love the Lord your God with all your heart, and with all your soul, and with all your mind, and with all your strength.' The second is this, 'You shall love your neighbor as yourself.' There is no other commandment greater than these." Then the scribe said to him,

"You are right, Teacher; you have truly said that 'he is one, and besides him there is no other'; and 'to love him with all the heart, and with all the understanding, and with all the strength,' and 'to love one's neighbor as oneself,'—this is much more important than all whole burnt offerings and sacrifices." When Jesus saw that he answered wisely, he said to him, "You are not far from the kingdom of God." After that no one dared to ask him any question. (Mark 12:28–34)

◈

Ecology is religious. There, I have said it! Everyone sit back. It is Earth Sunday, and this is the one Sunday each year when I can proclaim the good news of environmental ministry. Ecological issues are religious issues, and environmental issues are spiritual issues. Life is religious, and one's spiritual life is dependent upon a relationship with the Creator and with the creation. Without Creator and creation we have no life. All life is dependent upon the Creator in whom we live and move and have our being. The same is true with creation, for without a healthy ecological system we cannot live healthy lives. Without one we will not have the other.

In case you think that environmental issues do not belong in church—think again! If you are here today because you have a deep faith in God and consider yourself a Christian, then believe this: *You are an environmentalist.* You may not like the word *environmentalist,* because it often comes with baggage, but we can repack the baggage of the word to mean "a person who cares for others." If you do not want to be associated with environmentalism because it sounds liberal, democratic, and political, then call it something else. Call it "stewardship of creation." Call it "concern for future generations." Call it "mindfulness of one's behavior." Call it "loving others as I have loved you."

And remember, "In the beginning was the Word, and the Word was with God . . . and without him not one thing came into being" (John 1:1–3). Jesus was there "in the beginning." And all living things that came into being through the Word will also be reconciled to God through Jesus—not just you and me and other humans. *All things. All life.* Everything that God created and called "good." As Christians, you and I are called to be caretakers of God's creation. If we, the people who sit in pews and profess a love for God, do not care for God's creation, then who will? Care for creation is central to Christian faith. It belongs at the forefront, with love, justice, and peace. Care for creation is what we do when we obey the commandments to love God and love our neighbors as ourselves. Creation is not ours to exploit and to use up. Rather, creation is for us to preserve, nurture, and keep healthy for the next generations.

If you had not realized that your faith calls you to protect and love creation but you are willing at least to entertain the idea, then hold the thought. Here is something else to think about. The environmental community is not doing a very good job protecting creation. After thirty years, what might happen?

Listen to what one highly regarded environmental watchdog group has to say. According to the 2003 State of the World report by the Washington-based Worldwatch Institute, "The human race has only one, or perhaps two generations, to rescue itself." The report goes on to say that overuse of resources, pollution, and destruction of natural areas continue to threaten life on the planet, and conditions continue to deteriorate rapidly. Although there are some hopeful signs in regard to the fact that technical solutions to the problems have been found and—where there is political will—adopted, in most cases nothing is being done. The state of the world's natural life-support system is perhaps the most worrying indicator for the future, says the report. About 30 percent of the world's surviving forests are seriously fragmented or degraded, and they are being cut down at the rate of 50,000 square miles a year. Wetlands have been reduced by 50 percent over the last century. The State of the World report concludes with this statement: "The longer that no remedial action is taken, the greater the degree of misery and biological impoverishment that humankind must be prepared to accept."[1]

It is up to us, you and me and other communities of faith around this country, to take a leadership role in the protection of our land, air, and water, and consequently of our health as well. If people of faith do not take on this role, how can we expect others to? It is our responsibility. Remember that our baptismal vows denounce forces of evil that destroy creation.

We may not think that we matter, especially when the problems are not on our doorstep, but we do. Every one of us and every one of our behaviors matter. Our choices matter: the clothes we wear, the food we eat, the coffee we drink, the electricity we use, and the cars we drive. These behaviors all affect others, in many cases adversely.

Might we begin to live our lives in a way that shows our love for God? If we recognize God as the source and sustainer of everything, let us live that way. Some of us live in ways that suggest we care more about ourselves than our children or grandchildren. We can transform that behavior, however, and reflect our love for God and for each other by becoming aware of the ways in which our habits affect the world around us.

God loves us and God loves the creation, which, in many ways, was created to sustain us. Our role is to be in relationship with God in such a way that God, our Creator, might know our love. We live for God, do we not? Listen to this passage from the First Letter of John: "If we say that we have fellowship with him while we are walking in darkness, we lie and do not do what is true; but if we walk in the light as he himself is in the light, we have fellowship with one another, and the blood of Jesus his Son cleanses us from all sin" (1 John 1:6–7).

We must strive to make our relationship with God a harmonious one. If we walk in the light with one another and with all living things, we carry forth our faith. We must love the whooping crane and the forest for their own sake, not just for what they can do for us and not only for what use they are to us—use, yes, but exploit and plunder, no; sustainable use, conservation, and sharing rather than greed and hoarding.

We are destroying rainforests before we even know their value. Medicines and cures are being rapidly extinguished. As a young friend in Japan asked me at a conference, "Why do you adults destroy things that you don't know how to bring back?" She explained that she was raised not to take things apart if she did not know how to put them back together. I have to ask the same question: If God created these resources, do they not have a value in themselves? They could not have been created with the intention of being entirely destroyed. Were rivers meant to be damned or wetlands filled in?

Each of us has a working theology. Each of us has a place where we center ourselves on God, a place where God works through us. Our job is to live into that center. Some of our working theologies are in lesser developed stages than others. But if we live our lives for God, we do things that are pleasing to God. We love each other and we can, and mostly do, demonstrate such love in many different ways. Some people work with the homeless, some with the elderly and sick, some with children, some in prisons, and some of us are just nice people who are kind to strangers. Some pick up trash, and some feed the hungry. My working theology is to lead a life that demonstrates love of creation. In this way, I show my love for God; I drive a small car, have a compost pile in my backyard, walk when I can, reduce purchases of things I do not really need, and conserve both energy and water. What is your working theology? Where in your daily life do you show God your love?

If you have not found your niche, why not try showing God your love through living a sustainable lifestyle? Winston Churchill said, "We make a living by what we get; we make a life by what we give." Giving and loving God are what make us Christians. What good is it to be Christian if we do not in some way lead lives that show we are Christian? Leading by example is what Jesus called us to do. As Scripture says, "By this everyone will know that you are my disciples, if you have love for one another" (John 13:35). People will know us by the example we set.

Some of you may doubt the seriousness of environmental problems: global warming, the spread of disease, toxins in the water and particulates in the air, the high and rising rates of cancer and asthma. There will always be "doubting Thomases," but please do not be one. You can be one about other issues, but not about this issue. Do not wait until the hounds are at your door. You do not need to touch and feel what the scientists already know. Do not be afraid to believe them. The problems are real, and more study and delay will only allow things to get worse. According to the National Academy of Science, over 90 percent of the world's accredited scientists agree that human activities are destroying creation. They do not call it creation. For them, it is the planet, the living organism that sustains all life. For religious people, the earth is the body of God.

For religious people, the living organism that gives us life is the creation that God called "good" and gave us dominion over. This "dominion" is the same dominion that God has over us: one of love, compassion, and responsibility—not exploitation, pollution, and destruction.

Nature is different than it was when I was growing up. There are few places in the United States that we might call pristine. When we go hiking in the mountains now or enter a park to sit under a tree, we see soft drink cans or plastic bags. Trash covers our beaches and lies in the bottom of our rivers and streams, and once you see that bottle or can, the nature of nature is changed. When I am searching for signs of God in nature, I find the experience in some ways ruined by just one plastic bottle on the trail or in the bottom of a clear stream. The human footprint is everywhere—at least it seems to be so for me. I go into the wild for peace, for communion with the Divine, for a reminder of my relationship with God, and for quiet and to be alone. I seldom if ever find that anymore. There are snowmobiles racing through our national parks, airplanes and helicopters flying over, noise from cars, and, worst of all, the presence of trash everywhere. Is this love of God and neighbor?

There is hardly a natural anything left. We humans have our influence everywhere, and the most startling of all is what we are doing to the climate. We have influenced the climate. Fifty years ago no one would have thought that possible. Insurance companies can no longer claim that severe storms and falling trees are acts of God! The storm damage is the result of human behavior. The increase in carbon dioxide that we have put into the atmosphere has upset the balance that God put into place, and now the storms are far more severe and more frequent than ever before. We are influencing every aspect of what was once called nature or natural.

What this is leading up to is a question: If we destroy nature, what are we doing to our relationship with God? What does it mean when God is no longer in charge but we are? We have genetically engineered plants, cloned animals, changed the climate, and killed vast numbers of species that were sacred with their own intrinsic right to life. Bill McKibben, a writer and naturalist, asks, "Have we become God's equal in terms of what happens in the natural world or is there a natural world anymore?"[2]

I struggle with these issues, and I have no answers—only questions. And that really scares me, because I am a great fan of the theologian Paul Tillich, who said the answers are in the questions. If many of us are asking these kinds of questions, it implies that we are indeed destroying our natural world and ultimately ourselves.

What are we to do? For starters, do not doubt the seriousness of the ecological issues and the condition of the planet. Believe the scientists. Then let us start to live lives that demonstrate love for one another and love for God. We can do that by shifting what is in our own self-interest. Instead of the "bigger is better" and "more is better" attitudes, we can open our hearts to recognize the truth, namely, that more and bigger are not always better but are rather destructive and harmful, even to the owner. If we are going to look after ourselves, which most people seek to do, it is in our own interest to become conservationists.

It is most probably love that will transform us. If we can learn to love the natural world, we will protect it. And if we love one another, we will want future generations to share the bounty that we have had during our time here.

Let me share an experience I had last Friday afternoon. I left my office about six and went down to the recently restored wetland area by the bay. It had just stopped raining; the sky to the north was still stormy, but to the east the sun was out. The normally calm beach was being hit with medium-size waves, and the sound was wonderful. A large blue heron was standing like a statue in the lagoon. I walked along and took in all the amazing beauty around me. We are so blessed to live here. Our Presidio still has foxes and at least one coyote. I felt guilty taking in all the natural beauty that so few people get to see, much less live in the midst of. We can ski four hours away, surf, swim, bike on trails, hike within minutes of our homes, and do all this in such splendor. As I thought about what I would say to you today, it occurred to me that I should have rented a couple of buses and taken you all to a beautiful natural place and just asked you to love it and appreciate it. We do not harm what we love. If our hearts can be transformed to love what God has given us, we will become caretakers of the earth. We will become environmentalists. We will want to protect our air, land, and water, and we will become informed as to how to do that.

So let us bring our religious lives, our faith, and the natural world together into a working theology. Make the connection between ecology and faith and become a steward of creation, a good neighbor, a person who cares about the legacy we leave for the next generations, and, *without shame*, become an environmentalist. Practice the two great commandments—loving God and loving our neighbors as ourselves. If not us, then who?

Sally G. Bingham is pastor of environmental ministry at Grace Episcopal Cathedral in San Francisco and chair of the Episcopal Diocesan Commission on the Environment. She serves on the San Francisco Commission on the Environment and for two decades has been on the board of the Environmental Defense Fund. She is founder and director of the Regeneration Project, a nonprofit ministry responding to global warming that has been replicated in a number of states.

Notes

1. *State of the World: A Worldwatch Institute Report on Progress Toward a Sustainable World* (New York: W.W. Norton, 2003.), ed. Linda Starke.
2. Bill McKibben, *The End of Nature* (New York: Random House, 1989).

CONVERSION TO ECO-JUSTICE

MARGARET BULLITT-JONAS

THE REV. ROBERT W. TOBIN, rector of Christ Church (Cambridge, Massachusetts), invited me to preach on Earth Sunday 2004 on the theological foundations for earth care. The sermon's focus was on how a Christian becomes converted to eco-justice. The sermon sprang from my effort to make sense of my own spiritual journey. In May 2001, I was arrested in front of the Department of Energy in Washington, DC, during an interfaith prayer vigil to protest President Bush's energy policy and his intention to drill for oil in the Arctic National Wildlife Refuge. My decision to participate in non-violent civil disobedience came as a surprise to me. I am not "the type." I am an Episcopal priest. I lead retreats and teach courses on prayer. By temperament I am a peacemaker and reconciler. When a photograph of me being led away in handcuffs showed up in the *Boston Globe*, more than one startled person commented, "You're the *last* person I would have thought would get arrested!" In the end, you never know where God will lead you, but maybe the pattern of our journeys to eco-justice does have a recognizable shape. I hope that my sermon moves its readers to consider their own process of conversion and that it provides a theological underpinning that can sustain the work of eco-justice for the long haul.[1]

> Just after daybreak, Jesus stood on the beach; but the disciples did not know that it was Jesus. Jesus said to them, "Children, you have no fish, have you?" **(John 21:4–5)**

❖

> Meanwhile Saul, still breathing threats and murder against the disciples of the Lord, went to the high priest and asked him for letters to the synagogues at Damascus, so that if he found any who belonged to the Way, men or women, he might bring them bound to Jerusalem. Now as he was going along and approaching Damascus, suddenly a light from heaven flashed around him. He fell to the ground and heard a voice saying to him, "Saul, Saul, why do you persecute me?" **(Acts 9:1–4)**

❖

Every year, countless congregations across the country celebrate Earth Week by setting aside a Sunday to focus on God's creation. The truth is, I have not always been a big fan of Earth Day. I used to think of Earth Day as being kind of retro—a quaint throwback to the time when I was young and foolish and wore tie-dyed shirts and bell-bottoms. I used to think that Earth Day was for tree huggers, people who liked tinkering with solar-powered contraptions, or people who dreamed of living on a farm. Surely we had outgrown all that, I would tell myself—we who had entered the modern, electronic age in which most of us live in cities and are too busy and stressed-out raising families and working long hours to waste time on secondary things. Earth Day was for sentimental types. I had better things to do.

Today I look back on my supposedly sophisticated point of view as completely naïve. The environmental crisis has made me acutely aware of our dependence on clean air and healthy soil and our interdependence with all living beings. There is nothing sentimental about being alarmed that fully a quarter of the world's animal and plant species may be driven into extinction just a few decades from now. There is nothing sentimental about being upset that so many kids in inner cities now suffer from asthma caused by air pollution. There is nothing sentimental about being shocked that the rise of only a single degree in average worldwide temperatures—when a much greater rise is forecast in the years ahead—is already heating the deep oceans, melting glaciers, causing lethal floods and droughts, and changing patterns of bird migration.

In the Gospel of John, the risen Christ appears on the seashore and asks a poignant question as he watches his troubled disciples try in vain to catch some fish: "Children, you have no fish, have you?" The truth is, often enough *we* do not have fish. The United States Commission on Ocean Policy reports that pollution, overfishing, and poor management are jeopardizing the health of North America's oceans. Too often the fish we do have are contaminated with toxic chemicals like PCP or mercury. And it is not just fish stocks that are being rapidly depleted; researchers warn that human beings are gobbling up the world's natural resources so fast that at current population trends and rates of exploitation, by the year 2050 we will need two earths to cope with the demand.

No, it is not sentimentality that leads us to honor Earth Day and to care about the fate of the planet; it is hardheaded realism. We have no future if we poison, deplete, and destroy the very ecosystem on which our life depends.

The question that I have been wrestling with for several years is this: What needs to happen inside us in order for us to place care for the earth at the center of our moral and spiritual concern? What deep change in perspective, what significant shift in values, must we experience before we become willing to offer ourselves to the great work of healing the earth? Such a conversion makes a person like me turn from pooh-poohing Earth Day to cherishing it as a day to lift up our conviction that God loves the world God made and that

God calls us to be partners in the work of environmental justice and healing. Our conversion to eco-justice may or may not be as dramatic as what Saul experienced on the road to Damascus, but it can certainly go as deep, challenging us to a radical reorientation of our lives.

For Christians, "eco-conversion" often involves three steps or stages. The first stage, *creation*, is when we fall in love with the beauty of God's creation. We experience amazement, gratefulness, wonder, and awe. In this first stage of the journey, we discover how loved we are as creatures made in the image of God and connected by breath, blood, bone, and flesh to the whole of God's creation.

I do not take this first step for granted. It is a huge discovery to experience creation as sacred. I for one grew up in a city, and to some degree we city-dwellers are cut off from the natural world. We cannot see the stars at night; we cannot hear the spring peepers. Here in Boston our water may come from a source a hundred miles distant and our food from places six or seven thousand miles away. "Nature" can become an abstraction, nothing more than the weather that does or does not get in my way as I hurry into my car and drive from one building to the next.

What's more, many of us—as I did—grew up in a family riddled with addiction. Or we developed an addiction of our own. If you have ever been close to an addict, you know that addiction functions to disconnect us from the needs and rhythms of the body. In my own years of addiction, I paid no attention to my body's signals. I not only ignored my body—I openly defied it. It did not matter whether I was tired, sad, or angry, if I was lonely or anxious; whatever I was feeling, I stuffed it down with food. One night I had a dream that even the squirrels hated me. It was a telling dream, not only because it expressed an addict's self-hatred but also because it expressed the addict's deep disconnection from the natural world. The more thoroughly we cut ourselves off from our bodies, from nature, from our embodied humanity, the more we also cut ourselves off from God.

I began my recovery in 1982, and in the years that followed I gradually learned to honor the first bit of nature with which I had been entrusted: my own body. As I learned to listen to my body and to live within its limits, I also began to connect with nature. I began to see that God loved not only my body but that God also loved the whole "body" of creation. My prayer began to change. It was like turning my pocket inside out; whereas once I had found God mostly in silent, inward contemplation, now God began showing up around me—in the pond, the rocks, the willow tree. If you spend an hour gazing at a willow tree, after a while it begins to disclose itself and to disclose God. I began to understand the words of poet Gerard Manley Hopkins: "The world is charged with the grandeur of God." I began to understand the words of Genesis: "God saw everything that [God] had made, and indeed, it was very good" (Gen 1:31).

Creation is the stage when we discover the great love affair that is going on between God and God's world. We enter that stage when we experience God's love for us, and not only for us, not only for our own kind. Because God's love is infinite, this stage is one that we can never outgrow and never finish exploring.

The second stage is *crucifixion*. Nobody likes this part of the journey, but it is becoming harder and harder to avoid. The more fully we experience the ways in which the creation reveals the love of God, the more we cannot help seeing and sensing the relentless assault on the natural world: clear-cut forests, extinct species, vanishing topsoil, ocean "dead zones," disappearing wetlands, acid rain, an increasingly hot and unstable climate.

We try not to notice these things. We try to shrug them off or look away. But crucifixion is the place where God finally breaks through our denial. When we reach this stage we finally dare to feel the pain, to mourn what we have lost and what our children will never see. It is important to feel our protest and grief, because it is an expression of our love. We cannot sidestep this stage if we are to become truly human. I wonder what the church would be like if it became a genuine sanctuary, a place where we felt free to mourn, free to express our anger and sorrow about what is happening to the earth.

At the foot of the cross we express not only our grief but also our guilt, because if we are honest with ourselves, we must confess the ways that we ourselves benefit from the destruction of the earth. We must admit our own patterns of consumption and waste. When it comes to eco-justice, none of us—at least, not most North Americans—can stand in a place of self-righteousness, because we, too, are implicated. I wonder if Paul did not weep with penitence and sorrow during those three days of fasting when he could see nothing but the darkness of what he had done. He had reached his own inner cross, the place of self-awareness where God gives us grace to face our malice, ignorance, grief, and guilt. It is at the cross of Christ that evil and suffering are continually met by the love of God, and in a time of ecological crisis, we may need to take hold of the cross as never before.

In the first stage of eco-conversion, creation, we let ourselves fall in love with the beauty of God's world. In the second stage, we share in Christ's crucifixion, letting ourselves mourn creation's wounds and acknowledge our own deep grief and guilt. And in the third stage, we gradually come to share in Christ's *resurrection*. Filled with the love that radiates through all creation and empowered by the cross that like a lightning rod grounds all suffering and sin in the love of God, we come at last to bear witness to the Christ "who bursts out of the tomb, who proclaims that life, not death, has the last word, and who gives us power to roll away the stone."[2] When we are led to resurrection we move out into the world to participate in works of caring for creation. A sure sign of having entered this stage is when, through the power of the risen Christ, we become seekers of justice and agents of healing.

Our action can take many forms. God's creation needs healing at every level, so wherever you feel led to begin is a good place to start. Commitment to care for the earth will affect what we buy and what we refuse to buy, what we drive and what we refuse to drive, how we heat our homes, how much we reuse and recycle, whether we are willing to do something as simple as switch to compact fluorescent light bulbs, whether—and for whom—we vote, and whether we go even further and engage in public protest and civil disobedience.

The resurrected life is no solo affair. Ananias helped Paul to understand what was happening to him, and Paul in turn created small communities as he made his way around the Mediterranean, bearing witness to Christ "before Gentiles and kings and before the people of Israel" (Acts 9:15). The resurrected life is a life lived in community, filled with hope and fired by love. In the work of environmental care and justice, we need to find allies and to join a network so that our actions will be strategic and effective. Left to our own devices, it is easy to feel paralyzed and overwhelmed, because there is so much to do. Conversely, we can run around doing everything at once but be ineffective and burn out before we have accomplished a thing. As my brother-in-law wryly observes, "Don't haul water in a bucket full of holes."

Many Americans do mark Earth Day, but you know as well as I do that a lot of us want to ignore the environmental crisis, to deny its urgency, to deal with it some other time. I read somewhere that comedian George Carlin once remarked, "I don't believe there's any problem in this country, no matter how tough it is, that Americans, when they roll up their sleeves, can't completely ignore."

When we Americans get past our denial and actually take a look at the challenges we face, what may come next is despair—the awful sense that it is too late, that it has gone too far, that we will not be able to turn this around. I know of only two antidotes to despair: prayer and action. Prayer roots us in the first stage of that three-part journey, namely, in the love of God that extends through all creation. Prayer also gives us courage to enter the second stage, as we share Christ's crucifixion, mourn the losses, and feel the grief. And through the spirit of the risen Christ, we embark on the third stage: we are sent out to act, to do what we can to transform the world.

There is good nourishment to be had in a life lived like that. In the scene from today's Gospel, the depleted fishery is restored, the exhausted disciples are refreshed, and the risen Christ prepares and serves them a meal. The bread and fish that he gives them are a sign of God's abundance; they recall the multiplication of loaves and fishes, when everyone on the hillside sat down and was fed.

Here at this Communion table we too will be fed, we too will taste the marvelous generosity of the God who loved us—and all creation—into being. Conversion invites us to become people of prayer, people who take time to steep ourselves in the love of God. And it invites us to become people of action, too, people who try in every aspect of our lives—from what we eat to what we drive and how we vote—to move toward ecological sanity and sustainability and to honor our first and most basic God-given call: to become caretakers of the earth.

Margaret Bullitt-Jonas is priest associate of Grace Episcopal Church (Amherst, Massachusetts) and has been leading retreats around the country since 1986. Since 1992 she has been a lecturer in pastoral theology at Episcopal Divinity School, and she recently served as chaplain to the Episcopal Church's House of Bishops. Her published works include *Holy Hunger* and *Christ's Passion, Our Passions*, as well as the pastoral letter on the environment that was released in 2003 by the Episcopal bishops of New England. She serves on the leadership council of the interfaith network Religious Witness for the Earth.

Notes

1. Part of the sermon originally appeared in a presentation I made at Harvard Divinity School for the Costas Consultation in Global Mission 2002–2003, "Earth-Keeping as a Dimension of Christian Mission," February 28–March 1, 2003. Matthew Fox's Via Affirmativa, Via Negativa, and Via Transformativa helped inspire the three-part model that I propose.
2. This quotation is from "To Serve Christ in All Creation: A Pastoral Letter from the Episcopal Bishops of New England," sent to the Episcopal Churches of Province One on the Feast of the Presentation of Christ, 2003.

THE ISAIAH FACTOR

Prophetic Words That People Can Hear

STEVEN CHARLESTON

THIS SERMON WAS PREACHED DURING EARTH WEEK at Episcopal Divinity School in Cambridge, Massachusetts. In this sermon, my goal is to speak a word of common sense to those of us committed to environmental justice. The point is simple: We need to enliven our "story" if we want people truly to hear our message and to act on it.

> You will indeed listen, but never understand,
>   and you will indeed look, but never perceive.
> For this people's heart has grown dull,
>   and their ears are hard of hearing,
>   and they have shut their eyes;
>   so that they might not look with their eyes,
>   and listen with their ears,
> and understand with their heart and turn—
>   and I would heal them. **(Matt 13:14–15)**

❖

What is one of the best-known parables in the New Testament? There are probably three or four good answers, but surely the parable of the Sower and the Seed in chapter 13 of the Gospel of Matthew would be among them. Most Christians, even if they are only occasional churchgoers, have heard the story of the man who went out to sow. Some of his seeds fell on rocky ground, some in the thorns, some in good soil. The images of this parable are simple, direct, and very familiar. They communicate quickly with an audience that understands almost intuitively that the "seeds" are the words of the gospel. We get the message even before it is explained to us.

But there is a part of this story that often goes unnoticed. It is sandwiched between the image Jesus creates of the man tossing the seeds onto his field and the explanation he offers as to the meaning of this image. The disciples of Jesus ask him why he always tells stories when he is teaching. They want to know why he uses parables in the first place. In his answer, Jesus quotes a passage from Isaiah, which says, in effect:

> "Keep listening, but do not comprehend;
> keep looking, but do not understand."
> Make the mind of this people dull,
>   and stop their ears,
>   and shut their eyes. (Isa 6:9–10)

These strange and dark words have a different kind of message. In fact, I believe they are something of a parable in themselves, especially to those of us who are evangelists of environmental justice. Like the sower of seeds, we have been in the business of trying to spread the word about the threat to our earth. We have been seeking to communicate to as many people as we can about the truth of ecological destruction. We have sought converts to help us defend the integrity of all of God's creation. And in doing so, we have encountered a mystery that only a great prophet like Isaiah may be able to unravel: while everyone hears what we say, no one seems either to understand it or to want to do anything about it.

I do not think I exaggerate when I say that most advocates of environmental justice have a very common experience: We seem to tell a story that everyone agrees with but no one wants to act on. How many times have you had that experience? How many times after you have spoken to others about the urgency of environmental action have you received a warm response, only to watch it evaporate into benign neglect when it comes time to do something? The great irony of the environmental movement is that it is the one cause everyone agrees with but very few actually support.

People hear it, but they do not truly understand it. People see the need for it all around them, but they do not perceive their own place in being part of the solution. It may not be that their hearts are hardened on purpose, but the effects are the same: Environmental ministries find few fertile grounds for growth in the life of the church.

Why? Like Jesus, we may be tempted to ask our complacent audience, "Do you have ears but you cannot hear?" In fact, it may be that Jesus told his original story about how so many seeds fell on barren ground exactly because he had the same experience as so many environmental activists. It is frustrating to feel that you have a life-giving message with an urgent appeal but one that seems to motivate only a few deep responses. The reasons for why this is so may be as varied as the listeners themselves, but there is one common theme worth considering: When Jesus spoke to people about the importance of a spiritual life, they all agreed with him. But when he spoke to them about the changes they would have to make to live into that life, a great many simply stopped listening.

When you or I talk about the need for environmental justice, most people agree with us, but when we talk about the changes that will have to occur for this justice to be genuine, we can begin to hear the crickets in the auditorium.

The call to change is the heart hardener. Even in well-intentioned, supportive people, the call to change is often impossible to hear. This is why the prophets, like Jesus, insisted on the need for repentance. Repentance is the "tag line" on the end of the parable. It is the call to an action that takes the words of truth and starts them growing in human life. Without this repentance, this amendment of life, there is no growth, and the truth, even if it is spoken in the most eloquent language of urgency, dies slowly on fallow ground.

Environmental action is repentance. It is a change of life. The message most of us in the environmental movement preach is very much a gospel message because it asks people to live their lives in a different way. Our message is not just a montage of beautiful images from nature, a kind of *National Geographic* version of the Bible, but rather an insistent proclamation that human civilization must redirect its efforts by sacrificing comfort and privileges long enjoyed by a power elite—and do it for the sake of all creation. That message is not dissimilar from the one Isaiah taught, John the Baptist preached, and Jesus told in parables. It is the essential gospel message of repentance and change.

Is it any wonder, therefore, that it has such a hard time being received? As Jesus tells his disciples in verse 15, quoting from Isaiah:

> . . . so that they might not look with their eyes,
>   and listen with their ears,
> and understand with their heart and turn—
>   and I would heal them. (Matt 13:15)

That last word from Isaiah is the most important, both to Jesus and to you and me. The whole point and purpose of our environmental ministry is healing. We are not just in the business of advocacy or political action; we are very much engaged in a healing ministry.

As hard as it may be for us to get our message across, we must never relent, because to do so is literally a matter of sickness or health, of life or death. Our goal is to heal human beings from those things that keep them addicted to power and privilege. It is to help heal the isolation of humanity from the rest of creation. Our work is to bring healing to a devastated planet and all of its endangered inhabitants. We are healers, for whom change is not a question of being politically correct but rather of being healthy and whole. Repentance, for us, is recovery.

As most of us who are familiar with recovery from addiction understand, there are few ministries as difficult both to initiate and to sustain. Environmental action is intervention. In the healing work of the environmental mission, we confront others with a reality they would rather never face. It is not at all surprising that the response we most often receive is one of denial. While people may accept what we say on the surface, like the hard ground in the parable, they will not receive this message deeply enough to let it have an impact on their behavior. This fact alone tells us something important about the nature of our ministry: environmental ministry is addiction ministry. In many ways, we have more in common with people who work in 12-step programs than we do with political activists.

What strategies work best when dealing with addiction? That question may be one of the most helpful tools we have in generating an environmental ministry that works. If we place the responses we receive to our call for action into the context of an intervention, we begin to see why so many people have ears but cannot hear, and eyes but cannot see. The polite reaction we get to our message is designed to keep it on the surface level of equally polite denial. In other words, to admit that a problem exists is fine, as long as it does not have to exist for us personally. The challenge for us is to help people break through that denial to confront the reality for which they are personally responsible.

And how have we been trying to do that? If we are honest, much of the time we have been trying to do it with a flood of scientific information. We have been trying to break down the denial barriers by overwhelming them with a tide of scientific data. We tell people how fast the polar ice caps are melting, how many bird species are disappearing, and how toxic their water is becoming. In a sense, we try to heal them by reminding them of how sick they are. But are we honestly breaking down their barriers of denial and reaching the inner core of their addictions—all of which are the true sources for the lack of personal investment in ecological responsibility?

I think the answer is no. Statistics may present a valid picture of reality, but they are not very convincing emotional arguments against denial. We need another approach. We need the same approach Jesus used when he told his disciples why he chose to tell stories instead of delivering sermons.

Jesus told the story of the Sower and the Seeds because it was far more effective than trying to make his listeners feel guilty. Rather than moralizing at them, he invited them into a new way of thinking. Instead of making a frontal assault on their defenses, he went around the corner and surprised them by getting them to think for themselves. Parables are invitations. They are small models of new ways of thinking about old, familiar situations. They are grounded in everyday experience. They refer to the most common human experiences. They are stories that give the maximum number of people a chance to hear what is being said, because the real end of the story is always told by the hearer. In other words, we finish the parable ourselves and, by so doing, we become drawn into its meaning by giving it meaning.

If Matthew 13 has any value for those of us engaged in environmental ministry, it is as a parable about effective evangelism—not only evangelism for the gospel but for the cause of environmental justice. The hinge point is Isaiah's commonsense warning that most people will not be ready to hear what we have to say, even if they agree with us. The challenge is in the healing work of Christ to overcome that reticence through an act of repentance. And that repentance comes from an honest look at the denial that is common to all human beings caught by the power of addiction. For those of us sowing seeds of environmental action in the affluent communities of the northern hemisphere, that means facing our addictions to a level of privilege that cushions us from the need to change. Breaking through that denial zone, oddly enough, does not mean a frontal assault armed with facts and figures, but rather a holy act of subversion: inviting people to accept personal responsibility by helping them to see themselves in the environmental story. Most of all, it means letting them finish that story for themselves.

In the days to come, when you or I are called on once again to share our witness, I pray that we will take a moment and remember how Jesus placed Isaiah's prophetic words in the middle of one of the best-known stories in the New Testament. He did that in order to tell his disciples something important about gospel strategy. He wanted to teach them about the power of story to win hearts and minds. We need to remember those lessons if we want to avoid watching the eyes of our congregations glaze over every time we give a talk on environmental justice. We need to create modern parables that communicate deep truths in earth-centered language. We need to craft stories of everyday life with images easily accessible to everyday people. We need to illustrate an invitation to change with a call to repentance that sounds more like a promise than a prophecy. We need to get out of the way of the story and let our hearers decide what this means to them. If we do not, we will just be scattering seeds to the wind.

Steven Charleston is president and professor of theology at Episcopal Divinity School in Cambridge, Massachusetts. He has served as executive director of the National Committee on Indian Work at the Episcopal Church Center, director of the Dakota Leadership program, and Episcopal bishop of Alaska. Recent publications include *The Middle Way: A Congregational Resource for Studying the Windsor Report* and *Good News: A Congregational Resource for Reconciliation.*

THE CRY OF THE EARTH—
THE CRY OF THE HEART

JOHN CHRYSSAVGIS

THIS SERMON DRAWS CRITICAL CONNECTIONS between the cry of the heart (spirituality), the cry of the earth (ecology), and the cry of the poor (charity). It seeks to combine theological thought, spiritual practice, and social outreach. An early version was presented during the Costas Consultation on Global Mission at Harvard Divinity School in March 2003.

> For just as Jonah was three days and three nights in the belly of the sea monster, so for three days and three nights the Son of Man will be in the heart of the earth. **(Matt 12:40)**

◈

Why is it that, despite the alarming—indeed, truly terrifying—statistics and information we have at our disposal, we appear to be all the more distant from any solution? How is it that, while we are so much more articulate about the contributing factors—addressing the subject from so many and diverse perspectives—the situation is in some places even deteriorating? From an Orthodox spiritual viewpoint, I know that my church tells me to stop and reflect. That is, as I understand it, what I am called to do as an Orthodox theologian and clergyman.

I must then respond by doing what I am ordained to do: preach the death and resurrection of Jesus Christ, proclaim the power of silence and tears, and share the sacraments of life and death. I believe that it is just as critical to speak authentically from one's own perspective as it is to learn from one another's perspective. My personal perspective is the liturgy. In fact, that is precisely where my mind drifts when I hear the notion of "con-serving." I think immediately of serving at the altar of the world, of "con-celebrating" what Maximus the Confessor in the seventh-century called "a cosmic liturgy." In that worldview, everything bears a sacramental seal and a sacred significance.

There is a moment in the liturgy of the Orthodox Church when the deacon stands in the middle of the temple and, in almost apostolic conviction and fervor, chants aloud, "Let us stand well; let us stand in awe." The deacon is not reminding people to be upstanding; in fact, the deacon is saying, "Don't just do something; stand there!" Before we can act—and we should be humble enough to recall from time to time that it is our "acting" that got us into this mess in the first place!—we should refrain from acting. We should contemplate and meditate on the way we are living. If we are going to reverse the environmental crisis and change our lifestyle, we must first of all transform the way we perceive our world and ourselves; we must change our worldview, our "icon" of the world. This calls for a change of heart.

We must admit that our treatment of the earth is based on rigid assumptions and dogmatic presuppositions about the created world. "How the world works" will depend on "how the world looks"; it will reflect our worldview and world image. That is also my criticism of the term and concept of "stewardship," which implies a self-centered worldview—perhaps more efficient and more productive, but ultimately a worldview that is determined by our needs and desires. There is an inherent danger in presuming that the world somehow awaits our proclamation of good news. If we are going to bear good news, then we first of all have to hear what I call the cry of the heart.

THE CRY OF THE HEART

I choose to cut down a tree. I want to be creative and productive, yet I am creating a problem. So in making a table or cabinet, I have also—perhaps unwillingly, even unwittingly—prepared a coffin. The imagery is crude, and I apologize. The enterprise of cutting down a tree normally assumes a more subtle form: like the paper used for a book, the expenses for a household, the choice of a motor vehicle. In cutting down a tree, I have cut down also the level of oxygen. I have buried not just the tree and the earth, but life itself and, indeed, my very own child. I now behold my own soul and my own child lying in the coffin—the very earth's soul and existence. How dare I speak of hasty or romantic solutions when I am perpetuating the vicious cycle! Salvation is indeed healing. Yet how can I possibly speak of healing unless and until I have understood the hurt that I have inflicted?

Instead, I must first be silent. I must kneel silently. I must weep. I must want back my child. Tears are a crucial element of spiritual thirst for new life. This passionate desire for a change of heart— what my tradition calls "erotic desire" (eros)—is itself the overture to paradise. It alone can recover that which is lost. To adopt contemporary psychological jargon, I must grieve the loss, perceive the sin, sense the decay, sincerely want back my life, my child, and even the tree that I destroyed. I must ask for forgiveness. This is my only hope of resurrection. Paradoxically, it is death that becomes my teacher about life. That is the way of nature. Perhaps that is the way of God.

Then I own my sin; I assume responsibility. When they tell me there is a hole in the ozone layer, I may feel nothing unless I sense that hole, unless I grieve the missing link, unless I recognize my child—my child's child, the generations of children in the future— buried in that hole. Only then can God's hand reach out through the hole. Only then is this emptiness transformed into an openness that reflects the open tomb of Christ.

So it is only when I see in the face of the world the face of my own child that I can further discern in that face the very image of the risen Christ, the face of all faces. The eighth-century poet and artist John of Damascus observed that "the earth is the living face of God." Only then can I also recognize in each tree a face, and a name, and a time, and a place, and a voice, and a cry that longs to be heard.

Now I no longer act as if the world will always be there. I no longer relate to the natural world in a self-centered way, locked up in a selfish worldview, from which I can neither communicate nor even appreciate the way that nature enhances my soul. I know that I should not treat people like things. However, I need now to learn that I should not treat even things like mere things. Then the cry of the earth is planted deep inside me.

THE CRY OF THE EARTH

I am not, as you see, offering any solution. I am offering a cry, a confession, an expression of another, liberated worldview. If the cry of the heart is a painful admission of my wrongdoing in relation to the earth, then the cry of the earth itself is also a "groaning in labor pains" for liberation by the children of God (Rom 8:22–23). "Can we ask," wrote Augustine, "for a louder voice than that?"

The earth's cry arises and increases because we are primarily invested in producing for human consumption, in reducing the world and humanity to our needs. In such a reductionist worldview, we overlook the larger reality; we ignore the divine economy that incorporates everyone and everything, that embraces all beings and the whole world, that *allows space for all*—which is the literal meaning of the Greek word for "forgiveness" and "reconciliation" (*synchoresis*). Our economy should accommodate people and animals and trees in such a manner that is—again according to Maximus the Confessor— in harmony with or at least not in violation of the divine economy. Herein perhaps lies another weakness of the prevailing term "stewardship." The Greek equivalent to this term is *oikonomia*.

Yet *oikonomia* (or "economy")—and, by extension, *oikologia* (or "ecology")—belong properly to God. Ours is only the response to God's initiative of economy.

Industry and technology must acknowledge the dimension of mystery (*doxology*), we should be sensitive to the ultimate scheme of things (*eschatology*), and we must adhere to God's absolute concern for things (*providence*). Ecology is not an aspect of Christian vision or mission; it is not merely a dimension of Christian theology or spirituality. It is the crucial basis and the very method of all Christian life and practice. Our message is defective and hardly good news when it is not courageous and adventurous enough to appreciate the broader, universal relationship of the whole community—and not just the human community.

This broader reality, this greater economy, this more ecumenical or cosmic perspective reminds us that the context is always larger than you or I, always larger than any single denomination or faith; indeed, it is larger than the world itself! The earth will always be threatened when we impose a single-minded agenda. The proper response, the appropriate remedy for our excess consumption, is what the ascetic tradition of my church calls renunciation. It is the awareness that earth belongs to heaven, the acknowledgment that— to quote Ambrose of Milan—"neither the possessions of the earth, but the very sky, and the air, and the sea, cannot be claimed for the use of the rich few."

The cry of the earth is ultimately a call for humility. Pride, as we know, is a uniquely human attribute. All other species seem to know instinctively where they fit in the order of things. Human beings alone are unable to accept their proper place in the scheme of things; we alone just do not get it, not knowing when to stop, how far to go. We are to "serve and keep" (Gen 2:15), a phrase that I like to translate as "serve and preserve." It is a matter of doing with less, of traveling light. And we can always manage with a lot less than we imagine. Surely this is the "Sabbath principle." When we carry less, we are more sensitive to what is lacking in others. Then we become more attuned to the cry of the poor.

THE CRY OF THE POOR

We respond to nature with the same delicacy, the same tenderness (or lack thereof) with which we respond to people. The ecumenical movement has aptly coined the term *eco-justice*: all ecological activities, all economic programs, in fact all theological principles and spiritual practices are ultimately measured and finally judged by their effect on people, and especially on the poor (Matt 25:31). As Wendell Berry observes, "By some connection that we do not recognize, the willingness to exploit one [the earth] becomes the willingness to exploit the other [the human body]."[1]

We must allow room for the cry of the poor. We must hear the voice of the poor. We must affirm the dignity of the poor. We must assume responsibility for the consequences of our actions on the poor. Our market is based on exploitation and exclusion. Our technology pushes people aside and away, even outside. The first word in any ecological response comes less from the environment and certainly not from our theology; it comes from our attitudes toward the poor.

That is precisely what preserves us and protects the poor from paternalism or patronization. The poor do not simply have the same legitimacy; they have a greater legitimacy. To this point, the poor have "bought" what we have "sold" to them. They have listened to what we have said. They have patiently tolerated what we have offered in arrogance. Nevertheless, now the tables are turned; it is the suffering of the poor that should presently set the pace. It is their cry that determines the solution. It is their authority that speaks—just as it was death that taught us about life, and the tree that reminded us how to treat creation. And we have no excuse not to hear the cry of the poor. As we have been divinely assured, "You always have the poor with you" (Matt 26:11).

LOSS

If we lose the forest, we lose more than an aesthetic dimension of life; we lose an essential quality of life. We lose our imagination and inspiration; we lose the mystery of nature and life; we lose our sensitivity and soul. The most endangered species is not the whale or the forest; it is the earth that we share. The earth is our home (which is the meaning of *oikos* from which we have the term "ecology"); it is where all of us—whales, trees, and people alike—live and die.

Such is the cry of the heart. The world is not hungry simply for bread (Matt 6:10); it is hungry for a sense of holiness and mystery, for a spiritual vision that does not lose sight of the trees, or the poor, or the sacred. This in turn endows us with a sense of integrity for life and the natural environment. It bequeaths on us an understanding of the reconciliation of all people and all things. It implies a covenant between heaven and earth, so that God's will may be done "on earth as it is in heaven" (Matt 6:10).

That is the gift we have received, the promise of new life we have been pledged: "God said [to Noah]: 'This is the sign of the covenant that I make between me and you and every living creature that is with you, for all future generations. I have set my bow in the clouds, and it shall be a sign of the covenant between me and the earth'" (Gen 9:12–13). That is the treasure I am called to keep. Finally, that is the most precious gift I have to offer my children, and my children's children. It is, thankfully, far greater than any disgrace or destruction that I have wrought. It is the symbol of grace and life. How can I ever be grateful enough for this?

A native of Australia, John Chryssavgis received degrees from the Greek Conservatory of Music, the University of Athens, St. Vladimir's Theological Seminary, and the University of Oxford. He has served as personal assistant to the Greek Orthodox primate in Australia, was cofounder of St. Andrew's Theological College in Sydney, and in 1999 was appointed professor of theology at Holy Cross School of Theology. His published works include *Beyond the Shattered Image* and *Cosmic Grace, Humble Prayer*.

Note

1. Wendell Berry, "The Body and the Earth," *Recollected Essays, 1965–1980* (San Francisco: North Point Press, 1981), 304–5.

SCALES FELL FROM HIS EYES

JOHN COBB

THIS SERMON IS AN AUTOBIOGRAPHICAL REFLECTION on key conversions in my life brought about by the need to come to terms with transformations taking place in the culture.

> Meanwhile Saul, still breathing threats and murder against the disciples of the Lord, went to the high priest and asked him for letters to the synagogues at Damascus, so that if he found any who belonged to the Way, men or women, he might bring them bound to Jerusalem. Now as he was going along and approaching Damascus, suddenly a light from heaven flashed around him. He fell to the ground and heard a voice saying to him, "Saul, Saul, why do you persecute me?" He asked, "Who are you, Lord?" The reply came, "I am Jesus, whom you are persecuting. But get up and enter the city, and you will be told what to do." The men who were traveling with him stood speechless because they heard the voice but they saw no one. Saul got up from the ground, and though his eyes were open, he could see nothing; so they led him by the hand and brought him

into Damascus. For three days he was without sight, and neither ate nor drank.

Now there was a disciple in Damascus named Ananias. The Lord said to him in a vision, "Ananias." He answered, "Here I am, Lord." The Lord said to him, "Get up and go to the street called Straight, and at the house of Judas look for a man of Tarsus named Saul. At this moment he is praying, and he has seen in a vision a man named Ananias come in and lay his hands on him so that he might regain his sight." But Ananias answered, "Lord, I have heard from many about this man, how much evil he has done to your saints in Jerusalem; and here he has authority from the chief priests to bind all who invoke your name." But the Lord said to him, "Go, for he is an instrument whom I have chosen to bring my name before Gentiles and kings and before the people of Israel; I myself will show him how much he must suffer for the sake of my name." So Ananias went and entered the house. He laid his hands on Saul and said, "Brother Saul, the Lord Jesus, who appeared to you on your way here, has sent me so that you may regain your sight and be filled with the Holy Spirit." And immediately something like scales fell from his eyes, and his sight was restored. Then he got up and was baptized, and after taking some food, he regained his strength. **(Acts 9:1-19)**

The idea that scales sometimes fall from our eyes has taken hold in Christendom. It describes figuratively an experience that many have had. In this passage from Acts there is a double change. On the road to Damascus, in the figurative sense, we might well say that Paul had his most important experience of scales falling from his eyes. Until then he had not been able to see, or perhaps had not allowed himself to see, who Jesus was. Accordingly, he was angry about the great claims being made for Jesus, and he resolved to destroy this sect of Jesus' followers. On the road to Damascus, the scales fell from his eyes, and he saw that Jesus was what his followers declared him to be. That experience led to a drastic reversal of his life orientation. Understanding the meaning of what he had seen took him several days, during which time he fasted. During that entire time he was physically blind. There would probably be no Christian church today apart from the conclusions to which Paul came during those days.

The second change, the one in which the image of scales falling from eyes is actually used in the text, was minor in comparison, but nevertheless important. Physical blindness is not comparable to spiritual blindness in its destructive effects. It does not lead to persecuting those with whom you disagree. Nevertheless, if Paul had remained physically blind, his missionary work would have been greatly restricted. Whether a sustainable movement of Jesus' followers among the Gentiles, the movement of which we are a part, would ever have occurred without his recovery of physical sight, we can only guess. In any case, we can rejoice that the physical scales as well as the spiritual ones fell from his eyes.

I hope that you have had more than one experience of the scales falling from your eyes. This has happened to me repeatedly, and for each experience I am deeply grateful. I would like to share three such experiences.

THE FIRST EXPERIENCE

I went to the Divinity School of the University of Chicago after I got out of the Army soon after World War II ended. We were all aware at that time of the horrors the Nazis had inflicted on European Jews. We were sometimes critical of German Christians for not having resisted this evil system more strongly. Yet in my courses in New Testament and in church history, I do not recall having extended discussions of Christian anti-Judaism. I was vaguely aware that there had been pogroms and persecutions by Christians. But I made no connection, so far as I can recall, between Christian teaching and the treatment of Jews by Christians and, later, by Nazis and other European racists. I was hardly aware of the extensive anti-Semitism that pervaded American society and resulted in preventing Jews from escaping extermination at the hands of the Nazis.

Only a decade later did the scales fall from my eyes. I discovered that the pious ideas on which I had been nurtured had a shadow side that led to anti-Judaism. Somehow it had never occurred to me that my understanding of Jesus and salvation implied that the Jews were the enemies of truth and salvation. Since I had never been exposed to explicit Christian anti-Judaism, I had difficulty believing how widespread it had been. Nevertheless, rather rapidly did the scales fall from eyes. I saw that Christian teaching contributed massively to the Holocaust. I saw that some of that inflammatory teaching was still continuing and that my own theological formulations were not free of this danger.

A SECOND EXPERIENCE

I grew up in the mission field in Japan. I was somewhat aware as a child that Japanese women were subservient to Japanese men. But I was quite oblivious to the fact that American women, too, were limited by their culture and even by church teaching in what they could do. The single women missionaries I knew were strong and independent people who ran major institutions with great self-confidence. Missionary wives, like my mother, often held leadership roles alongside their husbands. Many of the Japanese Christian women I knew were also remarkably strong people. In school my general experience was that the girls outdid the boys academically.

In the early days of the feminist movement I began to hear women speak of how restricted they had been and how they were discouraged from excelling. They complained that in mixed groups their voices were ignored. Their opinions were simply not taken as seriously as those of men. At first, I was incredulous. But fairly soon the scales fell from my eyes. The patriarchal character of our culture, our history, and our church life became apparent to me. Since the facts were all around me and had been there all the time, I marveled that I had not noticed them—that I had filtered them out.

A THIRD EXPERIENCE

Here the scales fell from my eyes in the area of ecology. Like most people, I grew up with some emotional attachment to nature. I felt kinship to animals and hated to think of their suffering. Nevertheless, I was educated into supposing that all of this was basically sentimental. What truly mattered were human beings and their relations with one another. The really important issues are to be found in history, not in nature.

The power of this anthropocentrism was particularly manifest in my early theological work. I subscribed to a philosophy that emphasized the continuity and interconnection between human beings and other creatures. Yet I took my topics from the standard theological discussions of the day, heavily influenced by existentialism. This led to an exclusive focus on human beings and history. I wrote a book called *A Christian Natural Theology*. But in the book I dealt thematically only with human beings and God. In 1965, when I published that book, it did not occur to me how odd that was.

A few years later, the scales fell from my eyes. I was awakened to the seriousness of the ecological crisis. I read the famous essay by Lynn White Jr. on "The Historical Roots of the Ecological Crisis." In that essay, he showed how Christian teaching in the Western church had distracted attention from the natural world, treating it only as a means to human ends, an object of human exploitation. This freed the West to advance in science and technology and to develop the means of rapidly destroying the natural systems on which we all depend. I saw how the liberal Protestant tradition in which I had been educated intensified the alienation from nature and thus delayed recognition of the crisis and still inhibited the needed responses. I saw how my own work had fully acquiesced in this alienation.

This "ecological" instance of the scales falling from my eyes had a greater effect on my own work than had the other two. This was partly because the philosophy I had been using had great potential for guiding a healthy response to the crisis. In the other two cases, I saw that others were in a better position than I to lead. In this case of ecology, however, I could use my own philosophical tradition more inclusively than I had before as a means to contribute to that response.

Paul's experience on the way to Damascus was both similar and different from the personal experiences I have listed, which were typical of my generation. It was similar in the sense that he discovered, abruptly, how wrong he had been about the way things were. That happened to me in each of the three instances I cited. It was different, however, in the sense of being a more total reversal. I had not been intentionally devoting myself to anti-Jewish, patriarchal, or anti-environmental activities or teachings. My experience was one of realizing that something I had simply ignored was of great importance. Paul, on the other hand, had devoted great energy to destroying that to which he now knew he must give his life. It was different also in terms of its implications for change. My experiences led me to feel some responsibility for taking up in my teaching topics that I had previously ignored. Paul's experience made it immediately clear that he was to join the new movement and preach Jesus Christ and him crucified.

For some people in my generation, the new awareness brought about by the scales falling from their eyes did lead to truly dramatic changes. I knew one Christian theologian who rejected Christianity as inherently anti-Jewish and has stood outside the church ever since. But for most Christians, the new awareness of the crimes of Christians against Jews and of the responsibility of standard Christian teaching for poisoning this relationship leads only to modifications of practice and teaching. We try to make clear that Jesus and Paul were Jews and that to be Christian at all is to be a follower of Jewish teachers. We try to formulate the salvation we find in Christ in such a way that it does not deny that God's covenant with the Jews still stands. We try to criticize the endemic legalism of Christians without implying that the deep commitment of the Jews to the Torah leads to inferior results in Jewish life. We try to avoid using the word *pharisaic* in a pejorative way. And we try to relate to our Jewish neighbors in ways that assure them of our respect and our appreciative interest in their religious lives and communities. We deeply hope that these new patterns of teaching and relationship will deflect any tendency for the Christian faith to give rise again to anti-Judaism.

More common has been the radical response of women who realized that their whole conditioning in a patriarchal culture had blocked their true personal development and devoted great energy to liberating themselves and their sisters. This became for some of them as total a commitment as Paul's devotion to bringing the gospel to the Gentiles. Feminism has functioned not only as a modification of Christianity but also as a new religious movement disconnected from our patriarchal traditions. But for most of us, the awareness of the pervasive presence and prevalence of patriarchal habits and teachings has led to efforts to change our own habits and the teachings that have been transmitted to us. In personal relationships within and without the church, we try to attain full equality between men and women. We try to restructure the church so as to give leadership roles to women at all levels. We try not to use masculine pronouns when we are including women, or to use them exclusively when we speak of God. We seek the feminine metaphors in the Bible and in tradition, and we try to balance the masculine images with feminine ones. More significantly, we seek in women's insights new ways of relating to one another along with new ways to think about God, about other human beings, and about nature.

Awareness of the ecological crisis and its causes has similar results. For a few, the effect of scales falling from their eyes has led to total devotion to the preservation of the natural world. Much youthful idealism has been channeled into impressive efforts to save endangered species, stop destructive "development," and fight pollution. But for most of us here, too, this awareness has led to efforts to reform and modify our inherited traditions. We try personally to live in ways that are less destructive of the earth. We recognize that human population needs to be limited, especially in countries where per capita consumption is high. We seek governmental policies and actions that raise consciousness and protect the environment. In the church we lift up the obvious concern of biblical writers for the natural world and emphasize that God created it and saw that it was good in its own right, independent of its usefulness to human beings. We try to introduce more attention to the natural world into our liturgies. We try to make our church buildings and our practices within the church as sustainable as possible.

These three experiences, and we can all think of others, deeply affected my attitude toward my own Christian faith. I had grown up identifying being Christian with being good. If I discovered that something I had thought was Christian was not good, then I assumed it was not really Christian. Now I discovered that through most of Christian history, normative Christian teaching had contributed to the suffering of Jews and women and encouraged exploitation of the earth. I could add that Christian teaching about sexuality as basically evil led to a great deal of repression on the part of those who strove hardest to be faithful. The effect of Christian teaching on homosexuals was, and still is, far more brutal. I could not but wonder whether Christianity had overall done as much harm as good. In that case, was it good to be a Christian? Should I, perhaps, join the growing community of post-Christians, who may acknowledge the positive contributions Christianity has made but who see no reason to continue with a tradition that has so many flaws?

Perhaps I could say here that again the scales fell from my eyes. I realized how much I, and many others, I think, want to find some group or movement that is largely pure so that we can identify with that. But there are no movements or groups that are not profoundly flawed. We live in a profoundly flawed world and are surrounded by profoundly flawed individuals. We are ourselves examples of those profoundly flawed individuals, and we corrupt even the purest initiatives. In fact, we cannot really find in them even an initial purity.

Is the only reasonable response cynicism? If our religious traditions are all deeply flawed, should we not abandon the quest for the good? Does it not make more sense to look out for our personal interests with little regard to what this does to others? Many, indeed, have chosen this route. The quest for wealth and personal health and enjoyment has come to characterize our national character and that of much of the rest of the world as well.

But that is not a gain. Indeed, it threatens the human future and even the life of the planet. The deeper thinking to which my recognition of collective Christian guilt has led has actually heightened my sense of our collective need of the gospel both within the church and without.

We cannot find a historic community free of guilt for past crimes, nor can we find a new community free from present corruption. The question is not so much the past or present virtue of a community. It is more how it responds when the scales fall from its collective eyes and it sees how wrong it has been. Does it cling to its destructive ways? Does it pretend to itself that it has no responsibility for these sins? Do its members simply abandon it, so that they do not have to bear responsibility for what it has done? I would find it hard indeed to identify with a community that responded in any of these ways.

But I found that my community, the old-line Protestant one, followed a different course. It repented. Yes, we have committed terrible crimes against Jews, against women, against others, and against ourselves. But as we become aware of these crimes, we acknowledge them and seek to follow the difficult road of change. We try to change our teaching and our practice so that we will no longer contribute to anti-Judaism, to patriarchal domination of women, or to continued neglect of the needs of the earth. Our change is flawed. Not all of our members join in repentance. We have a long way to go, and we will never get to the end. Also, we will keep discovering additional crimes of which we need to repent. We hope we will have the strength to respond. We know that a repentant movement does not have the popular appeal of one that presents itself as pure. But we will not abandon this fundamental character for that reason. To do so would be to betray our Lord.

We know that collectively we are clearer about what we now reject than about how to reconstitute ourselves in a better way. For example, we reject anti-Jewish Christology, but what do we put in its place? That is not yet nearly as clear. We suffer from lack of such clarity, and we sin by our unwillingness to wrestle seriously together with our theological poverty. We continue to sin, but the continuing repentance signals that the one whom we try to follow is not identified with the anti-Judaism or the patriarchy or the anthropocentrism or the other things of which we have been, and continue to be, guilty. On the contrary, it is by him and his teaching that we judge that we have sinned.

Our repentance indicates that we are more committed to following Jesus than to the particular beliefs and practices that earlier generations developed in their effort to follow. In that lies hope. We do not need to abandon our faith. However distorted its expressions have been and still are, we can engage together in healing and up-building activity. We do not have to become cynical. We can believe that Jesus Christ remains the hope of the world. We can experience the scales falling from our eyes not only as repeated recognitions of our collective and individual sin but also as means to discern more clearly who Christ is and what it means to follow him.

Jesus called on all his hearers for *metanoia*. That means a profound change of mind. We have translated that as "repentance." We who repent in response to the scales falling from our eyes are true followers of Jesus.

Before his retirement, John Cobb was Ingraham Professor of Theology at Claremont School of Theology and Avery Professor at Claremont Graduate School. He is codirector of the Center for Process Studies. He has written many books, including *Is It Too Late? A Theology of Ecology*, *The Earthist Challenge to Economism*, and *For the Common Good: Redirecting the Economy toward the Community, the Environment, and a Sustainable Future*, an award-winning book he coauthored with Herman Daly.

A PASSION FOR THE POSSIBLE

A Message to US Churches

WILLIAM SLOANE COFFIN

THIS SERMON IS PART OF A COLLECTION called *The Passion for the Possible* (Westminster/John Knox, 1993). It shows the importance of seeing clearly the size of the ecological problems so that we are sure to measure fully the size of the needed solutions. It proposes the changes of mind and action we will have to make for humanity to develop a sustainable future. It is also a clarion call for US churches to have a vision of what is possible and to assume leadership in this endeavor.

> The heavens are telling the glory of God;
> and the firmament proclaims his handiwork. **(Ps 19:1)**

> "O! pardon me, thou bleeding piece of earth,
> That I am meek and gentle with these butchers!"
> **(William Shakespeare, *Julius Caesar*)**

Whatever befalls the earth befalls the sons of earth. Man did not weave the web of life; he is merely a strand in it. Whatever he does to the web, he does to himself. Continue to contaminate your bed and you will one night suffocate in your own waste. **(Chief Seattle, 1854)**

◈

We sit astride the world like some military dictator, some smelly Papa Doc. **(Bill McKibben)**

◈

While the heavens continue to tell the glory of God, the firmament *today* also proclaims sonic nefarious human handiwork—smog, acid rain, an immense hole in the ozone layer. Fortunately, since the first Earth Day in 1970, ecology has become a household word and environmental affairs a popular college major. Fortunately, too, more and more Americans are beginning to realize that the average American car driven the average American distance—10,000 miles a year—releases annually into the atmosphere its own weight in carbon.

The danger to the entire earth is immense. Scientists tell us that in the last three decades, carbon dioxide in the atmosphere has increased more than 10 percent. Since 1985 the damage to German forests caused by acid rain, the result of sulfur dioxide from burning fossil fuels, has risen from 10 percent to 50 percent; in Sweden, all bodies of freshwater are now acidic; from 1964 to 1979, acid rain killed half the mid- to high-elevation spruce trees in the state of Vermont, while one Tennessee's worth of the Amazonian rain forest is slashed and burned each year. As apparently there are more different species of birds in each square mile of that rain forest than exist in all of North America, we are silencing songs we have never even heard.

Then there is the "population bomb," as Paul Ehrlich in 1968 described the increasing rate of world population growth. It took a thousand years for the population of the world to double to five-hundred million in 1650. Then it doubled again, in only two hundred years, to one billion. The next doubling took only eighty years. Then, from 1930 to 1992—a mere sixty-two years— world population has gone from two billion to five-and-a-half billion, with six billion anticipated not long after.

Obviously, if we double energy efficiency but double also the number of energy users, we accomplish little. Unless significant corrective measures are quickly taken, it would appear that the entire human race is about to compound original sin with terminal sin.

Environmentalists sometimes accuse Christians and Jews of complicity in the destruction of the environment. They remind us that God told Adam to "have dominion over the fish of the sea and over the birds of the air and over every living thing that moves upon the earth" (Gen 1:28).

I doubt that many of us polluters have given a moment's thought to those words. The accusation is really another example of a very narrow reading of a very short biblical passage. When God also told Adam to "till the garden and keep it" (Gen 2:15), God could hardly have had in mind the careless, unbridled subjugation and exploitation so clearly attributable to sinful greed.

A far more serious accusation is that Jews and Christians no longer see nature at one with nature's God. No longer are our actions inhibited by wonder. To be sure, in church and synagogue we recite the psalms in which God and nature are seen to be inseparable: "When I look at your heavens, the work of your fingers, the moon and stars that you have established" (Ps 8:3).

We sing hymns based on these psalms, such as "The Spacious Firmament on High" or "Joyful, Joyful, We Adore Thee." But our adoration does not extend in any meaningful way to God's creation. Like almost all Americans—Native Americans being a great exception—we have divorced nature from nature's God. We view nature essentially as a toolbox. Nature may have beauty, but it has no purpose in its own right. It is there solely to serve human purposes.

I am convinced that unless in our own minds we re-wed nature to nature's God, we are not going to save our environment. Caution lest we exhaust our natural resources and kill ourselves in the process is not enough. What we need beyond caution is reverence. What we need beyond practical fears are moral qualms. Unless nature is "resanctified," we will never see nature as worthy of ethical considerations similar to those that presently govern human relations. And I am not at all optimistic. For not only are Christians poor stewards of God's creation, seriously challenging the Christian notion of stewardship are those who want us to think of ourselves as planet managers. And management today includes biotechnology, genetic engineering, a way to create new life. In conceptual and moral terms, genetic engineering may well be the most important scientific advance since the smashing of the atom. It suggests that if nature cannot put up with our numbers and habits, well, we will just have to change nature. We will create crops that can survive a much warmer climate, and we will alter human genes. And, of course, there is plenty of extra space in outer space where, as shuttle flights indicate, plants grow faster.

A lot of people are talking this kind of language. They are impatient with moral restraints. They rebuke us for panicking. They say we should be looking forward to our next "evolutionary exam." While I have many doubts about our passing this exam, I have few doubts about our having to take it.

Because medical cures, more and better food, and other good things are bound to result from advances in biotechnology, it feels wrong to oppose its advance. But that is the way so many of us felt in the 1950s when President Eisenhower extolled "atoms for peace." Few foresaw the way we would charge ahead with the production of nuclear power, with no real solution at hand or even in sight for the nuclear waste that we are now told will be radioactive for 25,000 years.

Because proponents of genetic engineering are intrigued by nature's possibilities more than they revere nature itself, they display more hubris than humility. Theirs is a perilous undertaking. If Christians cannot oppose it unconditionally, their spiritual qualms need very much to become part of the public dialogue. It has always been my hope that human beings might be clever enough to make things but wise enough to forgo doing so. Perhaps before funding any specific project in biotechnology, we should fund a study to consider the wisdom of it. I find compelling the words of Dennis Hayes, chairperson of Earth Day 1990. "The most fundamental human truth," he said, "is that although we humans routinely violate our own laws, we can't break Nature's laws. We can only prove them."

Far less complex and today more urgent is the need to start implementing something like Al Gore's "Marshall Plan" for saving the planet. From 1948 to 1951 the Marshall Plan cost close to 2 percent of the Gross National Product of the United States. A similar percentage today would be almost $100 billion a year. Our total nonmilitary foreign aid budget is presently about $15 billion a year, hardly comparable. But the need for a new Marshall Plan is altogether as great as was the need for the old.

We must, of course, stabilize world population and prevent famine. But it is simplistic to say that hunger results only from too many mouths to feed. China, for example, has more people than any other country. Yet in 1985 China produced enough grain to send surplus amounts to Ethiopia. In Holland, where there are three hundred people per square kilometer, there is no starvation.

Blaming overpopulation also ignores the need for large families. With no social security or pensions, our ancestors too had large families—enough hands to work the land and care for the home. Family planning in those days meant large families, as today it still does in third-world countries. Actually there is more than enough food to feed everyone. The trouble is, those who need it most can afford it least.

To increase food production in third-world countries, Gore and other experts underscore the need for literacy and education emphasizing simple techniques in sustainable agriculture, lessons to prevent soil erosion, planting trees, cleansing wells and streams. Extremely important is reducing infant mortality, for, as Julius Nyerere once remarked, "the most powerful contraceptive is the confidence by parents that their children will survive."

Obviously, birth control devices need everywhere to be available. In America it is important to recognize that the vast majority of those opposing abortion do not object to contraception. It is only to hold together their political coalition that they do not challenge the few who do. With a little more honesty Americans could help expedite the stabilization of world population.

To save the environment, Al Gore advanced an "SEI"—a Strategic Environment Initiative—to deal in America with waste reduction, recycling, conservation of soil, forestry, and energy. It is technologically possible today to construct cars that would go five times as many miles to a gallon of fuel, and to run on photovoltaic cells. Also, a single new energy-saving bulb, compared to a standard bulb, saves a half-ton of coal over its lifetime. And if storm runoff water in every city could be separated from waste water, sewage treatments would not be so overwhelmed as to dump sewage into rivers and lakes.

Following an earlier suggestion of former Soviet foreign minister Eduard Shevardnadze, Gore advocates an Environmental Security Council for the United Nations. Its primary purpose would be to share and stimulate the development of appropriate technologies, the kind that do not destroy the environment. Such a council could spawn a whole new generation of treaties and agreements such as the Montreal Protocol, adopted in 1987, which sought to reduce the amounts of CFCs and related chemicals that destroy the ozone layer in the atmosphere, and the subsequent Earth Summits in Rio de Janeiro and Kyoto.

It is a great mistake to talk, as many political leaders do, of balancing the needs of the economy with those of the environment. Any economy, national or world, is a subsystem of the ecosystem. Therefore, we cannot speak of growth as an unquestioned good. National banks and the World Bank should fund only such development projects as are ecologically sound. American industries should provide executive compensation for environmental stewardship as the enlightened among them still reward results in affirmative action.

I would love, with the wave of a wand, to declare the solar age "open," for solar energy is living off income. When you think that the vast majority of poor people live in the southern tier of this planet—in Central and Latin America, in Africa and Asia—and that the one thing they all have in abundance is sunshine, it breaks your heart that we have poured so many of our resources into weapons research and so few into the development of what eventually will be for billions of poor people a cheap, benign, and endlessly renewable source of energy.

America must convince itself that emergency measures require immediate implementation. If indeed we are stewards of God's creation, Christians have a big role to play. And the results could be dramatic, for the environmental point of view turns us away from the possessive individualism that has long been our secular credo and toward the interdependency that alone can save us. It was one thing for people to consume nature's surpluses. Today we are destroying the productive base of both present and future surpluses. Only together, all together, can we save that base. Only together can we eliminate toxic wastes in the atmosphere. Only together can we engage in the serious disarmament that will spring loose the funds to fight pollution. And because saving the environment is an enterprise so positive and so inclusive, its success is sure to help make the military impulse look ever more neurotic.

An ugly truth stares us in the face. Let us not wait until it hits us in the face. The churches are morally obligated to develop a locus, energy, and resolve to save the environment. Most of all, they can re-wed nature to nature's God, for only reverence can restrain our violence toward nature. It is primarily our lack of wonder that prevents our foreseeing and forestalling the havoc we will leave in our wake. In this "age of information," let us remember that "the greater the island of knowledge the greater the shoreline of wonder" (Huston Smith). Let us recall G. K. Chesterton's observation: "The world does not lack for wonders, only for a sense of wonder." Without wonder, we will never save life on the planet. God, I am sure, approves E. E. Cummings's preference: "I would rather learn from one bird how to sing than teach ten thousand stars how not to dance."

William Sloane Coffin (1924–2006), a Presbyterian minister, was a longtime peace activist. He was a CIA agent who later served as chaplain of Yale University, senior minister at the Riverside Church in New York City, and president of SANE/Freeze, the nation's largest peace and justice group. Among other books and articles, he wrote *Letters to a Young Doubter*, *Credo*, and *Passion for the Possible*.

WHOSE EARTH IS IT ANYWAY?

JAMES H. CONE

The earth is the LORD's and all that is in it,
the world, and those who live in it." **(Ps 24:1)**

We say the earth is our mother—we cannot own her; she owns us.
(Pacific peoples)

THE LOGIC THAT LED TO SLAVERY and segregation in the Americas, colonization and apartheid in Africa, and the rule of white supremacy throughout the world is the same one that leads to the exploitation of animals and the ravaging of nature. It is a mechanistic and instrumental logic that defines everything and everybody in terms of their contribution to the development and defense of white world supremacy. People who fight against white racism but fail to connect it to the degradation of the earth are anti-ecological,

113

whether they know it or not. People who struggle against ecological injustice but do not incorporate in it a disciplined and sustained fight against white supremacy are racists, whether they acknowledge it or not. The fight for justice cannot be segregated but must be integrated with the fight for life in all its forms.

Until recently, ecological justice has not been a major theme in the liberation movements in the African-American community. "Blacks don't care about the environment" is a typical comment by white ecologists. Racial and economic justice has been at best only a marginal concern in the mainstream environmental movement. "White people care more about the endangered whale and the spotted owl than they do about the survival of young blacks in our nation's cities" is a well-founded belief in the African-American community. Justice fighters for blacks and the defenders of the earth have tended to ignore each other in their public discourse and practice. Their separation from each other is unfortunate, because they are fighting the same enemy—human beings' domination of each other and nature.

The leaders in the mainstream environmental movement are mostly middle and upper class whites who are unprepared culturally and intellectually to dialogue with angry blacks. The leaders in the African-American community are leery of talking about anything with whites that will distract from the menacing reality of racism. What both groups fail to realize is how much they need each other in the struggle for justice, peace, and the integrity of creation.[1]

In this essay, I want to challenge the black freedom movement to take a critical look at itself through the lens of the ecological movement and also challenge the ecological movement to critique itself through a serious and ongoing engagement of racism in American history and culture. Hopefully, we can break the silence and promote genuine solidarity between the two groups and thereby enhance the quality of life for the whole inhabited earth—humankind and otherkind.

EXPANDING THE RACE CRITIQUE

No threat has been more deadly and persistent for black and indigenous peoples than the rule of white supremacy in the modern world. For over 500 years, through the wedding of science and technology, white people have been exploiting nature and killing people of color in every nook and cranny of the planet in the name of God and democracy. According to the English historian Basil Davidson, the Atlantic slave trade "cost Africa fifty million souls."[2] Author Eduardo Galeano claims that 150 years of Spanish and Portuguese colonization in Central and South America reduced the indigenous population from 90 million to 3.5 million.[3] During the twenty-three-year reign of terror of King Leopold II of Belgium in the Congo (1885–1908), scholarly estimates suggest that approximately ten million Congolese met unnatural deaths—"fully half the territory's population."[4] The tentacles of white supremacy have stretched around the globe. No people of color have been able to escape its cultural, political, and economic domination.

Blacks in the US have been the most visible and articulate opponents of white racism. From Frederick Douglass and Sojourner Truth to Martin Luther King Jr., Malcolm X, and Fannie Lou Hamer, African-Americans have wedged a persistent fight against white racism in all its overt and covert manifestations. White racism denied the humanity of black people, and even theologians debated whether blacks had souls. Some said blacks were subhuman "beasts."[5] Other more progressive theologians, such as Union Seminary's Reinhold Niebuhr, hoped that the inferiority of the Negro was not "biological" but was due instead to "cultural backwardness," which could gradually with education be overcome.[6]

Enslaved for 244 years, lynched and segregated another hundred, blacks, with militant words and action, fought back in every way they could, defending their humanity against all who had the nerve to question it. Malcolm X, perhaps the most fierce and uncompromising public defender of black humanity, expressed the raw feelings of most blacks: "We declare our right on this earth . . . to be a human being, to be respected as a human being, to be given the rights of a human being in this society, on this earth, in this day, which we intend to bring into existence by any means necessary."[7]

Whites bristled when they heard Malcolm talk like that. They not only knew Malcolm meant what he said but feared that most blacks agreed with him—though they seldom said so publicly. Whites also knew that if they were black, they too would say a resounding "Amen!" to Malcolm's blunt truth. "If you want to know what I'll do," Malcolm told whites, "figure out what you'll do."[8]

White theologians thanked God for being "truly longsuffering, 'slow to anger and plenteous in mercy' (Ps 103:8)," as Reinhold Niebuhr put it, quoting the Hebrew Scriptures. Niebuhr knew that white people did not have a leg to stand on before the bar of God's justice regarding their treatment of people of color: "If the white man were to expiate his sins committed against the darker races, few would have the right to live."[9]

Black liberation theology is a product of a fighting spirituality derived from nearly four hundred years of black resistance. As one who encountered racism first as a child in Bearden, Arkansas, no day in my life has passed in which I have not had to deal with the open and hidden violence of white supremacy. Whether in the society or the churches, at Adrian College or Union Seminary, racism was always there—often smiling and sometimes angry. Since writing my first essay on racism in the white church and its theology thirty years ago, I decided that I would never be silent about white supremacy and would oppose it with my whole being. Opposition to white supremacy is as important to me as fighting anti-Semitism is for Jews, patriarchy for women, class exploitation for the poor, and homophobia for gays and lesbians.

While white racism must be opposed at all cost, our opposition will not be effective unless we expand our vision. Racism and other evils, including the degradation of the earth, are deeply interrelated. It is important for black people, therefore, to make the connection between the struggle against racism and other struggles for life. A few black leaders recognized this need and joined the nineteenth-century abolitionist movement with the suffragist movement, and the 1960s civil rights movement with the second wave of the women's movement. Similar links were made with the justice struggles of other US minorities, gay rights struggles, and poor peoples' fight for freedom around the world. Martin Luther King Jr.'s idea of the "beloved community" is a potent symbol for people struggling to build one world community where life in all its forms is respected. "All life is interrelated," King said. "Whatever affects one directly affects all indirectly. . . . There is an interrelated structure of reality."

Connecting racism with the degradation of the earth is a much needed work in the African-American community, especially in black liberation theology and the black churches. Womanist theologians have already begun this important intellectual work. Delores Williams explores a "parallel between defilement of black women's bodies" and the exploitation of nature. Emilie Townes views "toxic waste landfills in African American communities" as "contemporary versions of lynching a whole people." Karen Baker-Fletcher, using prose and poetry, appropriates the biblical and literary metaphors of dust and spirit to speak about the embodiment of God in creation. "Our task," she writes, "is to grow large hearts, large minds, reconnecting with earth, Spirit, and one another. Black religion must grow ever deeper in the heart."[10]

The leadership of African-American churches turned its much needed attention toward ecological issues in the early 1990s. The catalyst, as usual in the African-American community, was a group of black churchwomen. These women, from Warren County, North Carolina, in 1982 lay on a road to block dump trucks carrying soil contaminated with highly toxic PCBs (polychlorinated biphenyl). In two weeks, more than four hundred protesters were arrested, "the first time anyone in the United States had been jailed trying to halt a toxic waste landfill."[11] Although local residents were not successful in stopping the landfill construction, that incident sparked the attention of civil rights and black church leaders and initiated the national environmental justice movement. In 1987 the United Church of Christ's Commission of Racial Justice issued its groundbreaking "Report on Race and Toxic Wastes in the United States."

This study found that "among a variety of indicators race was the best predictor of the location of hazardous waste facilities in the U.S."[12] Forty percent of the nation's commercial hazardous waste landfill capacity was in three predominately African-American and Hispanic communities. The largest landfill in the nation is in Sumter County, Alabama, where nearly 70 percent of its 17,000 residents are black and 96 percent are poor.

In October 1991 the first National People of Color Environmental Leadership Summit was convened in Washington, DC. More than 650 grassroots and national leaders from the fifty states, the District of Columbia, Mexico, Puerto Rico, and the Marshall Islands participated. They represented more than three hundred environmental groups of color. They all agreed that "if this nation is to achieve environmental justice, the environment in urban ghettoes, barrios, reservations, and rural poverty pockets must be given the same protection as that provided to the suburbs."[13]

The knowledge that people of color are disproportionately affected by environmental pollution angered the black church community and fired up its leadership to take a more active role in fighting against "environmental racism," a phrase that was coined by Benjamin Chavis, who was the director of the United Church of Christ Commission on Racial Justice.[14] Bunyan Bryant, a professor in the School of Natural Resources and Environment at the University of Michigan and a participant in the environmental justice movement, defines environmental racism as "an extension of racism."

Environmental racism refers to those institutional rules, regulations, and policies or government or corporate decisions that deliberately target certain communities for least desirable land uses, resulting in the disproportionate exposure of toxic and hazardous waste on communities based upon certain prescribed biological characteristics. It is the unequal protection against toxic and hazardous waste exposure and the systematic exclusion of people of color from environmental decisions affecting their communities.[15]

The more blacks found out about the racist politics of the government and corporations, the more determined they became in their opposition to environmental injustice. In December 1993, under the sponsorship of the National Council of Churches, leaders of mainline black churches held a historic two-day summit meeting on the environment in Washington, DC. They linked environmental issues with civil rights and economic justice. They did not talk much about the ozone layer, global warming, the endangered whale, or the spotted owl. They focused primarily on the urgent concerns of their communities: toxic and hazardous wastes, lead poisoning, landfills, and incinerators. "We have been living next to the train tracks, trash dumps, coal plants and insect-infested swamps for many decades," Bishop Frederick C. James of the African Methodist Episcopal Church said. "We in the Black community have been disproportionately affected by toxic dumping, disproportionately affected by lead paint at home, disproportionately affected by dangerous chemicals in the workplace." Black clergy also linked local problems with global issues. "If toxic waste is not safe enough to be dumped in the United States, it is not safe enough to be dumped in Ghana, Liberia, Somalia, nor anywhere else in the world," proclaimed Charles G. Adams, pastor of Hartford Memorial Baptist Church in Detroit. "If hazardous materials are not fit to be disposed in the suburbs, they are certainly not fit to be disposed of in the cities."[16]

Like black church leaders, African-American politicians also are connecting social justice issues with ecology. According to the League of Conservation Voters, the Congressional Black Caucus has "one of the best pro-environment voting records" in Congress. "Working for clean air, clean water, and a clean planet," declared Rep. John Lewis of Georgia, "is just as important, if not more important, than anything I have ever worked on, including civil rights."[17]

Black and other poor people in all racial groups receive much less than their fair share of everything good in the world and much more than their share of the bad. Middle class and elite white environmentalists have been very effective in implementing the slogan "Not In My Back Yard" (NIMBY). As a result, corporations and the government merely turned to the backyards of the poor to deposit their toxic waste. The poor live in the least desirable areas of our cities and rural communities. They work in the most polluted and physically dangerous workplaces. Decent health care hardly exists. With fewer resources to cope with the dire consequences of pollution, the poor bear an unequal burden for technological development while the rich reap most of the benefits. This makes racism and poverty ecological issues. If blacks and other hard-hit communities do not raise these ethical and political problems, they will continue to die a slow and silent death on the planet.

Ecology touches every sphere of human existence. It is not just an elitist or a white middle class issue. A clean, safe environment is a human and civil rights issue that impacts the lives of poor blacks and other marginal groups. We therefore must not let the fear of distracting from racism blind us to the urgency of the ecological crisis. What good is it to eliminate racism if we are not around to enjoy a racist free environment?

The survival of the earth, therefore, is a moral issue for everybody. If we do not save the earth from human destructive behavior, no one will survive. That fact alone ought to be enough to inspire people of all colors to join hands in the fight for a just and sustainable planet.

EXPANDING THE ECOLOGICAL CRITIQUE

We are indebted to ecologists in all fields and areas of human endeavor for sounding the alarm about the earth's distress. They have been so effective in raising ecological awareness that few people deny that our planet is in deep trouble. For the first time in history, humankind has the knowledge and power to destroy all life—either with a nuclear bang or a gradual poisoning of the land, air, and sea.

Scientists have warned us of the dire consequences of what human beings are doing to the environment. Theologians and ethicists have raised the moral and religious issues. Grassroots activists in many communities are organizing to stop the killing of nature and its creatures. Politicians are paying attention to people's concerns for a clean, safe environment. "It is not so much a question of whether the lion will one day lie down with the lamb," writes Alice Walker, "but whether human beings will ever be able to lie down with any creature or being at all."[18]

What is absent from much of the talk about the environment in first-world countries is a truly radical critique of the culture most responsible for the ecological crisis. This is especially true among white ethicists and theologians in the United States. In most of the essays and books I have read, there is hardly a hint that perhaps whites could learn something of how we got into this ecological mess from those who have been the victims of white world supremacy. White ethicists and theologians sometimes refer to the disproportionate impact of hazardous waste on blacks and other people of color in the United States and in the third world and even cite an author or two here and there throughout the development of their discourse on ecology. They often include a token black or Indian in anthologies on eco-justice and eco-feminism. It is "politically correct" to demonstrate a knowledge of and concern for people of color in progressive theological circles. But people of color are not treated seriously, that is, as if they have something *essential* to contribute to the conversation. Environmental justice concerns of poor people of color hardly ever merit serious attention, not to mention organized resistance. How can we create a genuinely mutual ecological dialogue between whites and people of color if one party acts as if they have all the power and knowledge?

Do we have any reason to believe that the culture most responsible for the ecological crisis will also provide the moral and intellectual resources for the earth's liberation? White ethicists and theologians apparently think so, since so much of their discourse about theology and the earth is just talk among themselves. But I have deep suspicion about the theological and ethical values of white culture and religion. For 500 years whites have acted as if they owned the world's resources and have forced people of color to accept their scientific and ethical values. People of color have studied dominant theologies and ethics because our physical and spiritual survival partly has depended on it. Now that humanity has reached the possibility of extinction, one would think that a critical assessment of how we got to where we are would be the next step for sensitive and caring theologians of the earth. While there is some radical questioning along these lines, it has not been persistent or challenging enough to compel whites to look outside of their dominating culture for ethical and cultural resources for the earth's salvation. One can still earn a doctoral degree in ethics and theology at American seminaries, even here at Union Seminary in New York, and not seriously engage racism in this society and the world. If we save the planet and have a society of inequality, we would not have saved much.

According to Audre Lorde, "The master's tools will never dismantle the master's house."[19] The master's tools are too narrow and bear the assumption that people of color have nothing to say about race, gender, sexuality, and the earth—all of which are interconnected. We need theologians and ethicists who are interested in mutual dialogue, honest conversation about justice for the earth and all of its inhabitants. We need whites who are eager to know something about the communities of people of color—our values, hopes, and dreams. Whites know so little about our churches and communities that it is often too frustrating to even talk to them about anything that matters. Dialogue requires respect and knowledge of the other—their history, culture, and religion. No one racial or national group has all the answers, but all groups have something to contribute to the earth's healing.

Many ecologists speak often of the need for humility and mutual dialogue. They tell us that we are all interrelated and interdependent, including human and otherkind. The earth is not a machine. It is an organism in which all things are a part of each other. "Every entity in the universe," writes Catherine Keller, "can be described as a process of interconnection with every other being."[20] If white ecologists really believe that, why do most still live in segregated communities? Why are their essays and books about the endangered earth so monological—that is, a conversation of a dominant group talking to itself? Why is there so much talk about love, humility, interrelatedness, and interdependence and yet so little of these values reflected in white people's dealings with people of color?

Blacks and other minorities are often asked why they are not involved in the mainstream ecological movement. To white theologians and ethicists I ask, why are you not involved in the dialogue on race? I am not referring primarily to President Clinton's failed initiative but to the initiative started by the civil rights and black power movements and black liberation theology more than forty years ago. How do we account for the conspicuous white silence on racism, not only in the society and world but especially in theology, ethics, and ecology? I have yet to read a white theologian or ethicist who has incorporated a sustained, radical critique of white supremacy in his or her theological discourse similar to his or her engagement of anti-Semitism, class contradictions, and patriarchy. In fact, many white religion scholars regard black theology's attack on white supremacy as racism in reverse. With sophisticated theological logic divorced from history, they skillfully make the affirmation of the "Black Christ" in a world of white supremacy appear to be the same as the "the Anglo-Saxon Christ" and "the Afrikaner Christ."[21] That is like saying that Malcolm X's racism was similar to George Wallace's.

To be sure, a few concerned white theologians have written about their opposition to white racism, but not because race critique was essential to their theological identity. It is usually just a gesture of support for people of color when solidarity across differences is in vogue. As soon as it is no longer socially and intellectually acceptable to talk about race, white theologians revert back to their silence. But as Elie Wiesel said in his Nobel Peace Prize acceptance speech, "We must take sides. Neutrality helps the oppressor, never the victim. Silence encourages the tormentor, never the tormented."[22] Only when white theologians realize that a fight against racism is a fight for *their* humanity will we be able to create a coalition of blacks, whites, and other people of color in the struggle to save the earth.

Today ecology is in vogue and many people are talking about our endangered planet. I want to urge us to deepen our conversation by linking the earth's crisis with the crisis in the human family. If it is important to save the habitats of birds and other species, then it is at least equally important to save black lives in the ghettoes and prisons of America. As Gandhi said, "The earth is sufficient for everyone's need but not for everyone's greed."[23]

James H. Cone is the Charles A. Briggs Distinguished Professor of Systematic Theology at Union Theological Seminary in New York and is the author of numerous books, including *Black Theology and Black Power, A Black Theology of Liberation, Martin & Malcolm & America: A Dream or a Nightmare?*, and *God of the Oppressed*.

Notes

1. See *Justice, Peace and the Integrity of Creation*, ed. James W. van Hoeven for the World Alliance of Reformed Churches Assembly, Seoul, Korea, August 1989; and Preman Niles, *Resisting the Threats to Life: Covenanting for Justice, Peace, and the Integrity of Creation* (Geneva, Switzerland: WCC Publications, 1989).

2. Basil Davidson, *The African Slave Trade: Pre-colonial History 1450–1850* (Boston: Little, Brown & Co., 1961), 80.

3. Eduardo Galeano, *Open Veins of Latin America: Five Centuries of the Pillage of a Continent* (London: Monthly Review Press, 1973), 50.

4. Adam Hochschild, "Hearts of Darkness: Adventures in the Slave Trade," *San Francisco Examiner Magazine*, August 16, 1998, 13. Louis Turner posits five to eight million in *Multinational Companies and the Third World* (New York: Hill & Wang, 1973), 27.

5. Charles Carroll, *The Negro a Beast* (St. Louis: American Book & Bible House, 1900).

6. Reinhold Niebuhr, "Justice to the American Negro from State, Community, and Church," in *Pious and Secular America* (New York: Charles Scribner's Sons, 1958), 81.

7. Malcolm X, *By Any Means Necessary* (New York: Pathfinder Press, 1970), 56.

8. Malcolm X, *Malcolm X Speaks*, ed. George Breitman (New York: Grove Press, 1965), 197–98.

9. Reinhold Niebuhr, "The Assurance of Grace," in *The Essential Reinhold Niebuhr: Selected Essays and Addresses*, ed. Robert M. Brown (New Haven, CT: Yale University Press, 1986), 65.

10. Delores Williams, "A Womanist Perspective on Sin," in *A Troubling in My Soul: Womanist Perspectives on Evil and Suffering*, ed. Emilie M. Townes (Maryknoll, NY: Orbis, 1993), 145–47; Williams, "Sin, Nature, and Black Women's Bodies," in *Ecofeminism and the Sacred*, ed. Carol J. Adams (New York: Continuum, 1993), 24–29; Emilie Townes, *In a Blaze of Glory: Womanist Spirituality as Social Witness* (Nashville: Abingdon, 1995), 55; Karen Baker-Fletcher, *Sisters of Dust, Sisters of Spirit: Womanist Wordings on God and Creation* (Minneapolis: Fortress, 1998), 93.

11. Robert Bullard, *Dumping in Dixie: Race, Class, and Environmental Quality* (Boulder, CO: Westview Press, 1990), 31.

12. "Report on Race and Toxic Wastes in the United States," in *Race and the Incidence of Environmental Hazards: A Time for Discourse* ed. Bunyan Bryant and Paul Mohai (Boulder, CO: Westview Press, 1992), 2. See also Bunyan Bryant, ed., *Environmental Justice: Issues, Policies, and Solutions* (Washington, DC: Island Press, 1995); and "African American Denominational Leaders Pledge Their Support to the Struggle Against Environmental Racism," *A.M.E. Christian Recorder*, May 18, 1998, 8, 11.

13. Robert Bullard, "Environmental Justice for All," in *Unequal Protection: Environmental Justice and Communities of Color*, ed. Robert D. Bullard (San Francisco: Sierra Club Books, 1994), 3–22.

14. Chavis is now known as Benjamin Chavis Muhammad and is currently serving as the national minister in Louis Farrakhan's Nation of Islam.

15. Bunyan Bryant, introduction to *Environmental Justice*, 5.

16. *National Black Church Environmental and Economic Justice Summit*, Washington, DC, December 1–2, 1993, National Council of the Churches of Christ in the USA, Prophetic Justice Unit. This is a booklet with all the speeches of the meeting, including the one by Vice President Gore.

17. See Ronald A. Taylor, "Do Environmentalists Care about the Poor?" *U.S. News and World Report*, April 2, 1982, 51–52; Bullard, *Dumping in Dixie*, 15; Deeohn Ferris and David Hahn-Baker, "Environmentalists and Environmental Justice Policy," in Bryant, *Environmental Justice*, 68; Dorceta E. Taylor, "Environmentalism and the Politics of Inclusion," in *Confronting Environmental Racism: Voices from the Grassroots* ed. Robert Bullard (Boston: South End Press, 1993).

18. Alice Walker, *Living by the Word: Selected Writings 1973–1987* (San Diego: Harcourt Brace Jovanovich, 1988), 173.

19. Audre Lorde, *Sister Outsider* (Trumansburg, NY: Crossing Press, 1984), 110.

20. Catherine Keller, *From a Broken Web: Separation, Sexism, Self* (Boston: Beacon, 1986), 5.

21. See especially Alan Davies, *Infected Christianity: A Study of Modern Racism* (Kingston, Ont.: McGill-Queen's University Press, 1988). Along with the "Germanic Christ," "Latin Christ," "Anglo-Saxon Christ," and "Afrikaner Christ," Davies also includes the "Black Christ" as a modern manifestation of racism. It never ceases to amaze me how white theologians call black people racists when we seek to find worth in history and culture. I know of no white people who have been oppressed by blacks affirming themselves. Compare that with the horrendous psychological and physical violence that whites have committed

against people of color. To call black resistance to white supremacy black racism is simply wrong.

22. The text of this speech is available at http://www.pbs.org/eliewiesel/nobel/index.html.

23. Cited in Leonardo Boff, *Cry of the Earth, Cry of the Poor* (Maryknoll, NY: Orbis, 1997), 2.

IN HIM ALL THINGS
HOLD TOGETHER

ELLEN F. DAVIS

THIS SERMON WAS PREACHED at Virginia Theological Seminary on October 22, 1997, in conjunction with the annual Sprigg Lectures, which that year focused on the challenge to Christian life and thought occasioned by the ecological crisis. The text for the sermon, Colossians 1:11–23, is one of the passages appointed in the Book of Common Prayer for a eucharistic service focusing on the theme "Of the Reign of Christ." The sermon refers directly and indirectly to that theme and to the texts appointed for it.

> May you be made strong with all the strength that comes from his glorious power, and may you be prepared to endure everything with patience, while joyfully giving thanks to the Father, who has enabled you to share in the inheritance of the saints in the light. He has rescued us from the power of darkness and transferred us into the kingdom of his beloved Son, in whom we have redemption, the forgiveness of sins.
>
> He is the image of the invisible God, the firstborn of all creation; for in him all things in heaven and on earth were created, things

visible and invisible, whether thrones or dominions or rulers or powers—all things have been created through him and for him. He himself is before all things, and in him all things hold together. He is the head of the body, the church; he is the beginning, the firstborn from the dead, so that he might come to have first place in everything. For in him all the fullness of God was pleased to dwell, and through him God was pleased to reconcile to himself all things, whether on earth or in heaven, by making peace through the blood of his cross.

And you who were once estranged and hostile in mind, doing evil deeds, he has now reconciled in his fleshly body through death, so as to present you holy and blameless and irreproachable before him—provided that you continue securely established and steadfast in the faith, without shifting from the hope promised by the gospel that you heard, which has been proclaimed to every creature under heaven. I, Paul, became a servant of this gospel. **(Col 1:11–23)**

When the lectionary stops abruptly in mid-thought, the preacher catches her breath with excitement, for she knows that whatever was left out is bound to be troublesome and for that reason eminently worth preaching. And so it is in this case. The portion of Colossians appointed for the theme "Of the Reign of Christ" stops in the middle of a discussion of how God is reconciling all things to himself through Christ. This morning I overrode the lectionary and let Paul[1] finish the thought so we could hear the crucial assurance: "You who were once estranged and hostile in mind," you, too, can be presented holy and blameless before God, "provided that you continue securely established and steadfast in the faith, without shifting from the hope promised by the gospel that you heard, which has been proclaimed to every creature under heaven."

"The gospel . . . which has been proclaimed to every creature under heaven"—it is easy to see why the lectionary stops short of that phrase, for it is truly wild. Think about it: "every creature under heaven." If we take that seriously, then are we to believe that the good news is meant not just for "every family, language, people and nation"[2] but also for badgers and rocks, fruit bats and giant sequoias? How can we take that seriously? It sounds flaky; it smacks of animism. Moreover, it is too far from our understanding of the Great Commission.[3] However strong may be our commitment to evangelism, who among us is prepared to answer to giant sequoias for our proclamation of the gospel?

On this point Bauer's Greek lexicon would seem to offer relief from our consternation. The Greek word translated "creature" is *ktisis*, and Bauer tells us that this is a wholly exceptional use of the word *ktisis*. Everywhere else in the Bible it appears as the generic word for "creature." Every single thing God ever made falls into that general category of *ktisis*. But in this one place here in Colossians, Bauer advises us, we must see *ktisis* as "limited to human beings."[4] And with that bit of advice, the wild statement is tamed. The gospel is proclaimed exclusively to human beings, just as we always thought.

I am normally a devotee of Professor Bauer and his team of lexicographers, swallowing everything they say and being grateful for it. My Greek is not good enough to warrant too many original ideas. But here I must venture to say that they are wrong, wrong to treat this as an exceptional use of *ktisis*, wrong to restrict its usage to human beings. Indeed, there is every reason *not* to make that restriction, for the whole point of the passage is that human beings cannot be firmly separated off from the rest of the creatures when it comes to the work of God in Christ.

In Christ, Paul (or whoever wrote Colossians) tells us, "all things in heaven and on earth were created, things visible and invisible," humans and powers of the spirit world, things animate and inanimate. "*All things* have been created through [Christ] and for him . . . and in him *all things* hold together" (vv. 16–17). "All things,"—*ta panta* in Greek—is repeated four times. All things hold together in Christ, and through Christ all things are reconciled to God. I do not pretend to completely understand that; this is mystical insight that reaches beyond my grasp. But this I know is true: Colossians presents us with a radical Christology, in which the doctrine of Christ and the doctrine of creation are inextricably intertwined. "He is . . . the firstborn of all creation"—incarnation and creation are finally inseparable, and the inclusion of every creature in the evangelical imperative follows from that. Because God made everything in Christ and for Christ, then it follows that everything needs to hear proclaimed the good news of Christ and actively claim its own place in the gospel story.

The creation is, then, a unity. Every creature—every person, every stick and stone and stallion and seahorse—is profoundly related to every other creature. This is the picture with which Colossians presents us. Yet we who live at this point in the world's history do not seem to require divine revelation in order to recognize the essential unity of creation. Scientific reports and the popular press have made us painfully aware that all of us on "this small blue dot" share a common fate. If the ship goes down, we all drown—a possibility we cannot discount. The solidarity of all creatures is something many of us are coming to acknowledge as a fact, and currently it appears to be a fairly grim fact. What difference, then, does the biblical witness make to us in this matter?

The Letter to the Colossians testifies to the unity of creation *under the universal lordship of Christ.* It shows us that all things hold together, not in bondage to a single threatening fate, but that all things hold together *in Christ.* The difference that biblical faith makes is the difference between accepting a sober fact—our common danger—and accepting an invitation to a party. The Christian participates in the solidarity of the creatures as one who is responding to an invitation to a gala banquet. That is Karl Barth's description of what it means for the Christian to accept the fact that she is a creature, no more and no less, and therefore an honored guest of the sovereign Lord of all the worlds. Thus, Barth describes the scene in the banquet hall: "There [the Christian] takes his place at the table, in the company of publicans, in the company of beasts and plants and stones, accepting solidarity with them, being present simply as they are, as a creature of God."[5]

Christians partying with plants and stones is not a vision of the reign of Christ that our lectionary encourages us to entertain. By abridging the passage, our lectionary, like Bauer's lexicon, backs away from Colossians' testimony that the gospel has indeed "been proclaimed to every creature under heaven." Why are we so reluctant to hear the biblical witness and claim our solidarity with all the creatures of God? Could it be that we are afraid? Afraid to sit down at the banquet table and open a conversation with the nonhuman creatures? Afraid that if we once open that conversation in the presence of God, the other creatures will find their voice and cry out against us? Afraid that the rivers we have dammed, drained, and poisoned will accuse us of culpable negligence? Afraid that the soil we have stripped of its hardwood forests, the seas we have drag-netted and depopulated, will cry out against us for our greed? Afraid that the mountains we are literally taking down to the ground—scraping out veins of low-grade coal and leaving behind vast piles of infertile rubble—will testify against us, that we have undone the work of God's hands, misused our God-given powers for evil, to satisfy our own selfish whims?

That would be an intelligent fear, well informed not only by modern science and the news media but also, and more significantly, by the Bible, where things that we call "insentient" do, in fact, have a voice. The prophets appeal to mountains and hills to give witness to the just judgment of the Creator (Isa 1:2; Deut 32:1). Then there are those "Fantasia" psalms that show a fully animated world: the sea shouting, the rivers clapping their hands, the mountains ringing out with joy, for God comes to "judge the world with righteousness, and the peoples with equity" (Ps 98:9). No wonder they rejoice. God's coming to judge the world is unambiguously good news for the nonhuman creatures. For in the day of judgment, all creatures will stand in immediate relation to the One who made them. For mountains and rivers, God's judgment means freedom; they are free at last from our doubtful mercy. The nonhuman creatures, then, clamor to hear the good news that our

Lord is coming in power and judgment. No wonder we hesitate to sit at table with them—who wants to be lambasted at dinner? Better to stay away, even if that means missing the meal that God has laid for all the creatures.

But the Letter to the Colossians shows us the one condition on which we may come into the banquet hall without fear of humiliation. We must accept one thing about the rules of this house: that the wine served here is the blood of sacrifice. Christ's blood poured out for the life of the world is the wine of fellowship that unites all the creatures. In stunning terms Paul sets forth the sole basis for reconciliation, after all the harm that we have done: "Through [Christ] God was pleased to reconcile to himself all things, whether on earth or in heaven, by making peace through the blood of his cross" (Col 1:20). "Making peace through the blood of his cross"—those words confound our rationalism, and if we can hear them, they draw us deep into "the mystery that has been hidden throughout the ages . . . [that] has now been revealed to [God's] saints" (1:26).

Through the blood of the cross, Jesus Christ is healing a breach that dates back nearly to the beginning of world history. The first chapters of Genesis disclose that the dangerous alienation between us and the other creatures originated not in modern technology but rather in the fallout from the first human disobedience. Alienation became a reality as soon as human beings had begun to seek their own way in the world, apart from God: "The LORD God said to the serpent, '. . . I will put enmity between you and the woman, and between your offspring and hers'" (Gen 3:14–15). But now Christ offers to heal that ancient enmity, "making peace through the blood of the cross." From the cross, the center point of all creation, Christ reaches out to embrace all things and reconcile them to God. Christ the firstborn of all creation, the most privileged of God's children, dying to draw the rest of us back to God—that is an image that has power to heal us from our profound estrangement and hostility of mind, if we can only grasp this one thing: The invitation to the feast of reconciliation is an invitation to sacrifice.

We are invited here, as the liturgy sublimely says, to be united with Christ in his sacrifice.[6] Instructed and emboldened by his sacrifice, we are charged to make it our own. Sacrifice literally means "making holy," sanctifying the world by accepting our lives as pure gift and offering back to God any and all of what God has given us. Strange and sad to say, it is easy to miss or misunderstand what the blood of the cross has to teach us about Christian discipleship. The crucial point is this: Christ's sacrifice does not make our sacrifice unnecessary. Rather, his sacrifice makes ours possible. If we are truly united with Christ in his sacrifice, then we are changed irrevocably, inducted into the strange inverse economics of the kingdom of heaven, where wealth is measured by how much you can afford to do without, comfort level by your ease in giving up.

Sisters and brothers, beloved in the Lord, we are invited now to the feast of reconciliation. If we speak with integrity and eat to our salvation, we commit ourselves to change, to *metanoia*, to new thought and action, bold and profound. What can we do, what can we give or give up, in order that our words and even more our lives may become a genuine and persuasive proclamation of this mystery long hidden that has now been revealed—the mystical solidarity of all creatures, held together in Christ, reconciled to God and one another through the blood of the cross? In our time may that mystical solidarity be made manifest, to God's eternal glory, lest we perish in our estrangement.

Ellen Davis is professor of Bible and practical theology at Duke Divinity School, where she has been active in fostering environmental commitments. She is the author of *Getting Involved with God: Rediscovering the Old Testament* and coeditor of *The Art of Reading Scripture* and *Wondrous Depth: Preaching the Old Testament*. She is currently working on a book, *"The Land I Will Remember": Biblical Interpretation and Ecological Responsibility*.

This sermon was subsequently published in the *Virginia Seminary Journal*, December 1997. It is reprinted here with permission.

Notes

1. Although Pauline authorship of Colossians is much debated, the traditional ascription is followed for rhetorical purposes here.

2. The phrase (from Rev 5:9) appears as a liturgical song (Canticle 18, Book of Common Prayer, 93) that is regularly appointed for a eucharistic service on the theme "Of the Reign of Christ." The congregation had therefore sung it after the reading from Colossians, shortly before the sermon.

3. Compare Matt 28:19–20. Behind the altar in the chapel of Virginia Theological Seminary, where this sermon was preached, appear the words, "Go into all the world and preach the gospel."

4. Walter Bauer, *A Greek-English Lexicon of the New Testament and Other Early Christian Literature*, ed. F. Wilbur Gingrich and Frederick W. Danker (Chicago: University of Chicago Press, 1979), 455.

5. Karl Barth, *Church Dogmatics* III/3 (Edinburgh: T&T Clark, 1975), 242.

6. Compare Eucharistic Prayer B, from the 1979 Book of Common Prayer: "We pray you, gracious God, to send your Holy Spirit upon these gifts that they may be the Sacrament of the Body of Christ and his Blood of the new Covenant. *Unite us to your Son in his sacrifice*, that we may be acceptable through him, being sanctified by the Holy Spirit. In the fullness of time, put all things in subjection under your Christ" (369; italics mine). This form of the Eucharistic Prayer was used at the service.

WHO WILL SPEAK FOR THE
SPIRIT OF THESE WATERS?

J. RONALD ENGEL

THIS IS AN EARTH DAY SERMON based on a public homily, "Lake Michigan as a Source of Spiritual Inspiration," delivered in 1989 at the Conference on Water and Spirit, Northwest Indiana Humanities Consortium, at the Indiana Dunes State Park.

> In the beginning when God created the heavens and the earth, the earth was a formless void and darkness covered the face of the deep, while a wind from God swept over the face of the waters. **(Gen 1:1–2)**

◈

> Let justice roll down like waters,
> and righteousness like an everflowing stream. **(Amos 5:24)**

◈

I

When I arrived at the University of Chicago to take up studies in 1960, I was worried whether anyone on the faculty would understand my enthusiasm for nature and the kind of work I wanted to do in what has since become known as the field of "environmental ethics."

On my first night in Chicago I attended a rally at Orchestra Hall for the antinuclear organization SANE, and one of the speakers was introduced as a professor at the University of Chicago Divinity School. I will never forget looking down at the stage from the upper balcony and seeing the tall, solitary figure of Joseph Sittler standing in the spotlight in the darkness as a hush fell over the audience. Sittler's speech consisted almost entirely of the poem "Advice to a Prophet" by Richard Wilbur. The prophet is advised to forego the alarming statistics of nuclear weapons that offer "the long numbers that rocket the mind," and even to forego warning of the death of the race—"how should we dream of this place without us?" Instead, the prophet is advised to "speak of the world's own change":

> What should we be without
> The dolphin's arc, the dove's return,
>
> These things in which we have seen ourselves and spoken?
> Ask us, prophet, how we shall call
> Our natures forth when that live tongue is all
> Dispelled, that glass obscured or broken,
>
> In which we have said the rose of our love and the clean
> Horse of our courage, in which beheld
> The singing locust of the soul unshelled,
> And all we mean or wish to mean.[1]

Not only were my personal worries about my studies alleviated that evening, but I had my first lesson in environmental ethics.

The roots of environmental ethics lie in our gratitude for the gift of life. In and through our experience of nature we create the world of interlaced meanings and metaphors that constitute our distinctive existence as human beings, the alchemy of the human imagination interacting with other unique actualizations of creative evolution. As Joseph Sittler later wrote, "Not in abstract propositions or dramatic warnings but in powerful, earthy images the poet makes his point. The point is single, simple, and absolute: human selfhood hangs upon the persistence of the earth, her dear known and remembered factualness is the matrix of the self."[2]

II

My favorite time of day is early morning. I go to the window of the office in my home on the twenty-first floor of our co-op apartment building in Chicago and work by the light of the sun rising over Lake Michigan. To walk from my darkened bedroom through the apartment to my office window is to experience each morning a new birth of the world.

I am reminded of Chicago artist Earl Reed's etching entitled "The Spirit upon the Face of the Waters." The etching is of Lake Michigan, but the image he depicts is the first day of creation as it was imagined by the poet who wrote the first chapter of Genesis.

This experience of beholding the bright blue lake with its infinite horizon, as though I were seeing the original waters out of which the earth was made, is a revelation that never fails to bring a catch to my throat. It is an experience that I share with millions of my fellow citizens across the world who feel a similar wonder before the lakes, rivers, and oceans of our beautiful blue planet as it rolls each day through the heavens. By such experiences we are bound in global fellowship.

I feel that fellowship with Carl Sandburg who, in 1894, at the age of sixteen saw Lake Michigan for the first time and wrote:

Out from the huddled and ugly walls,
I came sudden, at the city's edge,
On a blue burst of lake.

I share it with the residents of the settlement houses of Chicago who took the city's new immigrants on pilgrimages to the Lake Michigan shoreline so that they might catch a glimpse of the beauty of their new country—what one of their number, Amalia Hofer, described as "the glorious stretch of rolling blue just beyond." I share it with campers at the parks that ring Lake Michigan. I share it with early morning commuters driving into Chicago. I share it with friends and loved ones at Easter sunrise services and marriage services and on long walks along the shore.

To so experience Lake Michigan is to experience what historians of religion call a *hierophany*, which is when "something sacred shows itself to us." To experience Lake Michigan as a hierophany is to experience it both in itself and as more than itself, as a physical reality and as a medium of grace—a sacrament. Henry David Thoreau put it this way: "I can see, smell, taste, feel that everlasting Something to which we are allied . . . the actual glory of the universe."[3]

The history of religions is the history of hierophanies. We may therefore say without exaggeration that all of us who experience Lake Michigan as a hierophany share the "religion" or spirit of Lake Michigan. This is one of our unique windows onto the infinite.

III

Nothing in our spiritual experience of the lake contradicts what is literally true about it. Instead, it builds upon, deepens, expands, and complements our ordinary experience. According to modern science, water is the earth's most distinctive constituent. It set the stage for the evolution of life and is an essential ingredient in all life. It is, again in Thoreau's words, "the blood of the earth."

While this is true of water as such, it is even truer of freshwater. Although constituting less than 3 percent of the earth's total store of water, freshwater is the form most necessary to the procreation and survival of life. Lake Michigan is one of the largest bodies of freshwater on the face of the earth. It therefore functions as a primary reservoir in the life-giving circulation of water throughout the planet.

Our spiritual experience of Lake Michigan confirms and deepens this scientific truth. It is common testimony that through Lake Michigan we make contact with the recurring miracle of creation. But it is not only the miracle of original creation—the primordial creative processes of life—that we experience. It is also the miracle of regeneration, rebirth. The lake is the agency for the healing of the body and the purification of the soul associated for millennia with sacred rites of immersion in water. It is no accident that we refer to what the thousands of sun-tanned folks who crowd our beaches each summer are doing as "re-creation."

The ancients understood this. Tertullian, for example, wrote this in the second century of the Christian era:

> Water was the first to be commanded to bring forth living creatures. . . . Water was the first to produce what has life, so as to prevent our being astonished when one day it came to give birth to life in baptism. In forming man himself, God used water to complete his work. . . . Why should not that which produces life from the earth not also give the life of heaven?[4]

In my own experience of Lake Michigan, creation and re-creation are so fused that it is difficult to tell them apart. However tired or miserable I may be, Lake Michigan is there to renew me. Many attest to the fact that the lake "saves" them from the frantic routines of a market society, "centers" them spiritually, and bestows the benediction of "peace."

Chicago author Donald Culross Peattie worked for the *Chicago Daily News*. Once, after a night spent reporting the sins of humanity, he drove home along Lake Shore Drive at four a.m. Later he wrote, "From the east, from over the great cool lake, some mercy, newly sent once more, in spite of all our sorry yesterdays, was coming now to spread in radiance and freshness over all the city. In the waning dark I felt the offer of its purification."[5]

The power that creates is the power that redeems.

Is it any surprise that, face to face with this wild, free, pure manifestation of the sacred, face to face with such an overpowering symbol of cosmic creation and redemption, many persons over the years have discovered their life's vocation on the shores of Lake Michigan? Dorothy Day made her vow to serve the poor while walking in solitude on the lakeshore of Chicago. Illinois senator Paul

Douglas, alone on the beach one night, took an oath to save the Indiana Dunes from the spreading fires of industrialization. Author-naturalist Sigurd Olson learned the science of ecology on the shore-line of Lake Michigan while a student at the University of Chicago. In 1960, he revisited the dune beaches and asked himself whether his vocation as wilderness advocate was still worth pursuing. He later wrote:

> Imagine my surprise and delight to stand on the old beach once more watching the Surf rolling in from the north just as I remembered. The water was opalescent, the white caps marching in great rows as far as I could see. I looked toward the west and to the smoky concentration of steel mills. . . . I looked to the northwest to the twinkling lights and massive skyline of Chicago's loop. . . . The wave crashed at my feet and the roar of the surf was everywhere. *This was the moment of truth.*[6]

I cannot omit from my account of the hierophanies of Lake Michigan the passionate love that the lake evokes in us, our sense that wherever life my take us, Lake Michigan will always be a part of us, that we are forever bound to it and its Creator in a relationship of enduring affection.

Lake Michigan is a sacrament of the creative and regenerative powers of existence, the special window upon the universe we who inhabit this region have been given. It defines us, orients us, calls us, and tests us. It is an experience of what theologians call "common grace"—grace poured out through the natural world for all persons, irrespective of wealth, status, race, or creed. If anything is our common possession, inheritance, and responsibility, it is this lake. We would not be half the people we are without it.

IV

I wish I could leave it at that. But I cannot do so any more than I can go to my window in the morning and not remember Thoreau's aphorism "Morning is when I am awake and there is a dawn in me.

Moral reform is the effort to throw off sleep." What can I do this day to show that I am truly awake? How can I make my life a perpetual Lake Michigan sunrise?

This would be an utterly unfaithful speech if I did not point out that Lake Michigan is being abused and that this fact raises the most far-reaching and difficult questions for those of us upon whom she daily bestows her blessings.

I do not know all that is being done to Lake Michigan. I am not an expert in these matters. But recent reports indicate that toxic chemicals and metals—including seven chemicals included in the "dirty dozen" now subject to an international phaseout under a United Nations treaty—continue to enter Lake Michigan in dangerous amounts and threaten the health of humans and the ecosystem. Fish advisories remain in effect, and beaches continue to be closed.

I would ask us to pause and see these realities not as "another bit of bad news," which is how we are taught to think about evils such as war, pollution, and injustice. Rather, I invite you to consider their significance in light of what we have just said. This means moving from the sacramental to the prophetic dimension, from what theologians sometimes call a shift from "manifestation" to "proclamation." Richard Wilbur and Joseph Sittler were offering advice to prophets, advice that we ourselves should recall. They were telling us that prophecy should be grounded in our sacramental experience of the gift of life, but that it is nonetheless still prophecy. This requires us to confront moral transgression, name the agents and agencies responsible, and ask what actions we can take to change the situation.

In this light, these facts become not merely matters for debate among technical experts but matters of profound moral and spiritual import. To speak of *pollution* is to recall its original meaning of desecration—the defilement of what is holy. Great are the pressures not to do this, to limit our meditations on spirit and water to the good and to avert our eyes from the evil. Nothing would please the agents of moral transgression more than for us to dwell exclusively upon the aesthetic, mystical, beneficent aspects of our experience and to neglect the redemptive demands of the ethical and the political.

When the EPA charged United States Steel's Gary Works plant with dumping unacceptable amounts of sewage, oil, ammonia, cyanide, metals, and other pollution into Lake Michigan and the east branch of the Grand Calumet River, the company spokesman responded to the charge by stating that the "alleged violations are mostly technical in nature and not above acceptable levels." My immediate response was: I do not care what the technical considerations are! How can *any* amount of sewage, oil, ammonia, cyanide, and metals dumped into Lake Michigan be acceptable?

But there are other kinds of sacrilege. Shoreline development is booming. And as a result, access to Lake Michigan is becoming more and more a matter of economic privilege. Yet the hierophany of Lake Michigan is a matter of *common grace*.

It so happens that many of those persons who, over the years, have most powerfully borne witness to the spiritual meaning of Lake Michigan have also been those who have insisted upon equal access to the lake by all persons. In the words of landscape architect Jens Jensen, the lakeshore is a revelation meant for "all the people," but especially for the laborer and the poor. The plaque that commemorates the life of Paul Douglas in the national lakeshore reads in part: "Paul Douglas believed in open space as a source of spiritual renewal. . . . He felt that all citizens, rich and poor, should have access to that same source of strength, and he worked for the last twenty years of his life that here, at least, it might be so."

Surely, the hierophany of Lake Michigan must include justice for all.

We must carry this question of access one step further. I am often puzzled by those who believe that our lakeshore has been "saved." One hard look at most of the lakefront in the Wisconsin/ Illinois/Indiana/Michigan region will reveal that our dominant understanding of what constitutes access to Lake Michigan is sadly anthropocentric. It is access by human beings to Lake Michigan. It is not access by crustaceans, fish, waterfowl, amphibians, reptiles, mammals, native grasses, trees, and wildflowers. We are experiencing a lake that is shorn of its natural biota and is no longer a living system.

Is it not a vast injustice against the creation itself that the source of so much created goodness in the world is denied? Can we call our experience of the lake truly creative and redemptive if we experience it apart from our fellow human beings and our fellow creatures?

Might this not give us new understanding of the words of Amos: "Let justice roll down like waters, and righteousness like an ever-flowing stream"?

V

Who will speak for the spirit of these waters? Who among us has the poetic capacity to celebrate the sacramental quality of our experience of this lake and the moral courage to utter the prophetic word? Do the government agencies with which we have entrusted the care of this lake have the necessary authority, credibility, and wisdom to discharge their missions? Are our political leaders capable of placing the common good above special interests? Will the corporations finally act in such a way as to justify the freedom they have enjoyed for so many years in America?

Of all the institutions of our society, one would expect the churches, the synagogues, and the temples to be the clearest and most powerful voice for the spirit of these waters. Yet few religious voices have spoken out in prophetic defense of this lake. New winds are blowing in our religious communities. Christians are beginning to rediscover their biblical faith in the world as God's creation. But will they allow this place, this lake, to speak its revelation to them?

Can voluntary associations of citizens speak out to defend the lake? Do the conservation organizations that have fought so hard for the lake and to whom we owe an immense debt of gratitude also have the capacity to attend to the spiritual motivation of their activities? Do the schools, colleges and universities? Do the libraries and museums and hospitals? Do the professions? Do we? Do we have the capacity to change our lifestyles and our economic way of life? To rise to the vocation of prophetic citizenship? To hold our institutions accountable? To abstain from making the demands on the resources of the earth that cannot be made if the lake is to flourish and endure?

Who will speak for the spirit of these waters?

Ron Engel is senior research consultant with the Center for Humans and Nature and professor emeritus at Meadville/Lombard Theological School. He is the author of *Sacred Sands: The Struggle for Community in the Indiana Dunes,* which won the Meltzer National Book Award; coeditor of *Ethics of Environment and Development: Global Challenge, International Response;* coauthor of *Justice, Ecology, and Christian Faith: A Critical Guide to the Literature;* and author of over sixty articles in the field of environmental social ethics, history, and philosophy.

Notes

1. Richard Wilber, "Advice to a Prophet," in *Advice to Prophet and Other Poems* (Harcourt, Brace and World, Inc., 1959), 12–13.
2. Joseph Sittler, *The Care of the Earth and Other University Sermons* (Philadelphia: Fortress Press, 1964), 89.
3. Henry David Thoreau, *A Week on the Concord and Merrimac Rivers* (Princeton: Princeton University Press, 1983), 173.
4. Tertullian, *Tertullian's Treatises: Concerning Prayer, Concerning Baptism,* translated by Alexander Souter (New York: MacMillan, 1919).
5. Donald Culross Peattie, "A Breath of Outdoors," *Chicago Daily News,* Septermber 14, 1937.
6. Sigurd Olson, "Indiana Dunes Revisited," *The Isaak Walton Magazine,* January, 1966.

THE LORD'S PRAYER FOR EARTH COMMUNITY

DIETER HESSEL

THIS SERMON WAS PREACHED IN MARCH 2001 during a Savannah (Georgia) Presbytery Conference on "Preaching the Stewardship of Creation." The crisis of ecological destruction and social injustice is global as well as local, and it threatens the whole earth. The purpose of these reflections is to show that a faithful response to the environmental justice challenge can be discerned in the phrases of the Lord's Prayer.

> Happy are those whose help is the God of Jacob,
>> whose hope is in the Lord their God,
> who made heaven and earth,
>> the sea, and all that is in them;
> who keeps faith forever,
>> who executes justice for the oppressed,
> who gives food to the hungry.
>
> The LORD sets the prisoners free;
>> the LORD opens the eyes of the blind.

The LORD lifts up those who are bowed down;
the LORD loves the righteous. **(Ps 146:5-8)**

◈

When you are praying, do not heap up empty phrases as the Gentiles do; for they think that they will be heard because of their many words. Do not be like them, for your Father knows what you need before you ask him.

Pray then in this way:

Our Father in heaven,
hallowed be your name.
Your kingdom come.
Your will be done,
on earth as it is in heaven.
Give us this day our daily bread.
And forgive us our debts,
as we also have forgiven our debtors.
And do not bring us to the time of trial,
but rescue us from the evil one. **(Matt 6:7-13)**

◈

The prayer Jesus taught his disciples—a prayer that Christians worldwide repeat during worship—deserves fresh interpretation as a guide to living faithfully in earth community. Biblical scholars, theologians, and pastors throughout church history have offered helpful commentaries on the Lord's Prayer as a model for our *praying*. Building on that heritage and in response to our era's global crisis of ecology and justice, my purpose is to highlight resonant meanings of this spiritual treasure for our way of *living*.

The crisis of ecological destruction and social injustice looms very large in our time because it has become global, not merely local, and because it threatens the whole earth community as well as ecosystems and communities. A faithful worldview and consistent path of behavior to meet this challenge can be discerned as we become environmentally and socially mindful of what some of the phrases in the Lord's Prayer mean for being Christian.

We need to reread Jesus' prayer in light of the whole biblical story that calls us to love and to treat justly both neighbor and nature. To summarize all too briefly, the creation narratives in Genesis and the Sabbath ethic embodied in covenant law enjoin us not only to protect orphans, widows, and strangers but also to care for the land, to respect other creatures, and to protect their habitats, because the natural order and its many species possess inherent worth as the Creator's handiwork. Various psalms rejoice in the natural order as a place of divine presence for the common good. Analogies from nature are prominent in the Wisdom literature (and in parables that Jesus taught in that tradition). Also, the prophets highlight a causal link between social injustice and environmental degradation. Hosea declares that if we disregard covenant obligations to live rightly, "even the birds will die." The New Testament shows Jesus' love for nature, and the Apostle Paul proclaims that God in Jesus Christ redeems the whole creation, not just those who believe in him. The biblical story definitely calls us to restore creation for ecology and justice. The Lord's Prayer reinforces this orientation.

Still, many Christians who claim to love the Bible have not "heard" this message or recognized its eco-justice emphasis. A world-denying posture (expressed in some theologies and hymns) has led quite a few Christians to devalue the earth and to ignore the health of both nature and society, while focusing narrowly on their own salvation. They are not thinking in terms of "Your will be done, on earth as it is in heaven." Expecting this world to end soon, they care little and do little for the well-being of this planet, including all of its impoverished people, threatened species, and deteriorating ecosystems.

What Christians pray for, including the future they expect, does make a real public difference, as can be seen in the contrast between two late-twentieth-century US secretaries of the interior. One was James Watt, interior secretary in the Reagan administration, who espoused the world-denying view. The fundamentalist theology that shaped his thinking assumes that Christ is coming again soon. Consequently, we do not need to worry about the limits of renewable and nonrenewable resources; they were put here for human benefit on the way to eternal life. Standing the concept of stewardship on its head, this view implies that we may use natural resources rapidly since the end of the world is near. Influenced by this worldview (and by lobbyists for extractive enterprises), Interior Department policies during Secretary Watt's tenure favored exploitive use for today over preservation for tomorrow. I saw some of the results while touring Washington's Olympic Peninsula in the late 1980s, encountering one horrendous old-growth clear-cut after another (just behind thin screens of trees left next to the highway). In some of those devastated places, signs were posted—with mid-1980s dates and James Watt's signature—announcing in a misleading way that the abandoned clear-cut was now an effective Department of the Interior "reclamation" project.

The other interior secretary, with a sharply contrasting view of environmental responsibility, was Bruce Babbitt, who provided positive leadership during the Clinton administration to show respect for the created order, particularly for wilderness areas, and to restore ecosystem integrity in endangered places such as the Everglades. As a child, Babbitt attended a Catholic church in Flagstaff, Arizona, where he learned to appreciate the psalms and was fascinated by the Noah story, which permeated his consciousness to the extent that as secretary of the interior, he referred to Noah bringing animals onto the ark as the first Endangered Species Act. Babbitt noted, however, that inside the church building he attended as a boy, the blue and snowy San Francisco Peaks dominating the Flagstaff skyline did not seem to exist; those mountains never came up in the priest's homilies. Instinctively, Bruce knew that grand peaks reflect the sacred (in Hebrew, *El Shaddai* means "God of the mountains"). But it was left to his Hopi Indian friends to introduce him to sacred places in the San Francisco Mountains. Years later, as secretary of the interior, he showed great respect for many wild places and advocated policies to protect fragile ecosystems, as well as the rights of surrounding indigenous people.

This brings me, with eyes oriented to ecology and justice, to consider some fresh meanings of the prayer Jesus taught us. Let us discover guidance for living from this prayer, which addresses God and then offers both "you" petitions (concerning God's glory) and "we/us" petitions (concerning human needs).

OUR FATHER

By addressing God as "Father," Jesus dared to name God in a culture that assumed God was too holy to be addressed directly. By using the familiar and personal name Abba (Mk 14:36), Jesus presented God as a loving parent who knows our names. We can count on being heard by the One who knows, much better than we do ourselves, what we need (as distinct from granting whatever we want), throughout the vicissitudes of life. Personal relationship to a loving, just God is profoundly important to each of us as fragile, limited human beings in a vast, expanding universe and a highly conflicted world.

Addressing God as "Father" is two-sided: We know God both as a loving parent and as the creator of heaven and earth who originates, sustains, and completes the whole of reality. Theologian Paul Tillich cautioned that if we expect God to satisfy our wants and to forgive all for which we want to be forgiven, then our faith relationship will no longer be with the God who shows power, justice, love, and mercy throughout the whole creation. The "Our Father" situates us in the vast cosmos and the whole earth community where we encounter the mysterious divine ground of being. In this prayer, we are addressing the Birther and the Breathing Life of all.

Jesus spoke in Aramaic, not the Greek language in which the Gospels were later written. Neil Douglas-Klotz, author of *Prayers of the Cosmos: Meditations on the Aramaic Words of Jesus*, points out that the root *ab-*, which refers to the cosmic birthing of all creation, came to be used in Aramaic for one's personal father—*abba*. But the word still echoes its ungendered root meaning as "divine parent."

"Our Father in heaven," which richly connects us with our Creator and all the rest of creation, also says, "O Birther! Father-Mother of the Cosmos, you create all that moves in light." That image can be reinforced by slowly saying the Aramaic *Ah-bw-oo-n* as a meditative discipline. If the twelfth-century mystic Hildegaard of Bingen was correct in defining prayer as "breathing in and breathing out the one breath of the universe," then the "Body Prayer" of breathing suggested here is quite appropriate.

In the Lord's Prayer, we address and praise God, who creates, sustains, and redeems. With that firm knowledge, we then petition God to meet our basic needs.

YOUR KINGDOM COME

This petition anticipates the fulfillment of God's commonwealth expected by the prophets and inaugurated by Jesus. But what does that petition ask for? The prophets and Jesus projected harmonious peace among humans and the creatures. They also assumed that the commonwealth of God involves more than faithful believers; it encompasses the whole of nature along with all of humanity. Plants and animals belong in the kingdom, "the society for all under God's reign," as Daniel Day Williams defined it. All creatures are our kin; together we are a kin-dom. Signs of the divine commonwealth can be seen, therefore, wherever people care for creation and build sustainable communities based on right relations.

Meanwhile, the world seems to be going in the opposite direction, violating creature kinship and postponing healthy earth community. The Worldwatch Institute's annual *State of the World* reports show that we are experiencing rapid environmental deterioration along with huge and widening social disparities. At the end of the 1990s, despite a global surge in economic growth and significant gains in health and education, there were still at least 1.2 billion people trying to survive on less that a dollar per day. There are more now. Most of these people are malnourished, do not have access to clean water or health care, and bear the brunt of the AIDS crisis.

Another 2.5 billion people survive on an income of less than two dollars per day. Alongside this horrendous social failure is a much-touted story of economic success marked by a boom in global consumption and improvements in living standards. But in the process, humanity's ecological footprints have become more extensive and destructive, making a mockery of the rainbow covenant God made after the flood with "you [Noah] and every living creature that is with you, for all future generations" (Gen 9:12).

Agricultural lands are stressed on every continent. The world's oceans are in decline. Many fisheries are under threat. Coastal areas, including wetlands and beaches, are being eroded, and populations along coastlines are more vulnerable to intensifying storms. Coral reefs, which support many species, are being destroyed by direct human action or are sickened by toxic sediment washed into the sea. In the last fifty years, humans have removed half of the planet's original forest cover, which absorbs carbon dioxide, produces oxygen, anchors soils, regulates the water cycle, protects against erosion, and provides a habitat for millions of species. Increased burning of fossil fuels brings with it global warming and climate instability, a circumstance that poses serious threats to the well-being of earth community.

Yet in this deepening crisis we remain hopeful, knowing that Jesus announced the commonwealth of God in a bleak situation of oppression and hopelessness. In occupied Palestine, he called people to look for and live into the promised future. Now it is our turn to embody the petition "Your kingdom come."

Our actions will not deliver the kingdom, but we can point to or show signs of it. Bill Webber, a leader of the East Harlem Protestant Parish and later president of New York Theological Seminary, tells a delightful story in this regard. He was brought up in a Congregational church in Iowa where every Sunday the pastor prayed, "Help us to bring in the kingdom." Later at Union Seminary, Reinhold Niebuhr taught Bill that faithful humans do not actually bring in God's kingdom, though here and there humans offer signs of it. Webber knew that Niebuhr was right, but in his heart he continued to repeat the prayer of his Iowa pastor, because we are all called to show others the implications of the kingdom promise. In the words of theologian Sallie McFague, "If we want to say reality is good, we must help to make it so."[1]

Entering the kingdom here and now opens up a way of living faithfully that is embodied in the "we/us" petitions of the Lord's Prayer.

GIVE US THIS DAY OUR DAILY BREAD

Here we ask only for the bread we need today and tomorrow, not for a lot of extra sustenance or exotic foods. As manna-gathering Israelites learned long ago, hoarding stinks. "Sufficiency is the standard . . . [,] equality is the presumption, and sharing is the direction," Christian ethicist Larry Rasmussen reminds us.[2] Any society that has the resources to meet basic needs—food, shelter, clothing, health care, education, work, and festivity—and does not meet them fails the test of justice.

A just and sustainable society collectively restrains production, consumption, and reproduction so that every person and every kind can have sufficient sustenance, shelter, and space. Movement in that direction links us with the transgenerational and transnational community of those who do likewise.

FORGIVE US OUR DEBTS, AS WE FORGIVE OUR DEBTORS

We who accept undeserved forgiveness from God gratefully should reciprocate by forgiving others. This is an important guide for interpersonal relations. But this petition also points to collective and corporate responsibility, because we are all indebted to unfamiliar places, workers, and organizations, not just the persons we know who have helped us. How do we acknowledge and cancel those less obvious debts?

This "forgive" petition in the Lord's Prayer conveys a powerful image from the Jubilee tradition. As summarized in Leviticus 25, each seventh (sabbatical) year, and then again each forty-ninth (seven times seven) year, brings a social obligation to cancel accumulated debts on loans and to let the land lie fallow. In other words, the Lord's Prayer anticipates an economy that is forgiving—not exactly what we are used to! Commenting on this Jubilee image in the Lord's Prayer, New Testament scholar Sharon Ringe observes that the advent of God's reign is an event of liberation at the most basic level:

> Between the human present and God's future comes a proclamation of release. Those who would hear this petition as "good news" are those for whom "debts," whether before God or to other persons, result in a captivity that denies fullness of life. Among them would surely be the people considered outcasts by their neighbors, with whom Jesus so often enjoyed table community. Among them too would be those ensnared in the vicious cycle of literal indebtedness in the struggle to make of less-than-subsistence wages an adequate livelihood. Those for whom such a word would be bad news are those . . . who profit from the patterns of indebtedness that characterize business as usual. . . . In other words, the privileged people would have their pretense to status confronted and their self-made security threatened.[3]

What can we twenty-first century residents do to "forgive" oppressive debt? Each of us can make a difference locally in ways that acknowledge our own debt to the land by supporting sustainable farming and contributing to a land trust to preserve open space or special places. And we can become active in environmental and social justice organizations that advocate and embody conservation, preservation, worker rights, and animal protection. We can also join our denomination's organization that works for environmental wholeness with social justice, such as the Presbyterians for Restoring Creation.

And we can make a difference internationally by supporting debt relief, development assistance, and fair trade, which are so essential to the human and ecological health of poor countries. For many years, this has been a legislative emphasis of Bread for the World, an ecumenical advocacy organization based in Washington, DC. Poor countries especially are caught in the vicious cycle of ever higher loan payments that force their governments to drive subsistence farmers off the land in favor of export commodity growers, even as these same governments discontinue basic education, health, and social security programs. They need our help; distant as well as near neighbors are the debtors Christ wants us to forgive.

LEAD US NOT INTO TEMPTATION, BUT DELIVER US FROM EVIL

These final petitions bring to mind quite a list of temptations faced daily at home, at work, at play, in politics, and elsewhere. Meanwhile, contemporary history makes us all too aware of the threat of violent evil in a world of militarism and terrorism. These are complex subjects that deserve careful discussion in other sermons. Here I would just highlight our temptation to believe that we can and should have it all: more income, investments, creature comforts, energy consumption, family happiness, friendships, and vocational fulfillment—and, of course, bigger houses and cars. But such an expectation makes us acquisitive, anxious, and self-driven, in search of what one magazine calls "fine living," with obvious disregard for the common good.

Christianity at its best has a different posture. Reformation leader John Calvin proposed "frugality," or what others call "sufficiency" or "simplicity," as the norm for Christian living. It features moderation, thrift, efficient usage, liberal sharing, and satisfaction with having enough, so that there is more for others. To seek enough rather than demanding more for ourselves places us in a better future for creation's sake. In that spirit we are enabled to welcome human existence situated in the matrix of nature and to reduce our ecological footprint, with good effects for ourselves and for earth community.

Let us show what the prayer Jesus taught us means for individual and institutional living that really demonstrates care for earth and people. The Lord's Prayer becomes good news for earth community to the extent that those who say this prayer also try to embody its vision and values.

Dieter T. Hessel, a Presbyterian minister specializing in social ethics who now resides in Cape Elizabeth, Maine, is founding director of the ecumenical Program on Ecology, Justice, and Faith. He is author of *Social Ministry*, coeditor of *Earth Habitat: Eco-Injustice and the Church's Response*, and coeditor of *Christianity and Ecology: Seeking the Well-Being of Earth and Humans*, among other works.

Notes

1. Sallie McFague, *Super, Natural Christians* (Minneapolis: Fortress Press, 1998).
2. Larry Rasmussen, "Pentecost Economics," in Dieter Hessel, ed., *Social Themes of the Christian Year* (Philadelphia: Geneva Press, 1983), 236.
3. Sharon Ringe, *Jesus, Liberation, and the Biblical Jubilee: Images for Ethics and Christology* (Philadelphia: Fortress Press, 1985), 79–80.

FIRST THINGS FIRST

THEODORE HIEBERT

THE AIM OF THIS SERMON IS TO INVITE Christians to rethink the place of creation in biblical faith by considering the meaning and significance of the first verse of the Bible. It is a revision of a sermon preached at the St. Paul United Church of Christ in Chicago at a Sunday morning worship service centering on creation.

In the beginning God created the heavens and the earth. (**Gen 1:1**)

◈

It is all too clear that a healthy natural environment has not been a top priority in our society. On my way into work each day, I pass Chicago's most toxic waste sites, including a massive landfill just off the Bishop Ford Freeway. It is the highest point in the city of Chicago. I have discovered that scholars and commentators think that biblical society in this regard was not much different from modern society. Nature, they tell us, was not a top priority in biblical society either. My predecessor at McCormick Theological Seminary, the great biblical theologian G. Ernest Wright, saw nature in the Bible as a handmaid, a servant of history. Because of this view that nature is secondary in biblical faith, some ecologists have blamed the Bible for our current abuse of nature. They see our mixed-up priorities going back to the Bible's own skewed worldview.

In light of this predicament, I want to reflect about how our biblical traditions think about creation, about the world of nature, about what we today call the environment. In particular, I want to ask the Bible about its priorities. I want to ask how seriously the Bible takes nature. I want to find out what priority biblical society gave to its environment. And I want to find out whether the Bible got us started on the wrong foot right from the beginning or, conversely, whether the Bible's own priorities might have something to teach us about the environment.

But before we do this, I have an assignment for you. I teach in a theological seminary, so I am used to giving assignments, and I am afraid today you are going to get one. Here is your assignment; it is actually a kind of personal theological audit: Make a mental list of the first five words that come into your mind when you ask yourself who you think God is. Take the sentence, "My God is *blank*," and fill in the blank. Do not work too hard. Just pay attention to the first five words that pop into your head and in what order you think of them. This is like David Letterman's top ten list, only easier.

Now look at your mental list and notice the order in which the words came into your head. The order of the words in your list likely indicates a certain priority about what is most important or obvious to you about God. Here is how my list came out: love, just, compassionate, Savior, Creator. If I had not been composing this sermon about creation, I am not sure "Creator" would have made my top five. Does your list look anything like mine, or is it different? Whatever it looks like, keep it in mind, because I want you to compare it to the lists other Christians have made in the past.

First, let us take a look at one of the most famous lists made by the early church: the list found in the Nicene Creed. The Nicene Creed is a summary of the essentials of the Christian faith drawn up in the fourth century, and it is used regularly in some liturgies today. The Nicene Creed begins, "We believe in one God, the Father, the Almighty, maker of heaven and earth." According to those who framed this list, God is first of all one, not many; second, a father figure; third, all-powerful; and fourth, the Creator. In this classic list, God as Creator is fourth, one higher on the list than in my personal one, where it is fifth. How does this list compare to yours?

Now let us take a look at a much more recent list, found in an affirmation of faith prepared by the National Council of Churches in the United States for use in worship services just like this one— worship that focuses on creation and our role as Christians within it. This modern affirmation of faith begins like this: "We trust in God, whom Jesus called Abba, Father. In sovereign love God created the world good." According to those who wrote this list, God is first of all father; second, sovereign (that is, all-powerful); third, love; and fourth, the creator of the world. Even though the authors of this affirmation wanted to highlight God's role in creation, their list comes out not much different from the Nicene Creed. Here too, in this modern affirmation of who God is, creation takes fourth place.

Now let us compare these lists with the Bible's own list. The Bible's list, of course, begins at the very beginning: "In the beginning God created the heavens and the earth." This verse reflects a simple fact: In biblical faith—unlike more recent affirmations of faith—creativeness is the first character trait attributed to God— not the fifth, as in my own personal list, or the fourth, as in the Nicene Creed and in the affirmation from the National Council of Churches. When biblical writers sat down to collect and present to us, their heirs, all of their traditions and their theologies, their most sacred insights into the character of God, their most precious memories of their life together with God, what they put first out of all of these revelations was their recognition of God as Creator.

The power of the Bible's proclamation of God as Creator in its opening words can be grasped even more clearly if we look at these words more closely. In English translations, the word "created" is the fifth or sixth word in the sentence, but in Hebrew it is the second. The first word in the Hebrew text is *bereshit*, meaning "in the beginning." It tells us simply that this is the start of the list, so to speak, the beginning of everything that will be said about God. Then the second word in the Hebrew sentence—the second word in the Bible—is the verb "created." This verb is the first word in the Bible describing God and God's activity in the world. The third word of this sentence is the word "God," the subject of the verb "created," which precedes it. In Hebrew grammar, the regular rule is that verbs come before their subjects.

In spite of its grammatical correctness, this word order troubled some rabbis. Why, they asked themselves, would God not be mentioned until the third word in the sentence, which was, more importantly, the third word in the Bible? Should not God, the Bible's main character, be mentioned first, before anything else? I should interject here that biblical writers could, within the rules of grammar, vary the word order for effect or, as the rabbis later wished they had, for theological payoff. But they did not, and one rabbi explained it this way: God must, above all, be modest, and in order to reflect this modesty God must have seen to it that the first reference to God was not the first word in the Bible.

With all deference to the wisdom of the rabbis, I believe that the order of words in the Bible's first sentence is most likely the result of conventional Hebrew grammar. But I would like to point out that the result of this conventional verb-subject word order is that the Bible mentions God's activity as Creator even before it mentions God as the subject of that activity. Thus, both biblical faith and the grammar of that faith put God's creation first among all of the things said about God in the Bible. And the creation narratives that follow, which are so familiar to all of us, are simply magnificent illustrations of God's creative activity.

You might object to this. Perhaps you will not object to my claim that God's creative work was important in biblical faith. But perhaps you will object to my claim that because God's creative work is mentioned first, it is therefore biblical faith's top priority. After all, you might say, if you were one of ancient Israel's scribes and you took up the task of describing Israel's history with God, you would have to start at creation, because that is where everything began. But if you think about this, it is not necessarily so. In fact, we have biblical authors who started their "affirmations of faith," so to speak, at other places. One of these—the great theologian who composed what scholars now refer to as the Deuteronomistic History, the record of Israel's life with God found in the Old Testament books of Deuteronomy through Kings—started his account of God's activity in the world with God's appearance at Mt. Sinai and God's giving Israel the law. And we can turn to more recent examples. The Presbyterians, including those at McCormick Seminary where I teach, start their "affirmations of faith," for all practical purposes, with John Calvin's life and writings. The Mennonite Church, to which I belong, starts its affirmations with the Dutch Anabaptist Menno Simons, after whom we Mennonites in the United States are named, or with Conrad Grebel or with another one of the first Anabaptists.

If you ask why we all begin our affirmations of faith at such different places, I believe you will realize that these beginning points are not accidental or convenient or dictated by some external requirement such as chronology or literary genre or page length. Each starting point is selected because it is foundational. For the Deuteronomistic Historian, Mount Sinai was selected as the starting point because the law God gave there was to become the standard by which this historian-theologian explained everything that happened in Israel's subsequent experience. For Presbyterians, John Calvin is the starting point because his insights into God and God's activity in the world have been the foundation for Presbyterian theology ever since. And Mennonites start with Menno Simons or Conrad Grebel because Mennonites see in these men's lives and writings the foundational principles of faith for their own communities.

If we agree that starting points are foundational and not just chronological accidents, then we must take the Bible's starting point very seriously. If the Bible begins its affirmations about God with the affirmation that God is Creator, then we must take this as foundational for biblical faith. Creation is not the prologue to biblical faith, which finds its real center in the exodus from Egypt or in the law at Sinai or in the Davidic covenant, as many of our biblical scholars have believed. Nor is creation the handmaid or servant of biblical faith, as Ernest Wright put it. Rather, God's creation is the foundation and framework for biblical faith. It is the context within which everything else about God and about ourselves must be understood.

If we take the Bible's priorities seriously, there will be far-reaching implications for our thinking and our living. We will have to rethink our own priorities. We will have to reconsider our beliefs about who God is, who we are, and what the world is. If God is first and foremost Creator, then God is present not just in our hearts and souls, not just in our prayer meetings and churches. Rather, God is active and present in every aspect of the world of creation. If the starting point for our pilgrimage as human beings is God's creation, then we are not just Jews or Christians or Presbyterians or Mennonites. We are, before anything else, members of creation, citizens of the larger natural and biological community within which we were made. If the natural world in all of its complexity is God's first act, the foundational fact of God's world, then nature is not just material stuff, the "servant of history" in Wright's words. Instead, nature is the context for the life of faith, the framework for all of our theology and ethics.

As I mentioned a moment ago, it takes only one trip through south Chicago to my office to remind me that the health of creation has not been a top priority for our society. And I am sure each of you has these signposts of danger in your own neighborhoods. As things get worse and the health of our environment deteriorates, we need, more than ever, different ways to understand the world and our role in it. To this end, I commend to you the first verse of the Bible. It is here that our Scriptures affirm that biblical faith is grounded in creation. God is first and foremost the Creator. The world of nature is first and foremost God's world. And we as humans are first and foremost members of God's creation. Our calling is to take our membership in creation seriously.

Theodore Hiebert is Francis A. McGaw Professor of Old Testament at McCormick Theological Seminary in Chicago. He has also written essays on biblical perspectives on nature in various journals and for *The Oxford Companion to the Bible, The Anchor Bible Dictionary, Theology for Earth Community: A Field Guide, Creation and the Environment,* and *Christianity and Ecology,* the multivolume series on religions and the environment published by the Center for the Study of World Religions at Harvard. He teaches the course "Biblical Perspectives on Nature" with Barbara Rossing.

KNOWLEDGE, BUILDINGS, AND TREES

LAUREL KEARNS

THIS SERMON WAS PREACHED FOR EARTH DAY 2004 at Drew Theological School, just two weeks after I returned from leading a group of Methodist camp and conference and retreat center personnel on a trip to the Mayan highlands of Guatemala. The event was the honors convocation that recognizes the scholarly achievements of students. The chapel service was followed by a tree planting and a tree mourning ceremony in recognition of several oak trees that were over one hundred years old and that were about to be felled in order to build an extension to the seminary. The sermon therefore was partly about what I had been thinking about in Guatemala and partly about explaining why it mattered to many that those trees were being cut down. More than a hundred students, faculty, and staff participated in the tree ceremonies, much to the surprise of some, who thought I was a bit of a lonely tree-hugging eco-nut. This new wing of the building provides needed classroom space and, most importantly, an elevator that makes the building accessible to all. I had been on the building committee for several years, trying to make it a "greener" building. After giving this sermon, several other faculty members mentioned that their children, too, (according to their children's schools) thought and learned "differently."

> Then the angel showed me the river of the water of life, bright as crystal, flowing from the throne of God and of the Lamb through the middle of the street of the city. On either side of the river is the tree of life with its twelve kinds of fruit, producing its fruit each month; and the leaves of the tree are for the healing of the nations. **(Rev 22:1–2)**

◈

My nine-year-old son's brain works a little differently from most of his peers, and for this, most times, I am glad. In some context this could cause him problems, and yet it only seems a disability when compared with a narrow, normative model of learning and thinking. And with what seems currently to count as normal thinking, I think we need more "different" thinking! What this label really means is that he does not learn in a way consonant with the way educational systems are usually structured to teach. His brain structure and intelligences do not fit as well into the typical classroom setting. And although he is phenomenal (in his mother's modest opinion) with words and numbers, I can see how others like him might join the likes of Edison and Einstein in flunking at a regular school. We are lucky to be in a public school that stresses multiple intelligences and to work with incredible teachers who recognize his strengths and weaknesses.

Reading a lot of books to understand better his unique gifts has reinforced for me what we here already know, namely, that people learn through different avenues. And the concept of learning styles is different from the concept of multiple intelligences—that is, the recognition that some of us are musical and some are mathematical and some are visual, mechanical, linguistic, and so on. So I have been spending more than the usual amount of time thinking about learning and knowledge. In education, as in our society in general, we privilege certain types of knowledge and certain ways of conveying knowledge. We like words and we like books, and by now you students are swimming in words and books, not to mention paper and, I hope you know by now—trees! Here at Drew and in our lives in general, we spend a lot of time, indoors, dealing with words.

But classroom education is not the only way to learn. I hope you struggle to balance the type of learning that is privileged in our society with other ways to know and with other sources of knowledge, for there is a cost to pay for too heavy an emphasis on all of this book learning. Sometimes our belief that certain types of knowledge are more valuable than others cuts us off from learning from different sources. Although many of us at Drew try hard not to limit ourselves, nevertheless, books and words are still where our society thinks valuable knowledge is located. And so we easily forget to balance book learning with the lessons to be learned from cultures where books are not central, where knowledge is not always equated with reason and rationality—at least as we define it. We and the earth are paying the price for our imbalanced knowledge.

David Abram, an anthropologist, philosopher, and author of *The Spell of the Sensuous*, talks about the difference between our cultural knowledge system that is based in words, concepts, figures, and abstractions, and the cultural knowledge systems of oral cultures. He writes, "While the accumulated knowledge of our oral ancestors was carried in their stories, the stories themselves were carried by the surrounding earth. The local landscape was alive with stories!"[1] Unfortunately, in our culture, we have forgotten how to listen to the land, how to learn from the "natural" world.

Let me try to illustrate what I mean. I have talked with some of you before about why I moved to Australia for my sabbatical—namely, because I wanted to be shaken up about what I assumed I knew and therefore did not think about any more. In Australia, I would be challenged by not knowing the trees, birds, directions—basic things that I often take for granted here. I wanted to learn to be more mindful, more attentive, so that I could not subconsciously classify something as a robin or an oak and then just walk by, or assume that north meant cold and south meant warmth. This worked to some extent. In a different place and setting, I was open to asking all sorts of new questions, to hearing new things, to listening to the land. Just as I learned a lot about being human from observing the many moods of the ocean surrounding the island where I grew up, I learned many important things, such as some of the insights of this talk, from the more-than-human natural world in Australia and those who have been its caretakers for nearly 50,000 years.

But in general, we—and now I am using "we" to refer to Western cultures and Western-influenced worldviews—participate in a dislocated, portable, ungrounded system of knowledge in which what is learned in the abstract and universal is no longer locale-related, no longer geographically based. This has had mixed consequences. Because of our removal from land-based knowledge, we have assumed that we can know something in one place and apply it in another, and this has led to ecological disasters and regrettable cultural arrogance, as we have believed that what we do/think/want is what others do/think/want also. It has also led to some incredible scientific insights, including the knowledge that our ecosystems and survival are all interconnected, but this is a truth already well-known in many indigenous and other land-based cultures. This system of abstraction that leads us to talk of both trees and people as resources to be used has also allowed us to choose to forget what our cultures once knew—not just our connectedness to the land and all of creation but the more personal relationship between people, on the one hand, and the production of things, on the other hand. We have learned to represent complex relationships in fairly abstract terms that no longer relate to actual physical objects, contexts, conditions, and so on.

Perhaps we might say that many of us have lost the spiritual connection of things. A kind of forgetting and a taking-for-granted attitude—a mindlessness—are what allow us to move through incredibly complex situations without having to think about how, for example, the car works, what something is made of, and how/what the connection is between me and the multitude of people, places, and objects that surround me. These connections seem to be just too much to think about. Yet that is part of what the curriculum at Drew seeks to correct. We spend a lot of time trying to get you to think about the connections behind unjust circumstances and how you then are connected to those issues. And we do this as part of the Christian call to justice. We ask you not just to think but to think differently, and then to act.

Just as our culture's privileged ways of knowing and our every-day ways of knowing allow us to forget our connectedness, or never even to think about it, so do we also take buildings for granted. At Drew, we are expanding the seminary building with a new "greener" extension that we hope to use as another source of knowledge about our connections. Buildings and what they are made of are not "givens"; they cannot be taken for granted. What they are constructed of, where those materials came from, how they were produced and transported and how much energy was used, and so on, are all questions of justice that need to be asked.

In other words, in designing the new building, whenever possible, we chose to ask questions that are not often asked, questions, for example, about the full costs of products—economic, ecological, and social. To find answers, we hired "green" architects whose knowledge was more expansive. We tried to design a building that would teach by virtue of how it was different and that, by being different, would encourage people to know that there are better, more just ways of building a building. For instance, by using less electricity, which has clear economic benefits, we reduce our participation in the production of the gases that contribute to global warming. We reduce our contributions to the air pollution related to coal-produced electricity purchased by most of New Jersey. In so doing, we help a little to relieve respiratory problems, including—and for me, this brings it full circle—relief for the asthma that my son and so many children in the New York City metropolitan area suffer from. Having asthma may mean that children do not thrive or learn as well, as a result of the effects of struggling to get enough oxygen and of asthma medication. Our Western thinking, influenced by the linear teleology present in Christian theology, has tended to think in straight lines and to miss the connections, while the world around us constantly reminds us that we need to think in circles.

We have done something similar in the decision to serve Fair Trade coffee here at our school, recognizing that even from the food we eat and drink comes knowledge of our web of economic, political, ecological, and social connections. I do not know about most of you, but most mornings, I do not do much thinking about my cup of coffee or tea other than how soon I can get a cup. But there are a lot of people, and creatures, who are involved in my cup of coffee before it gets to me—insects, birds, growers, pickers, traders, shippers, roasters, and retailers—and they all take a price. In January 2003, most coffee growers were lucky to be getting about fifty-four cents a pound for coffee—and you know how much your local retailer, not to mention coffee shop, gets per pound! Coffee prices have fallen over fifty percent in the past three years. They are at historic lows, even though you would never know it in most cof- feehouses. Oxfam estimates that twenty-five million coffee workers around the world live in such poverty that they face starvation. I have just returned from Guatemala, with coffee on my mind more than ever. More than 200,000 people in the Guatemalan coffee industry have lost jobs in the last four years alone. In Central Amer- ica, the number stands at 600,000. Guatemala has the most unequal land distribution in all of Latin America, with less than 2 percent of the landowners controlling at least 65 percent of the farmland. Furthermore, in Latin America, as elsewhere, when coffee is sun- grown, as are the cheaper varieties flooding the market, there is a 95 percent reduction of the songbird population, the same songbirds that we hear outside our windows. Certified Fair Trade, shade grown, organic coffee guarantees farmers $1.41 a pound, does not use pesti- cides, and provides much needed habitat. It is a clear example of eco-justice for all of creation.

But whether it is the building or the cup of coffee, the issue is really about how much we choose to know and not know. We have forgotten that we have chosen to forget what we should and could know. We know that coffee does not grow in little bags, that trash has to go somewhere, and that someone made the clothing or shoes we are wearing. If we purchase things for a good, cheap price, we should know that people and the environment elsewhere are paying for it—that to buy perfect flowers for our churches and perfect fruits and vegetables for our tables means that people, animals, and ecosystems somewhere are paying the price of the pesticides that went into that perfect production. Yet how often we do not ask questions! Our culture and our economic system do not encourage the asking of such questions, and we are afraid that the answers might just disturb our comfortable North American lifestyles. We do not take into consideration what is called the ethical reach of a product.

Let me give one more example of choosing not to know. David Korten, a former World Bank employee and internationally known economist, writes:

> Nike shoes selling in the United States or Europe for $73 to $135 a pair are produced in Indonesia for about $5.60 by 75,000 girls and young women who are "independent contractors" paid as little as 15 cents per hour. . . . When asked about conditions at plants where Nikes are produced, John Woodman, Nike's general manager in Indonesia, [said] that although he knew that there had been labor problems . . . he had no idea what they had been about. Furthermore, he said, "I don't know that I need to know. It's not within our scope to investigate."[2]

Are we all that different when we walk into a store and buy something at the cheapest price, when we throw something out without taking some responsibility for our part in the whole cycle from production to consumer to the garbage dump? Have we decided not to know? There are costs to every product that must be acknowledged so that we pay what is really fair. To reduce those costs to people, to the creation, and to our collective well-being— that is why I am always on folks' case about reducing, reusing, and then recycling.

A moment ago I mentioned the concept of eco-justice for all of creation. As you all know, that is a difficult balancing act. In order to make our building handicapped accessible, it is necessary to chop down trees that have been here since before the school began. So I am suggesting that we have a ritual of mourning and rebirth, a saying good-bye and a planting of new life, in order to recognize that the all-inclusive community that the Drew Theological School strives to be *includes the forest.* As the Catholic "geo-logian" Thomas Berry comments regarding Abram's book: "The outer world of nature is what awakens our inner world in all its capacities for understanding, affection and aesthetic appreciation. The wind, the rain, the mountains and rivers, the woodlands and meadows and all their inhabitants; we need these perhaps even more for our psyche than for our physical survival."[3]

This is the recognition that, in addition to learning from books, we also learn from the more-than-human natural world, that we learn through all of our senses. Many Christians are scared of what they might learn, for learning from nature has been maligned as worshiping creation rather than the Creator. Upon learning that the whole earth is a connected ecosystem so that something like global warming affects all of us, some people chastise those who are trying to get churches and religious people to do something to make sure there is a habitable and just environment for our children and for their children and for all the other creatures who share the earth with us. Yet any review of our theological and biblical traditions demonstrates that we as Christians have always learned through the natural world, and we have felt God's presence there. For many of us, those trees that have stood by this building for more than one hundred years are also part of what we have learned at Drew. They have been for us exactly what Thomas Berry speaks about; they have healed our soul, brought us joy, taught us about being human, and have spoken in their own way to us of God. As David Abram commented in an interview about his book, "Everything speaks, just not in our language."[4] Take time to listen, to learn.

For me, this has been the guiding eco-justice vision of what we are about at Drew and of what we can become—to be still and listen and learn from all, to think differently, ask uncomfortable questions, be mindful of our interconnectedness, and then to act justly. That is the full circle of knowledge, buildings, and trees—justice for all of God's creation. Let us make sure then, as we go forth from here to say good-bye and hello to the trees, that as the Scripture today tells us, "the leaves of the trees are for the healing of the nations."

Laurel Kearns is associate professor of sociology of religion and environmental studies at Drew Theological School. Her teaching interests include the intersection of religion and the environmental movement and issues in the relationship between ecology and justice. She has written numerous essays in journals and collections. She has completed *Ecospirit: Religion and Philosphies for the Earth*, co-edited with Catherine Keller (New York: Fordham University Press, 2007).

Notes

1. David Abram, *The Spell of the Sensuous*, 20.
2. David Korten, *When Corporations Rule the World* (San Francisco: Berrett-Koehler, 1995), 115.
3. Thomas Berry quoted in David Abram's *The Spell of the Sensous: Perception and Language in a More-Than-Human World* (New York: Random House, 1996), jacket.
4. NPR Radio Interview.

THE SPIRIT SIGHING FOR
THE NEW CREATION

CATHERINE KELLER

THIS SERMON WAS PREACHED at Drew University. It reflects on the way the Spirit prays with sighs too deep for words and helps us to pray in solidarity with suffering humanity and suffering earth. Originally, the sermon was accompanied by Lynne Westfield and her didgeridoo, an aboriginal musical instrument that amplifies a nasal whine.

> We know that the whole creation has been groaning in labor pains until now; and not only the creation, but we ourselves, who have the first fruits of the Spirit, groan inwardly while we wait for adoption, the redemption of our bodies. For in hope we were saved. Now hope that is seen is not hope. For who hopes for what is seen? But if we hope for what we do not see, we wait for it with patience.
>
> Likewise the Spirit helps us in our weakness; for we do not know how to pray as we ought, but that very Spirit intercedes with sighs too deep for words. **(Rom 8:22-26)**

◈

We do not know how to pray as we ought. For we pray for this and for that—good stuff. We pray for results. Prayer helps. Lives full of prayer are often effective lives, effecting results. Communities that pray together, saying if not staying together, shape our reality positively, proactively. Any prayer is better than none. It calms and tunes us. We hope it tunes us to God—or God to us. But something is off. Something has been wrongly stated—overstated. Prayer is made into statement. Name it and claim it. Janis Joplin sang, "O Lord won't you buy me a Mercedes Benz? My friends all drive Porsches, I must make amends." Amen.

We do not know how to pray as we ought. But we here are experts in prayer; we write pastoral prayers; we lead communities in prayer. We are not praying for new commodities but for the new creation. We pray for great ends, for what we do not see: the justice that is not yet, the democracy to come, the ecologically sustainable, post-patriarchal, postracist, postwar, postalienation, spiritually harmonized new creation. Or do we see all too clearly in our minds' eyes what we hope for? Do we name it in prayer, as though God, prone to senior moments, must be reminded of what needs to happen? Of course, we are really talking at each other—educating and socializing (or is it programming?) the church. There is nothing wrong with that, really. These are meaningful liturgical traditions. These are ancient but still potent vocabularies of prayer. But something is off.

We do not know how to pray as we ought. So the Spirit helps us in our weakness, says Paul. I never really got this. If the Spirit has to help us to pray for the Spirit, and the Spirit is God, does this mean that in prayer we are not speaking to God at all but that God is speaking to God? That seems to make us into nothing but puppets on the knee of a master ventriloquist, or mouthpieces for some sort of internal conversation between the persons of the Trinity. I did not get it. This sounded like the Spirit interceding in a rather patronizing way: here let me pray for you; you are not doing it properly.

That very Spirit intercedes with sighs too deep for words. "To intercede" comes from *inter-cedere*, "to come between"; this Spirit *comes*, but not as a force from some external transcendence and not as a force of my own interior. This Spirit comes between—the divinity of the between—as an interstitial spirit between us and what we see as God. This is not about soliciting solutions from on high; it is not about mobilizing omnipotence on our behalf. *Sighs too deep for words.* This is the deep space of prayer. This is the space beneath and between words. This is the sign of the sigh. The Spirit sigh. This is the space of silence in which words break up, sink, and dissolve into the wordless. *Sighs too deep for words*—the gentle sighs of the deep. *Deep calls to deep*—a moan arising in our weakness, the wobbly washed-out spaces of our worst vulnerabilities. What is this depth? Do we not have the Word? Why should Christians ever be silent? Especially we Protestants: We protest, we preach, we proclaim.

For we do not know how to pray as we ought. The Spirit intercedes, interrupts. Breath—of *ruach.* A great wind. The breath not of one but of all. The breath of the creation. The *ruach* pulsing, oscillating, vibrating—as the verb *merephet* in Genesis 1:2 is quite properly translated—over the waters of the first birth. And now, the divine breath still vibrates through the creation—sounding something like a didgeridoo? The creation groans. The sign of the sigh—the groan, a suffering that is vibrant with potential even then, even now. The groaning in labor—we and the earth, our earthen bodies, flesh of the creation. Almost unspeakable, this maternity of the spirit. This *ruach* was feminine. Some early Christian hymns pray to her as divine mother. Still, all this unspeakable maternity got drowned by the speech about the father and the son. She became a rather bedraggled, flighty mediatrix, a lovey-dovey third person.

The creation groaning in birth pangs—from the beginning, spasms of spirit—God the Spirit vibrating in the wordless deep before the word, rhythmically entrained with the becoming world. If we let the sighs and the groans come through first, before the word, before all of our words about the Word, do we hear another tone of Word? Not a commandment, an order, a prescription, but a song, a poem of joyful creation.

A lament of dis-creation: Oh, how could we? Oh how powerful, how possessive, how poisonous have been our visible hopes.

I want a whole litany of sighs. (The didgeridoo may help us to pray!) We must let out the sighs—all of our sighs. If we hold them back they choke us. *Ruach* is in these sighs of our weakness.

Oh sigh of the self—with my own tremors of loss, of hurt, of fear, of inadequacy, of anger, of guilt, of shame, of cowardice, of unactualized potential, of wrongly actualized gifts, of wasted opportunities.

Oh groaning church, hurting, dwindling, dividing, breaking, threatening to fade before fulfilling our promise, a body sickening so many of its members, body of Christ sickening Christ.

Oh moan of humanity, trembling with the sighs of unassuaged torment, great waves of death and horror. No words touch these holocausts, these slaughters, these mass deaths intended and inadvertent. These daily diminutions, humiliations, one gender, one sexuality, one race, one class, still bloating at the expense of the one it marks as other, alter, subaltern.

Oh groaning planet, air and earth and water toxic, no space inviolate, earth sighing, shuddering, under assault from a single species, this gifted predator that preys on everything, that devours its home, that wars against itself.

What is there to say? *We do not know how to pray.*

Still, we are lured to hope, to hope for a world to come, to hope that from this visible, touchable, audible planet, this noisy planet that speaks through us, comes that which we cannot yet speak: the word not yet breathed, the spirit, the breath of the birth pangs. Divine Lamaze: If we breathe into our pain, breathe through our pangs, the birth of the new becomes possible.

Catherine Keller is professor of constructive theology in the theological and graduate schools of Drew University. Trained in process theology, she employs many interpretive approaches, such as feminism, poststructuralism, and ecojustice. Her published works include *Apocalypse Now and Then: A Feminist Guide to the End of the World, Face of the Deep: A Theology of Becoming,* and *God and Power: Counter-Apocalyptic Journeys.*

MATTER MATTERS

BARBARA LUNDBLAD

THIS SERMON WAS PREACHED at the Care for Creation Conference at the Lutheran School of Theology in Chicago. Joseph Sittler, who taught at LSTC as well as the University of Chicago, was an unseen presence at the conference. Many speakers, including myself, remembered his strong advocacy for the earth long before others had discovered the word *ecology*. My concern in this sermon was to make connections between care of the earth and justice for those who are poor and hungry; hence, two very different texts from Ezekiel and Luke shaped my preaching.

> Wherever the river goes, every living creature that swarms will live, and there will be very many fish once these waters reach there. It will become fresh; and everything will live where the river goes.
> **(Ezek 47:9)**

◈

And at [the rich man's] gate lay a poor man named Lazarus, covered with sores, who longed to satisfy his hunger with what fell from the rich man's table. **(Luke 16:20–21)**

◈

One of the newest parks in New York state is a few blocks from where I live in Manhattan. Riverbank State Park is aptly named, for it stretches out along the banks of the Hudson River on the edge of Harlem. Yet the park is not really on the banks of the river. It is above the river, but not on a hill. In fact, this park is not on the ground at all. This park, complete with trees, ice skating rink, running track, concession stands, swimming pool, and soccer fields is not on the ground. It is on top of a sewage treatment plant. One of the largest public works projects in this country, the expansive gray building with a park on top treats wastewater on its way to the Hudson River. While kids skate, the water flows. Beneath the bikes and trikes of summer, the water flows. Under the slam dunks, under the park bench where lovers kiss, under the playground laughter, the water flows and the Hudson River begins to come back to life. *Wherever the river goes, every living creature that swarms will live, and there will be very many fish once these waters reach there. It will become fresh; and everything will live where the river goes.*

You were not thinking about the Hudson River water treatment facility, were you, Ezekiel? The water in your vision is flowing from the temple, from the throne of God. This is the sacred river, the river shared by many cultures, the river flowing at the end of the Bible in the visions of Revelation.

> *Shall we gather at the river,*
> *The beautiful, the beautiful river?*
> *Shall we gather at the river that flows by the throne of God?*

We can try. But it is hard to gather on the shore of a metaphor.

This river is a metaphor, is it not, Ezekiel? Your vision comes from God and from what you have seen with your own eyes: the

Dead Sea, the memory of an oasis in a barren place, rivers teeming with fish. But Ezekiel, you did not expect us to take this picture literally. There is no river flowing under the temple door. There is not even a temple, let alone a temple door! This is the stuff of visions: promises in the midst of mourning, hope springing up from despair like your other vision of all those dry bones rattling to their feet, bone to bone, sinew to sinew, skeletons breathed back to life again— but not literally. And this vision is not literal either. God will purify and renew the people, not the river. Ezekiel, after all, was not writing a social statement on the environment.

But what if Ezekiel's vision was larger than he could see, even with his ecstatic wisdom? Did God offer visions deeper than the prophets could fully understand? Is God waiting for others to fill them in? To bring new meaning to them? Is there a river here after all? I have no wish to psychoanalyze Ezekiel, but I am intrigued and delighted by his mention of the marshes: "Its swamps and marshes will not become fresh; they are to be left for salt" (47:11). Was this an early plea on behalf of the wetlands? Surely Ezekiel did not know what Lutheran pastor Sharon Betcher knows, namely, that wetlands "which include marshes, bogs, sloughs, flood plains and swamps, are the richest ecosystems on earth. 75% of American bird species depend on roosting in wetlands; 90% of oceanic life begins in estuaries."[1] Don't mess with the marsh! Or is the marsh a metaphor?

A metaphor always points somewhere, moving us from the familiar to the strange, connecting words, images, and ideas to expand the way we see. Scripture is filled with metaphors from the created world: water flowing in the desert, flowers springing up in the wilderness, vineyards planted and ruined, mustard seeds sprouting into bird-nesting bushes, a shoot growing from a stump that was clean cut off. But often we pluck the metaphors far too quickly from their earthly roots. Ezekiel's river is not really a river. The metaphors go only one way—up, up, up to a spiritual world freed of matter. And they never come down to earth again.

Joseph Sittler spent a lifetime trying to bring us down to earth. He spoke the word *ecology* before it was in the newspapers or college catalogues. He connected the words *ecology* and *faith*. He wanted us not only to see the world but to *behold* the world and be changed. "With our minds we look at things," he said, "but in the spirit of our minds we behold things. To behold a thing means to regard it in its particularity—its infinite preciousness, irreplaceability, and beauty."[2] Dr. Sittler would urge us to behold the river. Wade in the water, children! For Sittler, theology was not a stagnant pool; theology is always moving like a river: "By theology we mean not only a having but a doing—not only an accumulated tradition but a present task which must be done on the playing field of each generation in actual life. One has a theology, to a greater or lesser extent, in order to do theology."[3]

Dr. Sittler invited pastors and teachers to engage new partners in our theological conversations. Such conversations are desperately needed for the well-being of our suffering planet and for the integrity of doing theology on the "playing field" of this generation. Our conversation circle needs to be expanded: Hebrew scholars and theologians, urban rangers and fishery experts, environmentalists and parish pastors, lovers of wetlands and seminary professors. All need to be in the same circle. Can Ezekiel's vision move back to earth as well as away? Maybe there is a river here after all. And if there is a river, maybe there is a table, too!

Is Jesus' story of Lazarus and the rich man a metaphor? Is there a rich man feasting sumptuously, never seeing, let alone beholding, Lazarus? Is there any table here, any food? Is this a parable pointing to heavenly promises beyond earth's miseries? Are all those banquets in Luke metaphors for an abundant spiritual life? Or did Jesus really mean that the blind and the lame, the poor and the maimed would eat at the table?

In her book *The Body of God*, Sallie McFague urges us to see the table, and the people. "Jesus' eating stories and practices suggest that physical needs are basic and must be met," she says. "Food is not a metaphor here but should be taken literally."[4] A bit later in the same chapter she insists, "The body of God must be fed."[5] In the church we have spent centuries focusing on the real presence of

Christ at the Communion table, but what about the real presence of food on the table for all of the world's people? Is that only a matter of politics, or is it doing theology? Is there a connection between the life-giving river and the poor man lying at the gate, longing for crumbs?

Bodies matter to God. Matter matters. Until we can proclaim that wondrous truth, ecology will be a sideline in our pastoring and preaching, our theologies and liturgies. But the gospel to which we return again and again is an embodied Word. This Word is not a metaphor. The cosmic, eternal Word became *flesh*. Christ's incarnation has brought the Word down to earth, blessing this earth as holy ground. Matter matters—wetlands and rivers, wheat fields and dough rising, people dancing in the aisles and people sleeping in the streets of our cities. Matter matters to God. We bring this strong biblical affirmation into the conversation circle. I am not an expert on global warming or complex ecosystems. Perhaps you are not either. But we believe the metaphors of faith are deeply rooted in this earth. God does not disdain matter in favor of a spiritual realm. Bodies matter to God. Matter matters. Or, as ethicist Larry Rasmussen has written, "The only viable earth faith is thus a biospiritual one. Earth ethics is a matter of turning and returning to our senses. The totality of nature is the theater of grace. The love of God, like any genuine love, is tactile."[6]

Wade in the water, children! "On the banks, on both sides of the river, there will grow all kinds of trees for food. Their leaves will not wither nor their fruit fail, but they will bear fresh fruit every month" (Ezek 47:12). Did you hear? There is not only water to refresh the parched earth but all kinds of trees for food—far more than crumbs for Lazarus and all his hungry sisters and brothers.

Everything will live where the river goes. Water flowing down over the baptismal font, splashing the acolyte holding the book, soaking the carpet all the way to the front door, then out into the streets, soaking into the water table, flowing even into the once-dying Hudson River. For the first time in years, people are fishing in the Hudson where 125th Street meets the river. Someone even pitched a tent in the cement parking lot not long ago when the weather turned warm. A few blocks north, children play in the park as the river runs by beneath them. Soon they will run home to eat— hopefully, they will find food on the table and a roof over their heads. And Lazarus, who had been lying on the church steps, comes in to sit with us at the table of God. "Pass the bread, please," he says.

"The body of Christ given for you, Lazarus." He takes and he eats. And he knows it is more than a metaphor.

Barbara Lundblad grew up on an Iowa farm and still has strong roots in that Iowa soil after twenty-five years in New York City, where she is the Joe R. Engle Associate Professor of Preaching at Union Theological Seminary. She is the author of *Transforming the Stone: Preaching through Resistance to Change.* Her Beecher Lectures will be published under the title *Marking Time: Stories Remembered at the River's Edge.*

Notes

1. Sharon Betcher, "An Ecofeminist Account of the Redemptive Value of 'Wet Land,'" *Living Pulpit* 2 (1993): 23.
2. Joseph Sittler, *Gravity and Grace* (Minneapolis: Augsburg, 1993), 16.
3. Ibid., 65.
4. Sallie McFague, *The Body of God: An Ecological Theology* (Minneapolis: Augsburg, 1993), 169.
5. Ibid., 170.
6. Larry Rasmussen, *Earth Community, Earth Ethics* (Maryknoll, NY: Orbis, 1996), 180–81.

MARRIAGE AS A "YES"
TO GOD'S EARTH

JAMES B. MARTIN-SCHRAMM

A SHORTER VERSION OF THIS SERMON was preached a few years ago on a farm in Wisconsin at the wedding of two Luther College graduates.

The LORD has established his throne in the heavens,
and his kingdom rules over all. (Ps 103:19)

◈

Then I saw a new heaven and a new earth; for the first heaven and the first earth had passed away, and the sea was no more. And I saw the holy city, the new Jerusalem, coming down out of heaven from God, prepared as a bride adorned for her husband. . . . Then the angel showed me the river of the water of life, bright as crystal, flowing from the throne of God and of the Lamb through the middle of the street of the city. On either side of the river is the tree of life with its twelve kinds of fruits, producing its fruit each month; and the leaves of the tree are for the healing of the nations. (Rev 21:1–2; 22:1–2)

◈

It certainly feels like heaven has descended to earth! The beauty of this early fall day is simply glorious. I know the two of you very much wanted to celebrate your wedding day outside on the land you love, surrounded by family and friends. The warmth of the sun, the quality of the late afternoon light, the rustling of the trees, and the songs of the birds all testify to the divine glory of God's dominion.

I know you two gave considerable thought to the texts you chose for today. They are unconventional and seldom used in marriage services, but they clearly reflect your personal, professional, and environmental commitments. As a physical therapist and an environmental educator, both of you have great compassion for those who are wounded, disabled, or endangered. These texts also reflect your knowledge about the life and work of Dietrich Bonhoeffer, a Lutheran theologian who was executed by the Nazis in 1945 for his work in a conspiracy to end the reign of Adolf Hitler.

What does Dietrich Bonhoeffer have to do with your wedding here today? Dietrich became engaged to Maria von Wedemeyer shortly before his arrest in 1943. For two long years in prison he yearned for the day when he and Maria could finally marry each other and live in a Germany freed from the tyranny of the Nazi regime.

In May 1943, one month after his arrest, Dietrich wrote "A Wedding Sermon from a Prison Cell" on the occasion of the marriage of his best friend, Eberhard Bethge, to his niece, Renate Schleicher.[1] I will not focus here on Bonhoeffer's conservative and culture-bound remarks about gender roles within marriage. Instead I want to focus on his timeless and important comments regarding the institution of marriage.

Bonhoeffer seizes on the significance of the vows we make in marriage and our positive affirmations of them. In a few moments you two will exchange such vows, and I will ask whether you accept these obligations. In response, you will answer, "Yes, I do." In the face of war throughout Europe and its devastating social and environmental consequences, Bonhoeffer seized upon this yes to life and love. He writes: "As God today adds his 'Yes' to your 'Yes,' as he confirms your will with his will, and as he allows you, and approves of your triumph and rejoicing and pride, he makes you at the same time instruments of his will and purpose both for yourselves and for others."[2]

Bonhoeffer emphasizes that God has established the institution of marriage so that not only the couple's life together may be blessed but that the lives of others may also be blessed. Bonhoeffer writes to the couple:

> Marriage is more than your love for each other. It has a higher dignity and power, for it is God's holy ordinance, through which he wills to perpetuate the human race till the end of time. In your love you see only your two selves in the world, but in marriage you are a link in the chain of the generations, which God causes to come and to pass away to his glory, and calls into his kingdom. In your love you see only the heaven of your own happiness, but in marriage you are placed at a post of responsibility towards the world.[3]

Three months later, in a letter to his fiancée, Bonhoeffer took this yes to life, love, and responsibility one step further. He argued that marriage requires faith:

> I don't mean the faith that flees the world, but the faith that endures *in* the world and loves and remains true to that world in spite of all the hardships it brings us. Our marriage must be a "yes" to God's earth. It must strengthen our resolve to do and accomplish something on earth. I fear that Christians who venture to stand on earth on only one leg will stand in heaven on only one leg too.[4]

I know both of you were immediately attracted to this comment by Bonhoeffer. His views about the purpose of marriage are a much-needed corrective for our age. Too many view marriage as a bulwark against the dangers of the world and as a sanctification of personal desires. Instead, Bonhoeffer argues that marriage is an institution created by God through which we might better serve the world and love our neighbors.

Historically the church has emphasized that marriage is the appropriate locus for the protection of a couple's loving unity, procreation, the rearing of children, and the experience of sexual pleasure. Bonhoeffer would dispute none of these, but above all else he regarded marriage as one of the "mandates" God has commanded so as to protect humanity and promote goodness in the world.[5] Ultimately, your marriage is not only about your love for each other but also about what you together can do for others, what you can do for God's earth.

Dietrich and Maria had chosen Psalm 103 as their wedding text. The psalm emphasizes God's "steadfast love and mercy" (v. 4) as well as God's "vindication and justice for all who are oppressed" (v. 6). This pairing of love and justice is central to the Judeo-Christian tradition. Today we realize that this scope of love and justice must extend to all creatures God has made, as well as the ecological systems that support life on this planet.

Psalm 103 also emphasizes human mortality. Adam is created from *adamah*. "For he knows how we were made; he remembers that we are dust" (v. 14). At a time when technology magnifies human power almost beyond imagination, we need to realize that the first human being was created from *humus*, from the soil of the earth, and to that earth we all will return. An earth-centered humility is central to Christian faith. This earth is our home.

Another important theme in Psalm 103 that resonated with Bonhoeffer and that is so relevant for us today is the welfare of future generations. The psalmist writes, "The steadfast love of the LORD is from everlasting to everlasting on those who fear him, and his righteousness to children's children, to those who keep his covenant and remember to do his commandments" (vv. 17–18).

This duty to future generations was one of the moral imperatives behind Bonhoeffer's work in the conspiracy. A similar willingness to risk our lives and security on behalf of future generations must characterize our lives together as Christians today. Faced with the reality of global climate change, the loss of biological diversity, and the degradation of environmental systems, each of us must do what we can to protect the welfare of future generations while we also work to help present generations. This is what it means to be a blessing to others.

The other text you chose for today is the first two verses from both chapters 21 and 22 of the book of Revelation. When Martin Luther was asked what he would do if he knew the world was going to end tomorrow, he said that he would go out and plant a tree. Luther said this for two reasons. First, he knew that the end time was up to God, and in the meantime he believed that God wanted us to live responsibly on earth. Second, Luther believed along with the author of Revelation that the new heaven and the new earth would descend from heaven. We are not going there, it is coming here.

Your choice to plant a tree during this marriage ceremony is a perfect illustration of your love for the earth and your confidence in the future. Given his interest in peace and the healing of the nations, I think Bonhoeffer would applaud your symbolic action today. May the fruit of all of our lives contribute to human reconciliation with others and with the earth.

Bonhoeffer teaches us that Christian faith is not about seeing a different world; it is about seeing this world differently. Christian faith leads us to see God at work redeeming the world by making the lame to walk, by healing the brokenhearted, and by lifting up those who have been cast off to perish on the margins. As persons baptized into Christ's body, all of us are part of this ministry of redemption. Marriage is an institution the church utilizes to further God's work in the world.

Certainly we have all gathered here today to celebrate and rejoice in your love for each other. And certainly we will witness your vows in a moment as you promise to love and support each other throughout your lives. But ultimately what is taking place today is not only about you and your future life together.

Your marriage is ultimately about how the two of you, together, can do more to participate in "the care and redemption of all that God has made" than what you can do alone. May God bless your lives together and the lives of others through your love for each other. May your marriage be a yes to God's earth.

James B. Martin-Schramm is an associate professor of religion at Luther College in Decorah, Iowa. He is the author of *Population Perils and the Churches' Response* and the coauthor of *Christian Environmental Ethics: A Case-Method Approach.* He has chaired the board of the Division for Church in Society in the Evangelical Lutheran Church in America.

Notes

1. Dietrich Bonhoeffer, *Letters and Papers from Prison,* ed. Eberhard Bethge (New York: Macmillan, 1972), 41–47.

2. Ibid., 42.

3. Ibid., 42–43.

4. Dietrich Bonhoeffer and Maria von Wedemeyer, *Love Letters from Cell 92,* ed. Ruth-Alice von Bismarck and Ulrich Katiz, trans. John Brownjohn (Nashville: Abingdon, 1995), 64. For a rich discussion of Bonhoeffer's earth-affirming faith, see Larry Rasmussen, *Earth Community, Earth Ethics* (Maryknoll, NY: Orbis, 1996), 295–316.

5. See Dietrich Bonhoeffer, *Ethics,* ed. Clifford J. Green, trans. Reinhard Krauss, Charles C. West, and Douglas W. Stott (Minneapolis: Fortress, 2005), 68–75, 388–408.

CAN THESE DRY BONES LIVE?

SALLIE MCFAGUE

THIS SERMON WAS PREACHED TO PEOPLE LIKE MYSELF—specifically, to two congregations of middle-class North American Christians—who need to hear some somber words about what our consumer lifestyle is doing to the planet and to other people.

> He said to me, "Mortal, can these bones live?" I answered, "O Lord GOD, you know." Then he said to me, "Prophesy to these bones, and say to them: O dry bones, hear the word of the LORD. Thus says the Lord GOD to these bones: I will cause breath to enter you, and you shall live." **(Ezek 37:3-5)**

> Then Jesus told his disciples, "If any want to become my followers, let them deny themselves and take up their cross and follow me." **(Matt 16:24)**

Do you not know that all of us who have been baptized into Christ
Jesus were baptized into his death? **(Rom 6:3)**

◈

Nature is dying, and we are responsible. The dodo bird takes her
last breath; an obituary is read for giant redwoods; Southeast Asia's
forests resemble a dog with mange. We too are experiencing
"extinction"—the extinction of experiencing nature. Ecological
worship services ought to be joyous affairs. We should be singing the
praises of God's creation, reveling in the delights of the world's
beauty. This is the relationship with nature we want. We like nature
calendars with photos of snowcapped mountains, baby elephants,
and old-growth forests. But nature is becoming sick, falling apart,
and dying all around us.

As a recent report on the state of our planet puts it:

> So far the world order emerging is one almost no one wants.
> Human numbers are growing, forests are shrinking, species are
> dying, farmland is eroding, freshwater supplies are dwindling,
> fisheries are collapsing, rivers are constricting, greenhouse gases
> are accumulating, soot is contaminating the air, and lead is conta-
> minating our blood.[1]

How can we rejoice in the face of this? We hear the endless,
depressing statistics: half of the world's wetlands are destroyed;
fifteen million African children are orphans because their parents
have died of AIDS; a quarter of the world's mammals are in danger
of extinction; and a quarter of the world's human population lives
in "absolute poverty" on less than a dollar a day.

How should we respond? What is a *Christian* response to this
death? Our Scripture readings suggest a threefold response. Very
briefly, I will indicate what this is. Paul's statement that baptism
means burial with Christ, the Matthean passage on the cross and
self-denial, and Ezekiel's valley of the dry bones share one thing:
dramatic, physical imagery relating death and life. Each in its own

189

way, these texts are saying, loud and clear and with brutal realism, that life—the life that matters—only comes through death. Romans claims that the old self must be crucified with Christ, Matthew says that to save your life you must lose it, and Ezekiel says that only a divine re-creation can resuscitate the dry bones.

These texts suggest a Christian response to the despair that settles over us when we listen to the depressing statistics about the earth, when we begin to allow the state of the planet to seep into our minds and hearts. Most of the time we do not admit the deterioration and death that are taking place around us. It is a slow death, after all—a species here, a species there; a report on global warming on the evening news sidelined by the latest glowing stock market figures; a picture in a magazine of a poor third-world woman gathering the last few sticks of wood to cook her family's dinner. We get used to this death by attrition; we adjust to it. We are, in fact, in denial that it is taking place and that we are responsible—not entirely responsible, to be sure, but substantially. We who live at the top of the food chain in every sense—as human beings in relation to all other plants and animals, and as first-world, privileged human beings in relation to other, poor human beings—are responsible for much of the deterioration and death that is taking place. We live the "abundant life," the high consumer life, sucking energy out of nature and diverting it in our direction at the expense of other less powerful human beings.

This is a harsh indictment, and it certainly does not apply equally to all of us affluent, first-world types. But if it is even partially true—and I know the shoe fits me fairly well—then a Christian response to nature's decay and death might be something like the following three steps.

First, let us listen to Paul. Baptism means a new life in Christ, but first one must die to sin. Paul does not mince words: Such a death is like being buried in the grave. The hold of sin—in our case, "ecological selfishness," wanting to have all of nature's bounty for ourselves—is so strong that only death will do the job. We are "enslaved to sin," addicted to consumerism; it is our definition of the abundant life. Paul's remedy is a brutal one, but one appropriate for addictions: We must experience the death of this sin. He is not suggesting a sprinkle baptism; in the early church the baptized were submerged, perhaps held under the water long enough to feel their breath getting short. Paul insists that we must be incorporated into Christ's death, that we must really change our location from our sinful place to the place of death *in order to* arrive at the place of new life. So, the first step is one of repentance, *metanoia*—confession that we have been in denial about our addiction to the consumer version of the abundant life and about the price it exacts from nature and less fortunate people. The first step is dying to our sinful life, our consumer life.

The second step in our response is suggested in Matthew's somber warning that the Christian life has a cruciform shape: Disciples must deny themselves, lose their lives. Is this the trade-off for the consumer life of which we have repented? It is not what we want. But it is not just Christianity that has a cruciform shape; reality does as well. Jesus did not invent the idea that from death comes new life. We see it all around us—for instance, in the "nurse" logs in old-growth forests that, in their decaying state lying on the ground, provide warmth and nutrients for new saplings. Raising the cruciform shape of reality to the central principle for human living is Jesus' contribution. To find abundant life (not consumer abundance, but real abundance), one must lose one's life. Self-denial, diminishment, limitation of that old life is necessary: "For what will it profit them if they gain the whole world but forfeit their life?" (Matt 16:26)

While I am not suggesting that the Matthean passage is about ecological selfishness and the need for consumer self-denial and limitation, I am suggesting that its basic premise of the Christian life as cruciform makes the passage open to that interpretation. In terms of the health and well-being of our planet, we need to lose one kind of life and gain another, and the other one, the new life, will continue to be cruciform in shape. It will involve limitation, emptiness, loss. Abundant life, cruciform-style, means sharing and giving—dare we say, sacrificing?—for others, for the health of other life-forms and the well-being of other people. It means limiting our needs, dying to our desires for more. It means practicing "the virtue of enoughness." Is this the abundant life, as John 10:10 puts it: "I came that they may have life, and have it abundantly"? Who wants it? Maybe none of us does.

But, interestingly, it is realistic; it is ecological; it is what the good life must mean in nature's terms, because it is in line with the way our planet works. Nature works through a complex system of interrelations and interdependencies, with its billions of individuals needing the others in the whole ecosystem and the health of the whole dependent on the functioning of the myriad different species and individuals. Nature cannot work well if one species destroys all the others in the fantasy that it can live the high life at the expense of the others; in fact, that species will eventually destroy itself. Case in point: Human beings cannot live a day without green plants, both to eat and to give them oxygen to breathe. Hence, cruciform living—living with limitation and sharing, living so others thrive, both human and nonhuman others—is nature's way; it is the abundant life in nature's terms. Thus, the life of the cross is realistic; it is the way of life for humans to live with other human beings and with nature. Does this joining of nature's way and the way of the cross make Christianity less novel, less radical? Perhaps less novel, but not less radical. For human beings to live in a cruciform way is extraordinarily difficult; those who manage to do it we call saints. The cross, then, is not an escape route to another world for chosen human beings; rather, it is a summons for human beings to live in a fashion that will be good for all of God's creatures.

Finally, can this happen? Can the dry bones live? Can our planet become healthy? The haunting, beautiful passage in Ezekiel makes an important point for a Christian response to our planet's decay. Here we have a new creation story. As with the other texts, the imagery is physical and radical, portraying movement from death to life. In a way that recalls the creation of Adam in Genesis 2, God forms sinews, flesh, and skin onto the dry bones, reconstituting them into living beings. But in this creation story, unlike the first one, God has two helpers: one is Ezekiel, who is the mediator of God's word that causes the bones to reassemble, and the other is nature (the "four winds"), which provides the breath that gives the bones life. The answer to the question "Can the power of life override the reality of death?" is Yes, with the help of God's partners—human beings and nature itself. In this story, resurrection is not a miraculous event for a few individuals but the gift of new life for all by God and with our help.

Ezekiel says that with God all things are possible, even the reconstitution of dry bones. In my mind's eye I see huge mounds of elephant bones, remnants of the ivory trade; I see the naked remains of an old-growth forest after a clear-cut; I see the shriveled legs of children with AIDS. Even these dry bones, Lord? Can they also live? Those who trust in the God of creation and of re-creation, the God of the cross and of the resurrection, answer yes—even these dry bones can live. But remembering the cruciform shape of reality and of the Christian life, we say, Yes—if we as partners of God will accept a *different* abundant life.

Sallie McFague is Distinguished Theologian in Residence at the Vancouver School of Theology in Vancouver, British Columbia. She retired from thirty years of teaching at the Vanderbilt University Divinity School in Nashville and is now a permanent resident in Canada. She has published in the area of theology and ecology, including *The Body of God: An Ecological Theology, Super, Natural Christians: How We Should Love Nature,* and *Life Abundant: Rethinking Ecology and Economy for a Planet in Peril.*

Note

1. Lester R. Brown et al., eds., *State of the World* (New York: Norton, 1999), 170.

THE COMFORTING WHIRLWIND
God and the Environmental Crisis

BILL MCKIBBEN

THIS SERMON WAS DELIVERED at the Unitarian-Universalist First Religious Society in Carlisle, Massachusetts, in March 2001.

Then the LORD answered Job out of the whirlwind:

"Where were you when I laid the foundation of the earth?
Tell me, if you have understanding." **(Job 38:1–4)**

◈

I wrote a book some years ago called *The Age of Missing Information*. I had gone out and found the largest cable television system in the whole world, which at the time was in Fairfax, Virginia, and had 100 channels. I got people in Fairfax to tape everything that came across those 100 channels. I took their tapes home to the Adirondacks and viewed all of it—roughly 2,000 hours of programming. The message, distilled down to its essence, which comes through that television all the time, is simple: "You are the most important thing on earth, the heaviest object in the known universe."

If you had to pick one message that was most effective for building a huge, strong economy, that would probably be it. It has worked incredible wonders. We have consumed and produced and raised our standard of living in ways that no one in any previous time or place could even have imagined. We have created what passes in physical terms for a utopia, where we live in comfort and convenience and security.

But if you wanted to create a message that was profoundly troubling from a spiritual point of view and one that made progress on issues of great importance, especially issues of the environment, you could not pick a better one than "You are the most important thing on earth. You are the center of the planet." This raises an old question: Where do we stand in relation to everything else?

This seems to me the question that animates Job. You probably know the book of Job as well as I do, so forgive me for running over it briefly. Job is a prosperous man, a good man, who always does his bit for the community and treats his family well. One day he wakes up and finds himself seemingly cursed by God. His cattle start dying of hoof and mouth disease, his children die, his property is taken from him, he ends up living in a dung heap at the edge of town covered with oozing sores. As one would in such a situation, he begins to question why this has happened to him. His friends, representing the orthodoxy of the day, come and visit, and they tell him it must be because he has sinned. He must have done something for which God is now punishing him. This was the standard operating belief of that day.

Job, surprisingly, will not take that for an answer. He keeps saying, "But I didn't do anything that bad. There must be some other explanation," and he audaciously demands an interview with God. Job wants God to justify God's self. Job demands this in increasingly belligerent language, and finally God appears. God appears speaking in a voice from a whirlwind. It is an amazing diatribe. Job has stirred up a hornet's nest. God is in a sarcastic mood and keeps asking him, "Well, where were you when I laid this whole thing out? Do you know how to stop the waves from breaking? Do you know where they should go? Do you know where I keep the hail and the snow? Do you hunt game for the lioness?" It is a beautiful piece of writing—probably the most beautiful and biologically accurate and sexy and crunchy piece of writing we have.

On the one hand its message is clear, I think: Job, and by extension the rest of us, are not at the absolute center of God's universe. We are one small part of a large creation, cut down to size in the course of God's diatribe. But that is not the only message. The other message is that this world of which we are a part is incredibly beautiful, full of meaning and sweetness and beauty.

> Do you show the hawk how to fly by stretching his wings to the wind? Do you teach the vulture to soar and build his nest in the clouds? He makes his home on the mountaintop. On the unapproachable crag he sits and scans for prey. From far off his eyes can spot it, his little ones drink its blood. The unburied are his. (Job 39:26–30)

These things, which are in some sense most vile to us, are clearly dear to God. This world is not always as we see it through our own particular lenses of justice and rightness.

> Then God asked Job, "Has God's accuser resigned? Has he swallowed his tongue?" Job simply says, "I am speechless. What can I answer? I put my hand on my mouth. I have said too much already. Now I will speak no more." (Job 40: 4–5)

That seems like a good answer in this situation.

That has always been one of the profound ways in which human beings have understood their relationship with the world—namely, that there is some force larger than us, which we perceive in the operations of the physical universe around us. That is one of the ways we have managed to remind ourselves to keep our hubris within at least some bounds. In our time, that answer is changing. That answer is disappearing. Human beings are putting themselves not only at the center in the sort of ways that we always have—in our pride and in our appetite—but also increasingly in the absolute chemical reality of the planet on which we live.

Take the example of climate change. Right about the time of the industrial revolution human beings began burning large amounts of coal, gas, and oil—carbon-based fuels. One result is the kind of pollution we are used to—smog over cities, for example; that is a minor effect. The major effect is that when we burn those fossil fuels, we release carbon dioxide into the atmosphere. Carbon dioxide is a colorless, odorless, nonpoisonous gas the concentration of which is higher in this room than it will ever be outdoors but a gas which by its molecular composition traps heat close to the atmosphere, heat that would otherwise radiate back out to space. The atmospheric concentration of carbon dioxide was about 275 parts per million before the industrial revolution. It is now about 385 parts per million, and it will be above 500 parts per million long before the middle of this century unless we do very dramatic things in the next few years to dramatically curtail our use of fossil fuels. If we do not, we have now been warned by scientists, whose data has grown ever stronger and more robust, exactly what to expect.

The Intergovernmental Panel on Climate Change, comprised of 1,500 climatologists from around the world, carry out an endless series of research and analysis on this problem. Their last five-year assessment, released in January 2001, reported that in this century we can expect to see the average global temperature increase about 4 to 6 degrees Fahrenheit. That would take it to levels higher than it has ever been in human history—indeed, than it has ever been. If everything tops out at the upper end of the parameter, we could see average global temperature increases as high as 11 degrees Fahrenheit.

Any of those changes are completely unacceptable. We know they are unacceptable because we have already increased the temperature about 1 degree Fahrenheit and have begun to see what happens when we do. For instance, the world gets a lot stormier, a lot wetter. That is because warm air, in the fashion that God designed this planet, holds more vapor than cold air. So an increase in temperature means a lot more evaporation in arid places and a lot more drought. That evaporated water has to come down somewhere, so in places where it is wet there is a lot more precipitation, a lot more flooding. Severe storms that drop more than two inches of rain in a twenty-four hour period have increased about 20 percent across this continent against the baseline. That is a very large increase in a basic physical phenomenon.

Consider what is happening to the cryosphere, to the frozen parts of the planet. Every glacier system in the world is now in rapid retreat, and remember this is just with a one-degree rise in average global temperature. By 2015 the snows of Kilimanjaro will have completely melted. Glacier National Park will have no glaciers by about 2030. The ice cap over the Arctic has thinned 40 percent in the last forty years. We have tremendous data on that because we ran nuclear submarines underneath the ice for a long time and we know how thick the ice has been; it's now almost half melted away. Those are unbelievably large changes in very fundamental elements of this planet in a very, very short time. They come with real consequences.

Forgive me for using harsh language for a few minutes, but I am going to. I have been working on these issues for ten or twelve years and have reached the point where I am unwilling to pussyfoot around them too much longer. These things are happening in large measure because of us. We in this country create 25 percent of the world's carbon dioxide. It is the affluent lifestyles that we lead that overwhelmingly contribute to this problem. And to call it a problem is to understate what it really is: It is a crime, a crime against the poorest and most marginalized people on this planet. We have never figured out, though God knows we have tried, a more effective way to destroy their lives. I spent much of last summer in Bangladesh, a wonderful country—vibrant, green, alive—that feeds itself even though there are 130 million people in an area the size of Wisconsin. The biggest problem is that it is low in the Bay of Bengal; it is a river delta. The Ganges and the Brahmaputra come pouring out of the Himalayas. They flatten and broaden out when they reach

Bangladesh. The country is half water. That is one of the reasons it is so fertile. Every year the rivers flood and lay this little beautiful layer of silt, and things just pop out of the ground.

But let's say the level of the Bay of Bengal rises just a few inches. (By every forecast, the level of the sea will rise by at least a foot in the next fifty years.) Then those waters cascading from the Himalayas have no place to go. They just back up and spread out all over Bangladesh. That is what happened in 1998. The water was a little higher than usual in the Bay of Bengal, and a lot of water was coming down out of the mountains. For about ninety days, about a quarter of the year, two-thirds of the country was in thigh-deep water or worse. That is just how people lived. They are incredibly adaptable and resourceful and did a heck of a lot better living in thigh-deep water than we would have. But they cannot do that year after year after year. They could not plant the rice crop. They were not food self-sufficient that year. And Bangladesh is just one on the list of a hundred places that will be similarly traumatized unless we make significant changes.

Our lifestyles are a crime against the rest of creation, against all the other interesting corners of God's brain, against the lion and the antelope and the vulture; you can just go on down the list. Think about coral reefs. I am sure some of you have taken vacations in the tropics and have swum around a coral reef. It is enchanting beyond belief, an ecosystem almost impossible to imagine in its jewel-like beauty and its gentleness. By current forecasts, coral reefs will probably disappear as an ecosystem by about 2050. As ocean water temperatures increase, the small animals that create the reefs die off. Once those corals begin to die, all the fish populations that they support die off and so on up the chain. In fifty years our only record of this world beneath the waves may be the films and pictures and things that we have made of them.

Imagine the polar bear—this incredible incarnation of the other, fiercest of our brethren, uninterested in us, not scared of us. The polar bears in large parts of northern Canadian are about 20 percent skinnier than they were ten years ago. As the ice pack melts, it becomes incredibly difficult to hunt seals, which is what polar bears do for a living. No pack ice, no hunting, no polar bears.

Our lifestyles are a crime against the future, against everyone who is going to come after us. If global climate change and its effects had happened several generations ago, how would we feel about the people who had done that to us? Can we imagine how people will one day consider us in this regard unless we do something soon?

Though our scientific system has done a tremendous job alerting us to the dimensions of climate change, we are not doing anything meaningful about it. Our political system, our cultural system, so far has yet to respond in any significant way. The reason that it has not responded goes back to the question with which we began. As long as we consider ourselves to be at the center of everything and our immediate comfort and gratification the most important of all tasks, it is extremely unlikely that our leadership will rise to the occasion and demand of us any real change.

In 2001, the Bush administration announced that it was not going to regulate carbon dioxide in any way, that in essence it was going to kill off the Kyoto Treaty, the one attempt internationally to deal with these questions. The reason? The administration's analysis had indicated that taking any steps would drive up the price of electricity, which would hurt American consumers. Well, they are correct. It is going to cost some money to transition from coal and oil and gas to a renewable energy future. It is going to cost some money, and the administration does not think we are going to stand for it. They might well be right.

So that is where you and I are right now. How do we get off this dime? How do we learn to stop putting ourselves at the center of everything and help our neighbors, our culture, our country understand the same thing? How do we rise to the obvious challenge that is put before us in our time, the challenge that is just as square-faced as the civil rights challenge was a generation ago or the challenge of fascism a generation before that.

I do not have any easy answers for you. In fact, I should probably just stop here, having alarmed you enough. Let me suggest, at the risk of getting in trouble, that there are a few beginning symbolic but powerful things we could start to do. This issue of drilling in the Arctic National Wildlife Refuge is coming before us today as a country. It has been presented as wilderness versus oil drilling, and it is true that drilling would harm that wilderness. But underneath that wilderness is a big pool of oil. If we bring that oil out and burn it we release more of that carbon dioxide into the atmosphere. We heat the planet a little bit more. We do a little bit more to contribute to making the Arctic Wildlife Refuge no longer a place of permafrost and caribou, but a place of muskeg swamp where no caribou will tread.

Let's try to bring this as close to home as possible, probably uncomfortably close. It is not just actions in Alaska. It is actions all around us that are important. There are symbols all around us: symbols like the huge houses we are building and do not need, or like the sport utility vehicles that have become so popular. I grew up in Lexington, Massachusetts, and I have been amazed when I have come back to visit in recent years. I live up in the Adirondacks, where it actually is sort of icy and we have bad roads, but no one has any money, so they just drive cars or maybe pickups. I was amazed to come back to Lexington a few years ago to see my folks and went down to the Stop & Shop to get a few groceries. It looked as if the 8th Armored Infantry had come to Lexington on maneuvers. The only logical conclusion you could possibly have drawn is that Lexington had suddenly been riven by three or four raging rivers one had to cross in order to get groceries. If you drive a normal car and a big SUV the same average distance for a year, in that one year the differential in the amount of energy you use, hence the amount of carbon dioxide you put in the atmosphere, is the equivalent of leaving your refrigerator door open for six years.

That is what we are talking about in realistic terms and in symbolic terms. What we are talking about are the endless levels of comfort and status and everything else at the complete expense of all around us. It is going to take us a long time to learn how to climb down a little bit from the heights on which we have put ourselves. We have been at this work for a very long time. All the witness of our religious gurus notwithstanding, we have done a good job of paying them lip service and going on about our ways. Now the signals from the physical world, from God's creation, tell us that we have gone too far and it is time to turn around. We will need each other's encouragement and help in doing that.

Our religious communities are deeply important. They are almost the only institutions left in our society that posit some goal other than accumulation for our existence here on this planet. Take good care of each other, but do not just take good care of each other— push each other a little bit, too. This work has to be done fast, it has to be done lovingly, and it has to be done not only with an eye on the temperature around us but with an eye on the temperature inside of us—on our understanding of who we really are, not who we have been told we are over and over and over again by all the images that flow through the cable or through the billboard or any of the other places that we increasingly have come to find our identity.

Bill McKibben is a former staff writer for the *New Yorker*. His books include *The End of Nature*, *Enough*, and *Deep Economy: The Wealth of Communities and the Durable Future*. McKibben is a frequent contributor to a wide variety of publications, including *Outside*, *Orion Magazine*, and the *New York Times*. He is a contributing editor to Earth Ministry's *Earth Letter* journal. He lives with his wife and daughter in the Adirondack Mountains of New York, where he is a Sunday school superintendent of the local United Methodist church.

"Dry Bones . . . Breath Came into Them and They Lived"

CYNTHIA D. MOE-LOBEDA

THIS SERMON WAS DELIVERED in conjunction with a public lecture for the annual Dale and Leone Turner Lectureship on Faith and Culture in Seattle. The lectureship for 2005 was charged with responding to the question of what it means to be church in the twenty-first century. The lessons for the fifth Sunday of Lent were Ezekiel 37:1–14, Romans 8:5–11, and John 11:1–45.

> [The LORD] led me all around them; there were very many [bones] lying in the valley, and they were very dry. . . . Then he said to me, "Mortal, these bones are the whole house of Israel. They say, 'Our bones are dried up, and our hope is lost; we are cut off completely.'" (Ezek 37:2, 11)

◈

Ezekiel recounted this vision to God's people in exile. The people of Judah—conquered by imperial Babylon, their city Jerusalem laid waste, their king blinded and his heirs killed—had been dragged off into exile. They were completely cut off from life as they longed for it to be. Their hope was lost.

Have you known—perhaps for moments, perhaps for years—that dried up place where hope is lost, where life is so painfully distant from what it should be that setting things right seems impossible? Have you known that place where hope dries up? I have known it. My sense is that as a society we dwell in that land today, although for the most part, we are too numb to know it. About this sensibility I will say more, but first journey with me briefly through time and space.

Imagine a world of splendor and abundance nestled in a tiny corner of a cosmos fifteen million years in the making. Dawn bursts forth every twenty-four hours, a sun called forth from the deep indigo of the sky, and songbirds sing with abandon, the voice of beauty. Fragrance wafts from exotic blossoms, from the tiniest and most delicate to exotic, voluptuous, deep purple extravaganzas. Drops of glistening water powder the land at the birth of each day. The air shimmers with fluttering leaves. Light rays dance. Luscious fruits hang from trees. In the soil, hearty grains emerge. Everywhere is breath. Life is birthing.

In this fecund circle of life, all that dies becomes sustenance for other creatures and elements. The weave of interdependence is breathtaking, beyond full comprehension: A radiant ball of energy from eons past sends energy, sufficient to meet the needs of all life-forms. What one gives off sustains the other. And the trees—the trees watch, hear, sustain, shelter.

It is a wild, raucous, birthing, fire-spewing, earth-quaking, communion of life, joined in the hymn of all creation, praising the Source and Sustainer of its being. The splendor of this world is exceeded by one thing only: the radiant love with which its Creator embraces it and courses through it.

In this world's most recent moments appear creatures of consciousness, self-aware temporally and spatially and able to reflect on their role in the world. As all the other creatures and elements, these "mud creatures" (the term used as a translation of the Hebrew word "adam" by Irenaeus of Lyons in the second century) are fashioned from the dust of stars long past. They are created as community and for community in a web of interrelated beings and elements upon which the human creatures depend for life itself.

The Holy One reveals to the human ones—the ones who claim to be in the image of their Creator—a lifework. They are called not only to praise God but to love. The work of the people, the *liturgia*, is to receive God's gracious gift of life-saving love and allow it to "abide in" them (the words are Martin Luther's) and work in them toward abundant life for all. They are created to be lovers—offering to God, self, others, and the entire creation the love that they are fed by the One who gives them life. For so doing, they are given, in the likeness of the Holy One, hearts of infinite compassion.

This is the household of God—in Greek, the *oikos*. The Holy One, hungering for its well-being, gave to the species called human, household rules (*oiko nomos*) and the intelligence to develop those rules in multiple ways as the complexity of their lives unfolded. The *oikonomos* (economy) rules are grounded in one firm foundation: The earth's bounty is to be shared. None may have too much if their "having" casts others into want.

And the Holy One declared, "I have set before you life and death, blessings and curses; choose life so that you and your descendants may live" (Deut 30:19).

They have chosen death. Unknowingly, unintentionally, unwittingly, blindly, they have chosen death. The human ones now threaten to destroy the earth's capacity to sustain life as we know and love it. Rejecting God's economy of life, powerful ones among them crafted new rules. The new rules enable a few—largely descendants of the tribes of Europe—to use far more than their share of the earth's bounty, to use it up, and to spew dangerous gasses into it. Ah, my God, what have we done? The species created to revel in God's shalom where none would exploit the other, and to serve it— that species now lives the opposite. They—we—live in strata. For those on the very bottom, notes Salvadoran priest Jon Sobrino, "poverty means death." On the top, according to a United Nations

Report, are 225 people who own as much of the world's wealth as nearly half of humankind. They and the strata in the "middle"—most of us here gathered—are "consumers," who consume the earth's bounty before it can be replenished. They—we—are toxic to our planetary home. If all people lived as we do, it would take five planets to provide resources and dump sites.

Churches in Latin America and in Africa cry out to the North Atlantic world: "The economic systems that provide your wealth create deadly poverty for many of us." Never will I forget Methodist bishop Bernardino Mandlate of Mozambique, speaking to people of the North Atlantic world. "Your wealth," he declared, "is covered with the blood of African children." Burned onto my heart is the voice of a Mexican strawberry picker who spoke to a delegation of US elected officials that I led. "Our children," she said, "go hungry, because this land which ought to grow corn and beans for them, grows strawberries for your tables." Not by our intent or will but by virtue of the social structures and public policies that shape our lives, we are complicit in both ecocide and economic brutality. Under our weight, in the words of the Apostle Paul, "the whole creation has been groaning" (Rom 8:22).

Why do we carry on with this? Why do we not wail in profound lament, cry out in anguish that our lives would bear such brutal consequences? Why are we not forging alternative ways of transporting ourselves, housing and feeding ourselves in ways that are not toxic to this planet and that do not require us to eat up the natural wealth of other lands and people. As the world's wealthiest society, how is it that we allow countless hard-working women and men to earn such meager hourly wages that they and their children—even here in wealthy Seattle—finally must take up residence in the streets? Why do we accept as normal the practice of paying senior executives hundreds of times what their poverty-stricken workers earn? Why do we not cry out in confession and repentance, protest, and devotion to more equitable and ecologically sustainable alternative economic structures? Why as a society are we not dedicating the best of our scientists, economists, business leaders, teachers, homemakers, church leaders, lawyers, and resources in all fields of human endeavor to renewable energy sources, fair trade instead of free trade, the end of sweatshops, streets devoid of gasoline-eating vehicles, bioregional small-scale agriculture, socially and ecologically responsible investment, a "triple bottom line" demanding not only financial but also social and ecological accountability from business, taxation of luxury items and large capital gains, debt cancellation for highly indebted poor nations? In God's name, I ask you, why? Why have we abdicated our moral-spiritual power to live toward God's gift of abundant life for all?

The reasons, of course, abound. Two are moral blindness and hopelessness. We flee from seeing the reality of unnecessary suffering in which our daily lives are implicated. Not seeing—moral blindness—is far more bearable. That failing, numbness sets in. Where numbness thaws, despair makes sense. We retreat into denial and defensiveness, overwhelmed exhaustion, or privatized morality. Holy outrage and lament are dead before born, and we hide our hopelessness regarding systemic evil under the comforting cloak of virtue in private life.

As a society, we have lost true hope. We are so far in exile, so cut off from God's economy of justice and abundance, that we no longer have a deep and real hope that it is possible! Where there is no hope, there are no cries of confession, repentance, lament, and holy outrage. Instead, we elude the demands of public morality, retreating into the relative ease of private virtue. We will be alive and good in personal kindness. However, when our sisters and brothers of the "majority world" (often referred to as the "third world") cry out in many tongues that their deadly poverty stems in part from the economic policies and practices that provide our wealth, in the face of these claims, we will be dry bones, "cut off" as Ezekiel says, from life as God would have us live it, our hope for it lost.

Dry bones of this land, listen ever so closely: And thus spoke God to Ezekiel, "Mortal, can these bones live?" Ezekiel, it seems, was not so sure. Things did not look good. "O Lord GOD, you know," he cried (Ezek 37:3)—a nice job of backing out from taking a stab at an answer himself.

God speaks through Ezekiel to the people in exile, the people whose hope has dried up, the people reduced to dry bones: "'O dry bones, hear the word of the LORD. . . . I will . . . put breath in you, and you shall live' . . . And the breath came into them, and they lived, and stood on their feet, a vast multitude. . . . 'I am going to open your graves, and bring you up from your graves. . . . I will put my spirit within you, and you shall live'" (Ezek 37:4–14).

This text from Ezekiel is a resurrection story, a gospel text. Ezekiel proclaims the promise through which all hope is ours. The promise that out of even the most devastating reality—where "our" lives are "covered with the blood of African children" and where our lives are destroying the earth's regenerative capacities—life rises up, flesh grows on dry bones, life triumphs, and eternal life begins now.

The gospel of Jesus Christ says more. *It tells us who we are and why we are created*: We are friends of God, empowered by God to receive her love and to live that justice-making, mysterious, and marvelous love into the world. Life was breathed into us for a purpose—we were given a lifework—to receive God's love, to love God with heart, mind, soul, and strength, and to love neighbor as self. Fed in community by word and sacrament, we are here to let God work through us, in us, and among us to bring healing from all forms of sin—systemic and individual—that would thwart God's gift of abundant life for all. Soul-searing, life-shattering destruction and death, and our complicity in it, is not the last word, in this moment or forever. The last word is resurrection, life raised up out of brutal death. We, the church, are to proclaim in our words and in our very lives this good news and to participate in it. This is our vocation as Christ's body on earth today. This is life breathed into dead, dry bones; it is hope restored.

It is not up to us to create that hope; God gives it. Our task is to accept God's promise of abundant life for all and our God-given lifework of helping to realize that end. That means swimming upstream against torrential forces of cultural and economic norms. In the second lesson for today, the Apostle Paul reveals a great deal about how we are given the moral-spiritual power to swim upstream. We have that power because, in Paul's words, "the Spirit of God dwells in you" (Rom 8:9). Just verses earlier he writes, "Hope does not disappoint us, because God's love has been poured into our hearts through the Holy Spirit that has been given to us" (5:5). That is, the Spirit of a God whose justice-making love will be stopped by no force in heaven or earth lives in us. Martin Luther said it well. Convinced that the most powerful courage known in humankind is generated by the Spirit living in the faithful, he preached that the Spirit brings "true courage—boldness of heart." "The Hebrew word for spirit might well be rendered 'bold, undaunted courage.'" That "bold, undaunted courage . . . will not be terrified by poverty, shame, sin, the devil, or death, but is confident that nothing can harm us and we will never be in need."[1] Furthermore, Paul instructs, we are to set our minds on that Spirit, rather than on the flesh. Now hear this, because it is of utmost importance. Within Pauline anthropology, flesh and spirit (*sarx* and *pneuma*) do not refer to a dualism of body and spirit or of the political realm and the spiritual realm. For Paul, "flesh" in this text refers to "life apart from the living Spirit of Jesus Christ," and "spirit" means "life rooted in that Spirit."[2]

As a society, we dwell in the valley of "dry bones." To us, as to our faith ancestors, God speaks through the prophet Ezekiel. As Ezekiel prophesied, God breathes into us and we will live. We will stand on our feet, a vast multitude to whom God offers hope and the Spirit of "bold, undaunted courage" to forge ways of being human on earth that enable just and sustainable communities and earth community for generations to come.

Cynthia Moe-Lobeda is on the faculty of Seattle University's Department of Theology and Religious Studies and the School of Theology and Ministry. In addition to writing numerous articles and essays, she is the author of *Healing a Broken World: Globalization and God* and *Public Church: For the Life of the World*, and coauthor of *Saint Francis and the Foolishness of God* and *Say to This Mountain: Mark's Story of Discipleship*. She lives in Seattle with her husband, Ron, a Lutheran pastor, and two sons, Leif and Gabriel.

Notes

1. Martin Luther, "Sermon for the Sixteenth Sunday after Trinity," in *Sermons of Martin Luther*, vol. 8, ed. John Lenker (Grand Rapids: Baker, 1983), 275–76.
2. Lisa E. Dahill, "Spirituality in Lutheran Perspective: Much to Offer, Much to Learn," *Word and World* 18, no. 1 (Winter 1998): 70.

THE CEDAR HAS FALLEN!

The Prophetic Word versus
Imperial Clear-Cutting

CHED MYERS

THIS SERMON WAS DELIVERED at Albright College in Reading, Pennsylvania, in 2005.

> Since you were laid low,
> no one comes to cut us down. **(Isa 14:8)**

◈

In mid-February 2005, a seventy-three-year-old nun was murdered by ranchers near Anapu, Brazil, because of her attempts to halt the illegal logging of the rainforest. Dorothy Stang, a Notre Dame Sister from Dayton, Ohio, was a faith leader, educator, and lobbyist on behalf of campesinos in the region. She was working on the Pilot Program to Conserve the Brazilian Rain Forest, which promotes environmental control to reduce deforestation and burning, and bolsters the economy by encouraging sustainable activities among poor peasants. "This is a hopeful project for the Amazon," Sister Dorothy wrote shortly after her name appeared on a death list in

2003, "but we are plagued by logging companies and ranchers destroying thousands of acres each year." She was walking to a meeting with a community group when confronted by her assassins. Witnesses said Stang pulled a Bible from her bag and began reading a passage to them. They listened for a moment, then fired six times, killing her instantly. I wonder what scripture she might have been reading in that terrible moment.

"Like the days of a tree shall the days of my people be," wrote Third Isaiah (Isa 65:22). This old wisdom acknowledges an essential symbiosis between human culture and the forests. It is echoed by contemporary ecological forecasters, who warn that the health of our forests is *the* key to global environmental integrity. Jan Oosthoek writes:

> The destruction of the world's forests is a major concern in our age. According to the UN 40% of Central America's forests were destroyed between 1950 and 1980. During the same period Africa lost 23 percent of its forests. With deforestation comes a whole range of environmental problems, among them severe flooding, accelerated loss of soil, encroaching deserts and declining soil productivity.[1]

The political and theological truth of this ultimatum was understood by Sister Dorothy, as well as by other forest-martyrs such as Father Nerilito Satur, a young priest murdered in Guinoyoran, Philippines, in October 1991 because of his opposition to illegal logging, or the more well-known Chico Mendes, head of the Brazilian rubber-tappers union, slain in 1988 for his organizing.[2] Their witness reminds us that forest preservation is a life and death struggle between communities who are reliant upon the forests and who value them spiritually, on the one hand, and the powerful interests who pillage old-growth forests for economic and political gain, destroying our treasured commonwealth, on the other hand. This, it turns out, is one of the oldest struggles in human history.

In indigenous cultures, the oldest and largest trees in the area were revered as the spiritual and social heart of the camp, offering witness to the past, shelter in the present, and continuity for the future. Such trees provide symbols for ritual as well as sustenance for daily life. According to the old ways from native California to Celtic Britain to the African savannah, the local great tree represented a sort of *axis mundi*, offering communion between heaven and earth. Elders would gather under its venerable branches in order to adjudicate community life: resolving conflicts, offering counsel, and telling sacred stories. The Bible too acknowledges the role of the sacred tree in the people's journey of liberation, from beginning to end: "Abraham planted a tamarisk tree in Beer-sheba, and called there on the name of the LORD, the Everlasting God" (Gen 21:33). "On either side of the river, is the tree of life . . . ; and the leaves of the tree are for the healing of the nations" (Rev 22:2).

Abraham (Gen 12:6–7; 18:1), Gideon (Judg 6:11), and Elijah (1 Kgs 13:14; 19:4) all had divine encounters beneath the shade of oaks. Although sacred trees are no longer acknowledged as the center of our Western consciousness or communities, they are still the living heart of the land—*if* we have eyes to see.

The cedars of Lebanon are eulogized throughout the Scriptures. Anyone who has visited modern Lebanon (from the Semitic root *lbab*, meaning "the white mountain" because of its snowy covering) may find it hard to believe that vast tracts of timber once grew throughout that now relatively barren region. Indeed, these highlands were once blanketed with hardwood cedar forests, referred to in the Bible simply as "the glory of Lebanon" (Isa 60:13). *Cedrus libani* average a height of more than a hundred feet and forty-five feet in girth, many with an age of more than a thousand years. Indeed, the Hebrew word for cedar, *e'rez* (Greek, *kedros*) is nearly homonymous with the word for the earth itself (*eretz*). The mountain slopes of the Levant were covered with massive cedar forests at the start of the third millennium BCE, but these had almost disappeared by the time of Jesus. David Haslam estimates that there may have been anywhere from one hundred thousand to one million cedars in the forests of Lebanon at the time Solomon's temple was built.[3] Today, however, less than 6 percent of Lebanon is forested, with cedars comprising less than 3 percent of that area. This most ancient of all sacred trees, then, represents a sort of sentinel, witnessing to the oldest legacy of environmental destruction in the history of civilization. As the nineteenth-century French poet Lamartine put it, "The Cedars know the history of the earth better than history itself."

The cedar was to the Mediterranean cultures of antiquity what the redwood was to nineteenth-century Americans coming to California. On the one hand, it was revered and the subject of countless literary paeans; on the other hand, it was mercilessly exploited as a strategic economic asset. Because most of the lowland areas of the Mediterranean and Fertile Crescent were logged out by the earliest city-states, the tall stands of hardwood in the Lebanon were coveted for their size and durability. Cedar wood resists rot and insects, is aromatic, polishes well, and has a close, straight grain that is easy to work with. Most importantly, ancient rulers typically undertook massive building programs to display their power and wealth and built large navies for conquest; for these projects they needed tall cedar hardwood, especially for ship masts and the bearing beams of great temples and palaces. Thus, the forests of the Lebanon were repeatedly the target of exploitation by successive empires. This legacy of deforestation is alluded to often in the biblical prophets. But the story is much older than the Bible; indeed, it is told in the oldest known literature in the world—the epic of Gilgamesh.

Written in Mesopotamia sometime in the third millennium BCE, some fifteen centuries before Homer, this epic concerns Gilgamesh, the ruler of the city-state Uruk. In a manner typical of ancient kings, he wishes to aggrandize himself with "a name that endures" by building "walls, a great rampart and a temple." He needs large amounts of timber, and so in the second episode of the epic, called "The Forest Journey," Gilgamesh sets out for the primeval forests—"to the land where the cedar is felled." But this forest was considered to be the garden of the gods, and it was protected by the chief Sumerian deity Enlil, who entrusted the ferocious demigod Humbaba to guard it.

Gilgamesh and his companion Enkidu cross seven mountain ranges (how archetypal!) before finding the cedars, and are awed by their initial encounter: "They stood quite still and looked at the forest, saw how high were the great cedars. . . . They saw also the Cedar Mountain, where lived the gods. . . . The cedar raised aloft its great luxuriant growth: What cool shade, what delight!" Nevertheless, Gilgamesh and Enkidu commence cutting down the cedars, while Humbaba howls in protest. A great struggle ensues, until finally Humbaba is slain. "For two leagues the cedars resounded. Then there followed confusion; for this was the guardian of the forest whom they had struck to the ground: he at whose words Hermon and Lebanon used to tremble. Now the mountains were moved . . . for the guardian of the cedar lay dead." When Enlil learns of the destruction of the cedar forest, he sends down a series of ecological curses on the offenders: "May the food you eat be eaten by fire; may the water you drink be drunk by fire."[4]

The Forest Journey cloaks a real historical pattern of ecological exploitation in the guise of a hero tale. But the myth also reflects keen anxiety too: There is a sense that once humans start exploiting the forests, nothing will stop them. So the chapter concludes with a chilling note: "So Gilgamesh felled the trees of the forests and Endiku cleared their roots as far as the bank of Euphrates." Indeed, the deforestation effected by Gilgamesh and his successors in southern Mesopotamia figured prominently in the decline of the Sumerian civilization, as analyzed most recently by Jared Diamond's *Collapse: How Societies Choose to Fail or Succeed*. The Euphrates, Tigris, and Karun rivers and tributaries began to fill with salt and silt, clogging up the irrigation canals. After 1,500 years of successful farming, a serious salinity problem suddenly developed, resulting in declining food production. So it was that the very building schemes that sought to strengthen the empire brought on its destruction.

It was the Phoenicians who used the cedars to build history's first great maritime nation, and their famous seagoing triremes ruled the coast of Lebanon from such ancient cities as Byblos, Tyre, and Sidon. They eventually came to control the lucrative international cedar market. As far back as 2800 BCE, the people of Byblos were cutting down cedar trees in the Lebanon to export to Egypt and Mesopotamia. The Egyptians used cedar sawdust for mummification; the resin, known as *Cedria*, for embalming and strengthening papyrus; and the oils as medicine. The biblical prophet Ezekiel writes at length about the Phoenician city-state of Tyre, its merchant marine grandeur, its militarism, its insatiable hunger for lumber (Ezek 27:2–11), and its eventual destruction by Yahweh (27:27–36). Ezekiel's elaborate taunt was appropriated centuries later by the political prisoner John of Patmos in his apocalyptic critique of Rome's oppressive international political economy in Revelation 18.

The Lebanon was eventually controlled by Egypt, and then successively by the Babylonian, Persian, Greek, and Roman empires. The highlands were so denuded by the time of the Roman emperor Hadrian that he felt obligated to install markers around the remaining forests, declaring them an imperial domain. But periodic exploitation went on for another two millennia. The last clear-cutting was done by the Ottoman Turks, who took all of the cedars growing within transport distance of the Hijaz railway in order to provide fuel for their wood-burning engines. Only the highest and most remote groves escaped damage. From antiquity to the present, then, the pattern was the same: As Benjamin Kasoff put it, "The forests of Lebanon were under constant siege."[5] No wonder then that the biblical prophets were forever warning Israel that the nearby forests were in danger: "I will prepare destroyers against you, all with their weapons; they shall cut down your choicest cedars and cast them into the fire" (Jer 22:7).

There are two main literary trajectories concerning the cedars in the Hebrew Scriptures. They represent the most common nature image, symbolizing beauty and strength (Ps 29:4; 92:12; Song 4:5, 8). They are the epitome of God's magnificent creation—"The trees of the LORD are watered abundantly, the cedars of Lebanon that [God] planted" (Ps 104:16)—although even their grandeur pales before the Creator's power (Ps 29:5–9). And they are a metaphor for Israel itself as the object of God's care (Hos 14:5–7).

But the cedars also have a unique political connotation in Scripture as well. During Israel's own short experiment with regional hegemony under the united monarchy, King Solomon's reign, like that of old Gilgamesh, was characterized by a lust after the cedar's hardwood. First Kings narrates in some detail how Solomon requested King Hiram of Tyre to supply cedar to build the first great temple and palace in Jerusalem (1 Kgs 5:6–10). Hiram's scheme to bring the logs to the sea from the Lebanon and float them down the coast in rafts is confirmed by a frieze depicting this very method found in the palace of Sargon at Nineveh (about 700 BCE). Solomon's treaty was a sweet deal between royal houses, with food going from one to the other in exchange for luxury imports (5:20). And all the logging was done by conscripted labor (5:13–15). This is not so unlike the political economy of bananas or coffee, zinc or uranium today, with the labor of poorly paid workers supporting a market controlled by highly paid profiteers, at an enormous (and unaccounted) environmental cost to the land itself. We might say, therefore, that there was blood on the cedar that figured so prominently in Solomon's temple and his own royal house.

And prominent it was. First Kings 6–7 describes both the temple and the "House of the Forest of the Lebanon" as paneled in cedar "from floor to ceiling," with dozens of beams and pillars. The cedar trade was one of many ways that Solomon aped the habits of other ancient imperial leaders (he is portrayed in Song 3:7 as a military chieftain surrounded by a phalanx of warriors, carried on a royal litter made of cedar). It was just such royal patterns of apostasy that earned the scorn of Israel's prophets, who viewed them as the reason the Israelite monarchy was doomed.

It is with considerable irony and even sarcasm that the prophets—well aware the cedars were a target of royal hubris—also speak of the tree as a metaphor for empire itself. The psalmist likens Egypt to a cedar that will be felled (Ps 80:8–12). Amos celebrates the downfall of the Amorites, "whose height was like the height of cedars, and who was as strong as oaks" (Amos 2:9). This rhetorical tradition is most fully developed in Ezekiel 31:

Consider Assyria, a cedar of Lebanon,
with fair branches and forest shade,
    and of great height,
    its top among the clouds.

All the birds of the air
    made their nests in its boughs;
under its branches all the animals of the field
    gave birth to their young;
and in its shade
    all great nations lived.

The cedars in the garden of God could not rival it. . . .

Therefore thus says the Lord God: Because it towered high and set its top among the clouds, and its heart was proud of its height, I gave it into the hand of the prince of the nations. (Ezek 31:3–11)

Jesus himself later alludes to this anti-imperial tree allegory in his famous mustard seed parable (Mark 4:30–32).

The metaphor of the "great height" of empire is of course an allusion to the ancient tale of Babel's tower: "Come, let us build ourselves a city, and a tower with its top in the heavens, and let us make a name for ourselves" (Gen 11:4). We hear clear echoes here of Gilgamesh's quest for an immortal name, and we see the archetypal project of imperial urbanism. This warning fable is a thinly veiled parody of Mesopotamian ziggurats, for *Babel* is a wordplay on the Babylonian word for "gate of the gods" and on the Hebrew word connoting "these people are deeply confused." Isaiah appropriates this motif in his taunt against the king of Babylon: "How you are fallen from heaven, O Day Star, son of Dawn! . . . You said in your heart, 'I will ascend to heaven. . . . I will ascend to the tops of the clouds, I will make myself like the Most High'" (Isa 14:12–14).

Zechariah's lament acknowledges that the forests were the first objective of imperial conquest:

Open your doors, O Lebanon,
    so that fire may devour your cedars!

Wail, O cypress, for the cedar has fallen,
>for the glorious trees are ruined!
Wail, oaks of Bashan, for the thick forest has been felled! (Zech 11:1–2)

Thus, the prophets longed for the day when, as Isaiah puts it, the very imperial powers who "lay the nations low" would be, in the justice of YHWH, themselves "cut down," like the ancient cedars they exploited:

For the LORD of hosts has a day
>against all that is proud and lofty,
>against all that is lifted up and high;
against all the cedars of Lebanon,
>lofty and lifted up;
against every high tower,
>and against every fortified wall;
against all the ships of Tarshish. (Isa 2:12–16)

This tradition is best captured in Isaiah's remarkable oracle specifically criticizing Assyria's denuding of the forests. The context is Israelite king Hezekiah's attempts to negotiate new alliances in the wake of King Sennacherib's defeat of Egypt in 701 BCE and Babylon in 689. In Isaiah 37 (compare 2 Kgs 19:8–28), the prophet warns Hezekiah *not* to seek political and military security in an alliance with Sennacherib:

This is the word that the LORD has spoken concerning [Assyria]:

She despises you, she scorns you—
>virgin daughter Zion;
she tosses her head—behind your back,
daughter Jerusalem.

Whom have you mocked and reviled?
>Against whom have you raised your voice
and haughtily lifted your eyes?
>Against the Holy One of Israel!
By your servants you have mocked the Lord,
>and you have said, "With my many chariots

> I have gone up the heights of the mountains,
>> to the far recesses of Lebanon;
> I felled its tallest cedars,
>> its choicest cypresses;
> I came to its remotest height,
>> its densest forest." (Isa 37:22–24)

Taking chariots up Mount Lebanon is like trying to drive heavy tractors deep into old-growth wilderness forest; it is difficult, but the imperial (or corporate) will to conquer eventually prevails. Isaiah understands that these forests are primarily a military objective. And today, war still is ultimately about resources—as is certainly the case in the US occupation of Iraq.

Little wonder, then, that Isaiah envisions the end of empire as a relief not only for oppressed peoples but for the forests as well:

> When the LORD has given you rest from your pain and turmoil and the hard service with which you were made to serve, you will take up this taunt against the king of Babylon:

> How the oppressor has ceased!
>> How his insolence has ceased!
> The LORD has broken the staff of the wicked,
>> the scepter of rulers,
> that struck down the peoples in wrath
>> with unceasing blows,
> that ruled the nations in anger
>> with unrelenting persecution.
> The whole earth is at rest and quiet;
>> they break forth into singing.
> The cypresses exult over you,
>> the cedars of Lebanon, saying,
> "Since you were laid low,
> no one comes to cut us down." (Isa 14:3–8)

What a remarkable image: trees taking up the chant of praise for the downfall of kings who clear-cut them! It is an extraordinary hymn to environmental justice. And eschatological redemption will include the reforestation of "desertified" lands resulting from millennia of clear-cutting: "The wilderness and the dry land shall be glad" because the "glory of Lebanon shall be given to it, the majesty of Carmel and Sharon" (Isa 35:1–2).

The Qadisha Valley in Lebanon has been the site of monastic communities continuously since the earliest years of Christianity. Early on, these communities claimed the role of "guardians" of the cedar forests, like Enlil of old. Thanks to them, and to modern environmentalists, the last remaining twelve stands of cedars in Lebanon were inscribed as a UNESCO world historic site in 1998. The most famous stand is named the "Cedars of the Lord" (*Arz el Rab*) and lies about eighty miles from Beirut, near the birthplace of the great Lebanese poet Kahlil Gibran. About 375 cedars—some over two thousand years old, are in a mile-high, sheltered glacial pocket of Mount Makmel. This small, surviving grove bears silent witness to clear-cutting that began some five thousand years ago, and it is a reminder both of the fragility and endurance of the creation, and of the duty of people of faith and conscience to guard it.[6]

The mythic fight between Gilgamesh and Humbaba and the prophetic rants against clear-cutting both narrate the imperial conquest of nature and the cultures that lived symbiotically with it. This war has been repeated in every generation since, in every corner of the globe, to satisfy civilization's ever increasing appetite for material growth. It is the oldest conflict on the planet, and it continues today, but now it includes also rivers, aquifers, mountains, tundra, the ozone layer, even our own genetic makeup. Countless endangered or extinct species are the toll in this war. But in destroying nature, we are in fact cannibalizing our very life-source, just as the Sumerians did. As Evan Eisenberg, in his brilliant book *The Ecology of Eden*, puts it: "Civilization depends upon wilderness; the inverse does not, however, apply."[7]

What then might this tradition of fierce prophetic eco-justice mean for us? When Julia Butterfly Hill sat in a northern California redwood for two years in the late 1990s to prevent old-growth logging, she did not rely on support from churches. Indeed, most Christians would have dismissed her as a wrongheaded idealist. But from the biblical perspective, she was acting squarely in the prophetic tradition, as were the forest martyrs I mentioned at the beginning of this sermon. This latter group did not die in vain: Chico Mendes became internationally famous, bringing the plight of the rain forests to worldwide attention. In the Philippines, the EarthSavers Movement gives an annual award in honor of Father Satur to those defending the environment, and many Catholics have become active in nonviolent resistance to illegal logging. Just one week after Dorothy Stang was gunned down, Luiz da Silva, the president of Brazil, responded to the outcry by ordering the creation of two massive Amazonian rain forest reserves.

The struggle goes on in North America too. For example, since 1999, the Anishnabe of the Grassy Narrows community in Ontario, Canada, have sustained a nonviolent blockade at two key logging roads to prevent government approved clear-cutting in violation of their treaty rights. Traditional warriors are putting their bodies in front of the logging trucks, supported by other First Nations and by Christian Peacemaker Team volunteers.[8]

"My love is as the cedars," wrote Kahlil Gibran in *A Tear and a Smile*, "and the elements shall not conquer it."[9] The historic struggle between the exploiters and defenders of the forests continues, and upon it, in a very real, ecological sense, hinges the fate of our world. The Bible takes sides in this contest on behalf of the trees, a suppressed tradition that the church must recover. So let us listen to the story the cedars have to tell. If we have ears to hear, we will seek to embody Isaiah's ethic of resistance and hope:

When the poor and needy seek water,

I will make the wilderness a pool of water,
    and the dry land springs of water.
I will put in the wilderness the cedar,
    the acacia, the myrtle, and the olive;
I will set in the desert the cypress,

the plane and the pine together,

so that all may see and know,

all may consider and understand,

that the hand of the LORD has done this. (Isa 41:17–20)

Ched Myers works with Bartimaeus Cooperative Ministries in southern California. An activist for peace and justice, he is the author many articles and books, including *Binding the Strong Man: A Political Reading of Mark's Story of Jesus*, coauthor of *Say to This Mountain: Mark's Story of Discipleship*, and *The Biblical Vision of Sabbath Economics*.

Notes

1. Jan Oosthoek, "The Role of Wood in World History," 2000, accessed at http://www.forth.stir.ac.uk/~kjwo1/essay3.html.

2. On Father Satur, see Joseph Franke, "Faith and Martydom in the Forest," *Witness* 88, no. 8 (March 14, 2005), accessed at http://thewitness.org/article.php?id=785. On Mendes and his movement, see the 1994 documentary by John Frankenheimer, "The Burning Season: The Chico Mendes Story," and the book by Andrew Revkin, *Burning Season: The Murder of Chico Mendes and the Fight for the Amazon Rain Forest* (Washington, DC: Island Press, 2004).

3. David Haslam, "The Cedars of Lebanon: An Engineer Looks at the Data," 1998, accessed at http://web.ukonline.co.uk/d.haslam/mccheyne/cedars.htm.

4. Gilgamesh, translated by John Gardner and John Maier (New York: Vintage Books, 1984).

5. Benjamin Kasoff, "Cedars of Lebanon and Deforestation," 1995, Trade and Environment Database, accessed at http://www.american.edu/projects/mandala/TED/cedar.htm.

6. See Rania Masri, "The Cedars of Lebanon: Significance, Awareness, and Management of the *Cedrus Libani* in Lebanon," November 1995, International Relief Fund, accessed at http://almashriq.hiof.no/lebanon/300/360/363/363.7/transcript.html.

7. Evan Eisenberg, *The Ecology of Eden* (New York: Random House, 1999).

8. See the story at the Christian Peacemaker Teams' Web site: http://www.cpt.org/canada/can_asub.php.

9. Kahlil Gibran, *A Tear and a Smile* (New York: Alfred Knopf, 1914).

THE GLAD SOIL REJOICES

A SERMON PREACHED ON THANKSGIVING Sunday, November 23, 2003, at the First Church (Reformed Church in America) in Albany, New York.

> Do not fear, O soil;
>   be glad and rejoice,
>   for the LORD has done great things!
> Do not fear, you animals of the field,
>   for the pastures of the wilderness are green;
> the tree bears its fruit,
>   the fig tree and vine give their full yield.
>
> O children of Zion, be glad
>   and rejoice in the LORD your God;
> for he has given the early rain for your vindication,
>   he has poured down for you abundant rain,
>   the early and the later rain, as before.

The threshing floors shall be full of grain,
   the vats shall overflow with wine and oil.

I will repay you for the years
   that the swarming locust has eaten,
the hopper, the destroyer, and the cutter,
   my great army, which I sent against you.

You shall eat in plenty and be satisfied,
   and praise the name of the LORD your God,
   who has dealt wondrously with you.
And my people shall never again be put to shame.
You shall know that I am in the midst of Israel,
   and that I, the LORD, am your God and there is no other.
And my people shall never again
   be put to shame. **(Joel 2:21–27)**

◈

Some time ago I received an offer from a company for some kind of new computer software. As part of their sales pitch they said that their product was so exciting that others, by comparison, were "about as interesting as looking under a rock." I was offended. I happen to think that looking under a rock can be pretty exciting. In fact, I think that no human-made invention, no matter how many bytes or bells and whistles, can hold a candle to the intricacies and wonders of God's creation. So I rather enjoy looking under rocks, and I think I stand in pretty good company.

We all know Charles Darwin as the nineteenth-century scientist who wrote *On the Origin of Species* and proposed the theory of evolution. But do you also know that Darwin spent forty-four years of his life, on and off, studying earthworms? He was fascinated by them. He kept them in jars in his apartment. He and some of his contemporaries calculated that on average there were 53,767 earthworms in each acre of land. In many parts of England, he figured, the worm population swallowed and brought up ten tons of earth each year on each acre of land. Earthworms were not only creating the planet's thin layer of fertile soil; they were constantly turning it inside out. They were burying old Roman ruins; they were causing the monuments of Stonehenge to tilt and topple. In what is a marvelous understatement, Darwin concluded, "Worms have played a more important part in the history of the world than most persons would at first suppose."[1]

Earthworms are by no means the only fascinating creatures beneath our feet. Charles Kingsley once wrote to a friend whom he was planning to visit. "Don't be anxious to entertain me," he said. "Put me down under any hedgerow and in two square yards of mother earth I can find mystery enough to keep me occupied for all the time I stay with you." But we do not need even two square yards of earth; much less will do. Annie Dillard writes:

> In the top inch of forest soil, biologists found an average of 1,356 living creatures . . . including 865 mites, 265 springtails, 22 millipedes, 29 adult beetles and various numbers of 12 other forms. . . . Had an estimate also been made of the microscopic population, it might have ranged up to two billion bacteria and many millions of fungi, protozoa, and algae—in a mere *teaspoonful* of soil."[2]

These creatures are not only fascinating; they are creatures whose lives sustain so many other lives on this planet, including our own. Harvard entomologist E. O. Wilson writes:

> The very soils of the world are created by organisms. Plant roots shatter rocks to form much of the grit and pebbles of the basic substrate. But soils are much more than fragmented rock. They are complete ecosystems with vast arrays of plants, tiny animals, fungi, and microorganisms assembled in delicate balance, circulating nutrients in the form of solutions and tiny particles. A healthy soil literally breathes and moves.[3]

"Let everything that breathes, praise the Lord," said the psalmist. This means that the very soils beneath our feet are, in their own way, choirs of creatures singing their insect hymns, microbial chants, and fungal anthems in praise to the God who made them.

How dependent, how absolutely dependent we are upon these creatures! They could live very well without us, but we would perish without them. One spring while I was digging in the garden with my son, I picked up a handful of soil, held it up, and said, "Look, David, everything you are or ever will be; all the books that you will ever read, all the music and art in the world, your teachers, your family, your friends—it all depends on this."

Gary Paulsen says it even more vividly:

> Everything we are, all that we can ever be, all the Einsteins and babies and love and hate, all the joy and sadness and sex and wanting and liking and disliking, all the soft summer breezes on cheeks and first snowflakes, all the Van Goghs and Rembrandts and Mozarts and Mahlers and Thomas Jeffersons and Lincolns and Gandhis and Jesus Christs, all the Cleopatras and lovemaking and riches and achievements and progress, all of that, every single . . . thing that we are or ever will be is dependent on six inches of top-soil and the fact that the rain comes when it's needed and does not come when it's not needed; everything, every . . . single . . . *thing* comes with that.[4]

What a wonderful, precious gift is the soil beneath our feet! And how good it is to know that ours is a God who loves and cares for the soil. "Do not fear, O soil; be glad and rejoice, for the LORD has done great things!"

Today, especially, on Thanksgiving Day, we give praise and thanks to God who provides for us. We give thanks for a creation that delights in its Creator and for a Creator who delights in creation. "Be glad and rejoice, O soil. . . . Do not fear animals of the field."

But there is also a more solemn, more challenging word from Joel, and if you were listening carefully you may have caught it. It is in verse 25, where God says through the prophet: "I will repay you for the years that the swarming locust has eaten, the hopper, the destroyer, and the cutter, my great army, which I sent against you." According to Joel, God not only sends the rain and causes the land and the animals to be fruitful; God also sends the locusts that destroy the crops. In fact, the first chapter of the book of Joel is a rather graphic description of a locust plague that decimated the land, and Joel sees this too as coming from the hand of God. This plague, says Joel, is a warning, a call to repentance.

It is one thing to acknowledge God as the loving creator and generous provider when things go well—when the soil, the crops, and the animals rejoice. At such times it is not difficult to have hearts overflowing with thanksgiving. But it is another kind of faith to be able to say that somehow, even in the bad times, when the rain fails and the crops whither, when sorrow comes on top of sorrow, that somehow behind these events, too, is the hand of God.

This is part of what we mean by *providence*. The Heidelberg Catechism explains it this way: the belief that God "so upholds and rules the world that leaves and grass, rain and drought, fruitful and unfruitful years, food and drink, health and sickness, riches and poverty, and everything else, come to us not by chance but by God's sustaining hand."

I am not sure that even the Reformers would assert that every event, every circumstance, is one that God directly wills. It seems to me that God in God's love for us and for creation has given creation a measure of freedom. There are some things we bring on ourselves through our own folly or ignorance or downright orneriness. And sometimes accidents happen. And when someone we know has suffered a devastating loss, we need to be especially careful not to hide behind the doctrine of providence. Sometimes we can be too quick to say, "I'm sure that there must be a reason for this." Perhaps there is. But sometimes it is more honest, and perhaps more caring, to admit that we cannot see how this tragedy could be the will of God, and that we, with them, at least for now, must live without answers and simply share their pain and their loss.

But the doctrine of providence does affirm—and the faith to which Joel calls us challenges us to believe—that ultimately God's purposes for creation are not thwarted, that God created this world in love, that God wills creation's fruitfulness, and that God made you and me and all creatures, including the creatures beneath our feet (even the locusts!) for good and delight. God wills that soil, animals, and humans live without fear and rejoice in the God who made them. For us this means that, although God may not will every sickness and every loss, we nevertheless trust that through them and from them God is working out God's purpose—so that even out of the tangled skeins of tragedy God will weave goodness.

That is not a faith we can impose on others. In the midst of our own sorrows, we may struggle to affirm it ourselves. I only know that this is the kind of faith that has sustained God's saints in their darkest hours—and not only sustained them but enabled them to live thankful, joyful lives. It is the faith that good is stronger than evil, that love is stronger than hate, that light is stronger than darkness, that ultimately, God's good purposes for us and for all creation will prevail—so that even in the midst of want or sorrow or loss or plague, we trust that nothing, absolutely nothing, will separate us from God's love.

Rejoice, O soil, in the God who made you. Fear not, animals of the field, for God provides for you. Give thanks, O people, for the God whose abiding love will never let you go.

John D. Paarlberg is a graduate of Hope College and Yale Divinity School. Prior to becoming the senior minister of the First Church in Albany, New York, he served congregations in Holland, Michigan, and in North Syracuse, New York, and as the minister for social witness and worship for the Reformed Church in America.

Notes

1. Quoted in Scott McVay, "A Siamese Connexion with a Plurality of Other Mortals," *The Biophilia Hypothesis*, ed. Stephen Kellert and Edward O. Wilson (Washington, DC: Island Press; Covelo, CA: Shearwater Books, 1993): 13.

2. Quoted in Elizabeth Achtemeier, *Nature, God, and Pulpit* (Grand Rapids: Eerdmans, 1992), 27.

3. E. O. Wilson, *The Diversity of Life* (Cambridge, MA: Belkamp Press of Harvard University Press, 1992), 308.

4. Gary Paulsen, *Clabbered Dirt, Sweet Grass* (San Diego: Harcourt Brace, 1992), 23.

FIRST AND EVERLASTING COVENANT

LARRY RASMUSSEN

THIS SERMON WAS PREACHED for commencement at Capital University in 2003.

> Then God said to Noah and to his sons with him, "As for me, I am establishing my covenant with you and your descendants after you, and with every living creature that is with you, the birds, the domestic animals, and every animal of the earth with you." **(Gen 9:8–10)**

◈

A beautiful world, still beautiful beyond the singing of it, is slowly being destroyed. Yes, by dint of good work and nature's stubborn resiliency, some communities of the living world are in good repair. But overall, the earth's life-systems are in decline. Soil erosion exceeds soil formation; carbon emissions exceed carbon fixation and apparently make for more extreme storms and varied weather; species extinction wildly exceeds species evolution, this time at the hands of the one species that never really thinks of itself as a species among species—namely, us—ocean fish catches exceed ocean fish reproduction; forest destruction exceeds forest regeneration; and in far too many locales, freshwater use exceeds aquifer replenishment. So the comment of Hans Blix, the chief United Nations inspector in Iraq, ought not surprise us:

> To me the question of the environment is more ominous than that
> of peace and war. We will have regional conflicts and use of force,
> but world conflicts I do not believe will happen any longer. But the
> environment, that is a creeping danger. I'm more worried about
> global warming than I am of any major military conflict.[1]

We do not call this gradual but ominous degradation "violence," because we do not truly feel it. We feel little in the way of intimacy, kinship, and neighborliness with the rest of nature. We do not consider ourselves bone of its bone and flesh of its flesh, though we indeed are. Try holding your breath for five minutes, or going without water for a week, or refraining from nourishment, or foregoing the life of the five senses altogether, and see whether or not you are a good animal who belongs to the community of life.

But the prophets did call the earth's degradation "violence," and we had better listen with cocked ears. Consider Isaiah:

> The earth lies polluted
>   under its inhabitants;
> for they have transgressed laws,
>   violated the statutes,
>   broken the everlasting covenant.
> Therefore a curse devours the earth,
> and its inhabitants suffer for their guilt.
>
> The wine dries up,
>   the vine languishes,
>   all the merry-hearted sigh.
>
> The city of chaos is broken down,
>   every house is shut up so that no one can enter.
> There is an outcry in the streets for lack of wine;

all joy has reached its eventide;

the gladness of the earth is banished. (Isa 24:5–7, 10–11)

This covenant, which is deemed to be everlasting, is the first one, and breaking it banishes the gladness of earth. When the vines languish, the merry-hearted sigh—so bundled together is our life with the rest of the community of life. That covenant, proclaimed to Noah when creation was almost undone and only an ark of life survived, was the covenant between God and the earth. It was broken by escalating human violence from Cain to Lamech, enough violence and injustice to make God regret the first creation and try again. Here is that first covenant:

> Then God said to Noah and to his sons with him, "As for me, I am establishing my covenant with you and your descendants after you, and with every living creature that is with you, the birds, the domestic animals, and every animal of the earth with you. . . . This is the sign of the covenant that I make between me and you and every living creature that is with you, for all future generations: I have set my bow in the clouds, and it shall be a sign of the covenant between me and the earth. . . . When the bow is in the clouds, I will see it and remember the everlasting covenant between God and every living creature of all flesh that is on the earth." (Gen 9:8–10, 12–13, 16)

Ask the average pew-sitter whom the first covenant was with, and the answer you will likely get is Abraham and Sarah and their descendents. We jump to that because we think covenants are always between God and human beings or among human beings themselves. Our Christianity turns on an axis that runs between God and humankind only. Our temples of worship move all holy ground indoors and use human artifacts to represent all sacred things. And even when we are sober enough to honor all ground as truly holy ground and all creation as truly sacred, we jockey into position as the good steward, the trustee who represents God to the rest of creation and rules from an appointed place of dominion. It hardly occurs to us that this is the preabolition notion of steward. The

Christian slaveholder was the good steward of his slaves. We got rid of that, mostly. But we did not get rid of nature as our slave—living property at our command over which we are stewards who make all the decisions with a view to our interests.

Or ask the average pew-sitter what the very first commandment is. You will not likely get the right answer. It is "Be fruitful and multiply." But to whom is it first said? Fish and birds!

> So God created the great sea monsters and every living creature that moves, of every kind, with which the waters swarm, and every winged bird of every kind. And God saw that it was good. God blessed them, saying, "Be fruitful and multiply and fill the waters in the seas, and let birds multiply on the earth." And there was evening and there was morning, the fifth day. (Gen 1:21–23)

Likewise, we do not much observe that the reason given by God for human earth creatures in Genesis 2 is "to till and keep" the garden. The Hebrew word here, 'bd, is the word meaning "to serve." It is the same word that in Greek is used by and about Jesus as one who serves. The human is, by vocation, the servant of the land, and in this second creation account the primary identification of *ha adam* (the "earth creature" or the "earth being") is with *adamah* ("topsoil"), from which Adam is made, as are all other creatures, and to which Adam and all else will return. You are topsoil; from topsoil you, just like the other creatures, came, and to topsoil you, and they, will return. Your task in life, as the human earth creature— Adam—is to serve and to conserve, to till and to protect, or to till and to keep, the land. "To till and serve" is not quite the first commandment, as I have noted. But it is the first one to human earth beings, and it comes long before Moses and Sinai. It comes at the dawn of our species and is our primordial calling and command. "To till and keep the garden," "to obey such an everlasting covenant," "to renew the face of the earth"—this is why we are here.

Ask the average pew-sitter who it is that is created next, after Adam, and the answer you will likely get is "Eve." In due course that is true, but in Genesis 2 all the animals are created first, right after

Adam, as God witnesses the earth creature being alone and seeks a fit partner for it. Read Genesis 2:18–20 and ask yourself: What is the logic embedded here, that "every animal of the field and every bird of the air" might be the appropriate partner for Adam? They might be Adam's companion and partner because they too are all from *adamah* and return to it, and they, each and every one, are all recipients of the very same breath of God that gives Adam life. They are kin in the community of life.

Next, ask the average pew-sitter what tree is in the midst of the garden. The answer you will likely get is "the tree of the knowledge of good and evil." That tree gets all the press; however, it is the wrong answer. The right answer is: "Out of the ground the LORD God made to grow every tree that is pleasant to the sight and good for food, the tree of life also in the midst of the garden, and the tree of the knowledge of good and evil" (Gen 2:9). The tree of life is at the center of the garden, at the very axis of the world. There the Bible begins, just as the Bible ends with this same tree of life, now in the renewed or redeemed world of New Jerusalem and along the banks of the rivers of crystal waters flowing from the throne of God. The tree of life bears its fruit for every season, and the leaves of the tree are "for the healing of the nations" (Rev 22:2).

But read on in Revelation. John of Patmos is an outrageously jealous author who closes the book of Revelation by saying that if you mess with a single jot or tittle of his prophecy, God will get you! And what is the worst that can happen? Hades, Sheol, Hell? No. Rather, God will remove your share "in the tree of life and in the holy city" (Rev 22:18). You will, in different words, be utterly cut off and alienated from that to which you belong—body, soul, and mind.

Of course, there are other themes in these familiar creation accounts. We are made in the image of God. And the command to humans, too, is to be fruitful and multiply. The command is also to rule and have dominion. A friend of mine says, "These commandments to be fruitful and have dominion we have kept with a vengeance. It is high time to move to those we have not kept to such excess."

But why do we raise up these themes and not the others? Why do we filter out themes of utter kinship while we systematically live out the themes that set us apart and over? This is apartheid-thinking at the species level: We think we are a species apart that can develop separately from the rest of the community of life.

Let me say this differently. We filter reality in the apartheid fashion the way we do not because we are poor students of Scripture. That may be true, or it may not be. We do so because of our whole way of life. We did not arrive at the decline of most every major life-system because we conveniently overlooked half the verses of Genesis. We overlooked the verses because they did not fit the mark of our way of living, namely, building a world that never even bothers to ask what the *whole* community of life—other humans and the more-than-human world—requires for its renewal and regeneration.

Of course, not all of us do this in the same degree. About 70 percent of environmental degradation has nothing to do with people's individual feelings about nature or their education and intelligence. It has to do with the patterns and systems (the way of life) of the richer nations and their imitators elsewhere.

Bill McKibben paints a picture that should stick with us. How big are we? McKibben asks, meaning the size of human claims on the earth. This is not so simple, he goes on to explain. Not only do we vary greatly in how much food and energy and water and minerals we consume, but each of us varies over time. William Catton, McKibben recounts, once tried to calculate the amount of energy human beings use each day. In hunter-gatherer times it was about 2,500 calories, all of it food. That is the daily intake of a common dolphin. A modern human being uses 31,000 calories a day, most of it in the form of fossil fuel. That is the intake of a pilot whale. And the average American uses six times that—as much as a sperm whale. We have become, in other words, different from the people we used to be—not kinder or unkinder, not brighter or stupider; our natures seem to have changed little since Homer. We have just gotten bigger. We appear to be the same species, with stomachs of the same size, but we are not. It is as if each of us were trailing a big

Macy's Thanksgiving Day Parade balloon around, feeding it constantly. Now each of us needs not only a little plot of cropland and a little pasture for the meat we eat but also a little forest for timber and paper, a little mine, a little oil well. Giants have big feet. Some scientists in Vancouver tried to calculate one such footprint and found that although 1.7 million people lived on a million acres surrounding their city, those people required 21.5 million acres of land to support them: wheat fields in Alberta; oil fields in Saudi Arabia, Kuwait, and Iraq; tomato fields in Mexico. Those balloons above our heads can shrink or grow, depending on how we choose to live.[2] *How we live*—that is what is at issue in keeping or violating the first and everlasting covenant.

Let the deep traditions of Christian faith speak to how we live. A sacramental apprehension of the whole creation is an orientation toward life that finds simply repulsive our turning all things, now even air and water as well as topsoil—*adamah* itself—into commodities, property to be bought and sold as though it had no life and value of its own and no claim upon our lives. Christian asceticism is a second long tradition—the tradition of learning to say yes and to say no in a way that loves the earth fiercely in a simple way of life, a life of material simplicity and spiritual richness, a life disciplined against consumerism. Yet another long tradition is the prophet's riveted attention to institutionalized habits that make some rich and others poor, some adding lot to lot while others lack a livelihood, some enjoying fine wine while others dare not drink the water, yet must. In sum, *how we live* is the issue, the issue at the heart of keeping, or violating, the first and everlasting covenant.

Friends, this pale blue dot, tiny little earth afloat in the vast sea of space, seven land masses bent over a great round water, does not belong to us. We belong, with all else, to it and its community of life. Until we get that right, the forests and the seas, the air and the water, and those species in them, will all languish. And we as a precious part of the web of life itself will suffer. That is the present warning label attached to what is deemed to be the first and everlasting covenant, the covenant between God and every living creature of all flesh, between God and the earth. Life—all life—is a precious gift. Till this gift and serve it, embrace it, cherish it, mother it.

Larry Rasmussen is a Christian ethicist whose present work seeks to provide a moral and theological reorientation to address the earth's distress as the result of unsustainable uses of human power. He is the author of many articles and books, including *Moral Fragments and Moral Community: A Proposal for Church in Society*, *Earth Community, Earth Ethics*, which won the 1997 Louis Grawemeyer Award in Religion, and *Dietrich Bonhoeffer: Reality and Resistance*.

Notes

1. "Hans Blix's Greatest Fear," *New York Times*, March 16, 2003.
2. Bill McKibben, "A Special Moment in History: The Future of Population," *Atlantic Monthly*, May 1998, 56–57.

BLESSING THE ANIMALS

DAVID RHOADS

THIS SERMON WAS PREACHED at a service of the "Blessing of the Animals" in Augustana Chapel at the Lutheran School of Theology at Chicago on St. Francis Day, 2006.

> And God said, "Let the waters bring forth swarms of living crea-
> tures, and let birds fly above the earth across the dome of the sky."
> So God created the great sea monsters and every living creature
> that moves, of every kind, with which the waters swarm, and every
> winged bird of every kind. And God saw that it was good. God
> blessed them, saying, "Be fruitful and multiply and fill the waters in
> the seas, and let birds multiply on the earth. . . .
>
> And God said, "Let the earth bring forth living creatures of
> every kind: cattle and creeping things and wild animals of the earth
> of every kind." And it was so. God made the wild animals of the
> earth of every kind, and the cattle of every kind, and everything that
> creeps upon the ground of every kind. And God saw that it was
> good. **(Gen 1:20–25)**

◈

And [Jesus] said to them, "Go into all the world and proclaim the good news to the whole creation." **(Mark 16:15)**

◈

Through [Jesus] God was pleased to reconcile to himself all things, whether on earth or in heaven, by making peace through the blood of his cross. **(Col 1:20)**

◈

First, I want to address you varieties of dogs and cats that are here today. And I want to speak with you fish and ferrets and hamsters and parakeets and snakes brought here today by your human companions. You are here for your own sake, and you also represent all those who are not here today, animals of every kind—cattle and goats and horses and elephants and bees and cougars and crocodiles and puffer fish and eels and insects—so many we cannot begin to name them all.

I want to announce the good news to all you creatures. I want you to know that God loves you. God loves you for your own sake and not because of what you can do for humans. You are good in yourselves. The good book tells us that when God created you—fish of the sea and birds of the air and creatures of the land—God looked at all God had created, and God saw that "indeed, it was very good!" (Gen 1:12, 18, 21, 25, 31)

When God created you, God blessed you. God told you to "be fruitful and multiply and fill the earth" (Gen 1:28). God created you in huge swarms and in great diversity. God wants all of you to survive and to thrive on the earth.

God created the world for you, so that you have what you need to live. The psalmist tells us that God made the rain to water the trees, the trees for you birds to nest, the grass for you cattle to graze, and the crags as a refuge for you mountain goats (Ps 104:14–24). God wants you to receive your "food in due season" and to be "filled with good things" (104:27–28).

The Bible tells us that when the flood came, God rescued each of you through Noah in the ark. And God made a covenant with you fish of the sea and birds of the air and domestic animals and all animals on the earth to protect you for the future (Gen 9:8–17). God made the first "endangered species act."

Just like us, you are called to worship God. The hills are to clap their hands. The fields are to exalt (Ps 148). You cattle and dogs and cats are to praise God by being who you are and exalting in it. John the seer had a vision in which he heard the entire creation—everything in heaven, on the earth, under the earth, and in the sea—cry out in praise: "To the one seated on the throne and to the Lamb be blessing and honor and glory and might forever and ever" (Rev 5:13).

We human animals need to confess to you that we have systematically mistreated you, depleted your numbers, destroyed you, slaughtered you, crowded you out, neglected you, treated you as commodities in our quest for comfort and ease. We have not seen you as God's creatures. We have not shown proper reverence or respect. Against God's will, we have not set limits upon ourselves so that you might live and thrive. For what we have done, we are sorry!

You who are here today are so fortunate because you have human companions who care for you. But so many of your cousins are threatened with extinction: snow leopards and timber wolves and green sea turtles and condors and paddlefish and fin whales among so many others. We humans may so crowd out or deplete these kin of yours such that not a single one of them will ever again exist on the earth.

When we diminish you and destroy you in these ways, we not only compromise your ability to survive, but we also stifle your capacity to praise God. Along with all creation, you are groaning in labor pains, waiting for the revelation of children of God who will care for creation and make provisions for you to thrive (Rom 8:19–23).

Now I want to address you human creatures. I want to announce the good news to you also. God loves you. God loves you for your own sake and wants you to thrive. When God made you, God saw that this too was good.

God said also to you, "Be fruitful and multiply, and fill the earth" (Gen 1:28). Yet we have already done this! So we need to stop, because God did not mean for us to crowd out the rights of other creatures to multiply also. In developed countries, we have become like an infestation—taking over land and destroying habitats and devouring species and infiltrating homes and migratory routes of so many other animals—and we need to learn our limits.

God even created us humans with a special responsibility, namely, to exercise dominion (Gen 1:28). This does not mean that we are to exercise domination over other creatures or to exploit them. Rather, we are to delight in other creatures, as God does, and care for them. Our love for creation is the only basis for our right use of creation. We are to take responsibility for all creatures, to serve their needs, and to work to preserve them.

We are to do this not with a sense of superiority but in solidarity with all other creatures. We were created to be together, to be companions to one another, to thrive together. All animals are our cousins, our kin. And God made a covenant with us and with all other animals together. Admit it, we humans are also animals, primate mammals.

Jesus, too, was a mammal. Jesus lived to care about all who were oppressed and made vulnerable and marginalized by society, and right now that includes most creatures, not just humans. Jesus died in order that God might reconcile to God's self "all things" in creation (Col 1:20).

In response to God's love, we are freed to behave in ways that enable all of life to thrive together. You do not need to prove anything. You can set limits on yourselves. You can simplify your lifestyle so that others may survive and thrive. You can become aware of your actions on other creatures and curtail your activity. You can act to establish safe homes and habitats for those animals that are endangered.

Now I want to address all of you creatures together. I had a vision in a dream one night. I was in the front row of a cathedral during a service of Communion. I saw the priest passing bread to the first person at the Communion railing. As I looked, the next figure at the railing was a snake! It was curled at the bottom with its back arching up over the rail and with head straining forward to receive the grace of Christ. The next figure was another person. Next was a raccoon with paws up on the Communion railing who was leaning forward to receive the grace of Christ. Then I saw a bird perched on the corner of the railing eating bread crumbs.

As I finished surveying this scene in my dream, suddenly the sidewalls of the cathedral fell away and outside was thick foliage and jungle on each side with all manner of wild animals roaming around. In this moment, it seemed as if the walls of separation had been removed and there was a seamless web of all creation praising God and exalting in the grace of Christ.

From the time I awoke from that dream until this day, I have never been able to think of worship in the same way again. I see all of earth as the sanctuary in which we worship, and I see myself invoking, confessing, giving thanks, praising God, and offering myself in solidarity with all of life. May that vision also become your vision.

You who are here today are very fortunate. You have a relationship of love and care and loyalty between yourselves and your companions. You model how all relationships between humans and other animals should be. We wish to project this relationship as the model for our human relationship with all animals. May we care about all animals as we care for our companions at home.

David Rhoads teaches New Testament at the Lutheran School of Theology at Chicago. He has published *Mark as Story: An Introduction to the Narrative of a Gospel* with Donald Michie and Joanna Dewey, *The Challenge of Diversity: The Witness of Paul and the Gospels,* and is the editor of *From Every People and Nation: The Book of Revelation in Intercultural Perspective.*

HEALING OUR "AFFLUENZA"

Jesus, the Rich Man, and Eternal Life

BARBARA ROSSING

THIS SERMON WAS PREACHED at Holden Village, a Christian retreat center in the Cascade Mountains of Washington.

> As [Jesus] was setting out on a journey, a man ran up and knelt before him, and asked him, "Good Teacher, what must I do to inherit eternal life?" Jesus said to him, "Why do you call me good? No one is good but God alone. You know the commandments: 'You shall not murder; You shall not commit adultery; You shall not steal; You shall not bear false witness; You shall not defraud; Honor your father and mother.'" He said to him, "Teacher, I have kept all these since my youth." Jesus, looking at him, loved him and said, "You lack one thing; go, sell what you own, and give the money to the poor, and you will have treasure in heaven; then come, follow me." When he heard this, he was shocked and went away grieving, for he had many possessions.
>
> Then Jesus looked around and said to his disciples, "How hard it will be for those who have wealth to enter the kingdom of God!"

And the disciples were perplexed at these words. But Jesus said to them again, "Children, how hard it is to enter the kingdom of God! It is easier for a camel to go through the eye of a needle than for someone who is rich to enter the kingdom of God." They were greatly astounded and said to one another, "Then who can be saved?" Jesus looked at them and said, "For mortals it is impossible, but not for God; for God all things are possible."

Peter began to say to him, "Look, we have left everything and followed you." Jesus said, "Truly I tell you, there is no one who has left house or brothers or sisters or mother or father or children or fields, for my sake and for the sake of the good news, who will not receive a hundredfold now in this age—houses, brothers and sisters, mothers and children, and fields with persecutions—and in the age to come eternal life. But many who are first will be last, and the last will be first." (Mark 10:17-31)

◈

What are your wounds? Are you sick with a fever like Peter's mother-in-law? Do you live with some other chronic disease like the Apostle Paul with his thorn in the flesh—diabetes, AIDS, or addiction? Are you paralyzed by a relationship that is broken? Is there a terrifying demon—mental, spiritual, or physical—that will not let you go? A few years ago I had a terrible hiking accident, and the scar on my leg still reminds me of that wound, but it also reminds me of the skill and care of medical people who brought me back to health with their healing touch.

The early chapters of Mark's Gospel give a veritable catalogue of wounds and of Jesus' healing. There is a familiar pattern to the opening lines of many of the healing stories: Jesus passes by a village, and a sick person or parent of a sick child runs up to him and falls down before him with a specific request. You see the pattern in the very first story of healing in Mark's Gospel: "Make me well," the man with leprosy requests as he falls to his knees before Jesus (1:40). "Heal my daughter" is the appeal of Jairus as he falls at Jesus' feet (5:23). All of these supplicants come to Jesus with a request for healing.

The story of the rich man who comes to Jesus in Mark 10 also follows the pattern of a typical healing story. This rich man's woundedness and Jesus' prescription for healing can speak to us and to our ecological situation today. Like these other supplicants, the man in the story in Mark 10 runs up to Jesus on the road and "falls on his knees." Here Mark uses the same word, *gonypeteo*, as in the story of the man with leprosy in Mark 1:40. Like other supplicants, this man has a request: "Good Teacher, what must I do to inherit eternal life?" Here, however, his request seems not to fit the pattern of the typical healing story in Mark. With his question about eternal life, this man does not seem to be asking for healing, nor does he appear to be sick. But is he indeed sick? Might he be sick without knowing it?

Cut to a doctor's examining room. A woman sits on the table in her skimpy little hospital gown. She clutches her purse nervously on her lap as she waits for the doctor to appear. The woman is actress Jackie O'Ryan from the soap opera *All My Children*, but here she is starring in a little drama called *Lives of Our Days*, complete with suspenseful soap opera music. As she sits on the table fiddling with her gold jewelry and purse, in walks the doctor with the grave news: "I'm afraid there is nothing physically wrong with you."

"Then why do I feel so awful, so bloated and sluggish?" she asks. "Nothing gives me joy anymore—not the clothes, the house, the raise. Doctor, I'm frightened. Can't you give me a pill?"

"There is no pill for what you have. I'm afraid you're suffering from affluenza."

"Oh my God," she reacts. "Why me? Is it fatal?"

"It's catastrophic. It's the new epidemic."

"Is there a cure?"

"Possibly."

So begins John de Graaf's hit film *Affluenza,* which aired several years ago on public television. In this humorous yet hard-hitting documentary, National Public Radio host Scott Simon narrates an expose of our culture, of our insatiable appetite for more—which the producers define as truly an epidemic that is making us and our world ill. A combination of the words *affluence* and *influenza, affluenza* is defined on the show's Web site as "1. An epidemic of stress, overwork, waste and indebtedness caused by dogged pursuit of the American Dream; 2. An unsustainable addiction to economic growth."

Unlike the woman on the examining table, the rich man in today's Gospel text does not know he is sick. He does not list his symptoms, but this man clearly has an advanced case of affluenza. Having inherited the family fortune, an enormous landholding, he now wants even *more*: He wants to inherit eternal life. So he kneels before Jesus with the request.

Jesus gives him the standard prescription: "You know the commandments: You shall not murder; You shall not commit adultery; You shall not steal; You shall not bear false witness; You shall not defraud. . . ."

Wait a minute. What was that last commandment about "defrauding"? That's not in the list of the Ten Commandments as we learned it in catechism class. Here Jesus has replaced the more familiar Old Testament commandment against coveting with the word "defraud." Is Jesus implying that if a rich person is so rich it may well be the result of having defrauded the poor? If so, this is an interesting economic zinger.

The rich man does not seem to notice this shift. He confidently assures Jesus that he is a paragon of health as far as God's laws are concerned: "I have kept all these since my youth." He sits on the examining table expecting a clean bill of health, as we do when the doctor has gone through the checklist of items (Do you smoke? Do you ever go outside without sunscreen? Do you ever drive without your seat belt?).

Jesus looks at this man—gazes "into him" as the Greek puts it— and Jesus loves him. This is a wonderful moment of healing. Jesus can see the sickness in this self-righteous man, his great lack, yet Jesus still loves him, as he loves each of us with a wonderful, unexpected love that gazes deep into our souls, that loves us and our world unconditionally. It is this gaze of love that heals the rich man and heals each of us.

Healing stories in Mark's Gospel typically continue with a command to do something, often beginning with the Greek command *hypage*: "Get up" or "Go your way." Little does this rich man realize that the doctor is about to write out the toughest prescription imaginable. Because Jesus loves this man, Jesus lovingly invites this man to follow him, to take the next step to accept his healing—namely, to move to embrace eternal life by letting go of his possessions and by making restitution to the poor.

"You lack one thing," Doctor Jesus offers by way of diagnosis.

"Get up," Jesus tells him, using the same words he uses with so many others as he completes the process of healing them from their diseases—to the man with leprosy (1:44), to the paralyzed man (2:9, 11), to the Gerasene demon-possessed man (5:19), to the woman with the flow of blood (5:34), to the Syrophoenician woman (7:29), and to the blind Bartimaeus (10:52). "Get up. Sell what you own and give to the poor, and you will find treasure in heaven." Follow me. This will be health to you; this will be eternal life.

Jesus invites the rich man into community, into a new way of life. The tragedy of this story is that the rich man cannot swallow that pill. He cannot take the cure. Even though Doctor Jesus has looked at him and loved him, this man leaves grief-stricken, weeping, *alone*, apparently to resume his illness. He is apparently so addicted to his possessions, to his great wealth and inheritance—so sick with affluenza—that he misses out on being an heir to eternal life. He misses out on the community of the gospel.

Are we sick? Have we been stricken with an epidemic? Environmental writer Bill McKibben thinks so. He defines our culture's insatiable hunger for more as a sickness. The sickness metaphor is helpful, I think, because it helps us see the health threat that our way of life poses, both to ourselves and to the world.

How does the story in Mark 10 end? The rich man goes away, unable to take the cure. But perhaps his weeping offers hope for healing. Weeping can do that; it can open us to the cries of the world and to our own desperate need for change.

I will never forget the weeping of four poor Honduran farmers who shared their stories with us at Holden Village. The joy these campesinos found in the gospel—in eternal life—was a testimony to everyone. Shyly, softly, they laid bare their childhood trauma of abject poverty. They told of the shame of not having shoes until the age of seventeen, the shame of not having anything to eat when it is lunchtime, of being told day after day that you are nothing. One of them, Jorge, lived from age 10 to 14 as a slave to a rich man. Miguel has become a primary school teacher, but he is still very poor, and his heart goes out to the poorest children in his classroom. He told of one of his students who had no pants to wear to school—a story that clearly struck a chord in the three other men, for all were softly weeping, wiping their eyes with huge white handkerchiefs as Miguel described his student.

One of the questions of today's Gospel text is this: How does the weeping of four poor campesinos—who know the shame of not having pants and who cannot even buy medicine for their children when they are sick—connect to the weeping of the rich man in the Gospel story who cannot let go of his possessions? How do the wounds of our affluenza and overconsumption connect to the wounds of impoverished people throughout the world? And how does their weeping connect also to what Brazilian theologian Leonardo Boff calls the "cry of the earth"? Is there a connection by way of our weeping that can help us find healing for the world?

In issuing his prescription of "Go, sell your possessions and give to the poor," Doctor Jesus seems to be saying there is indeed a connection. Doctor Jesus appears to be diagnosing as fraudulent the very system—in his time and also in our time—that perpetuates a chasm between rich and poor in the world while also endangering the planet's future, a system that is making us all sick.

We cannot inherit eternal life while clinging to the disease of affluenza. But there is hope. There is love. As Jesus gazes lovingly into each one of us, he offers not only the diagnosis but also the gift of eternal life. "Follow me," Jesus says to each one of us, as he said to the rich man.

"Lay aside your possessions," Jesus says. Give them away; divest yourself! These possessions are killing you. They are making you feel bloated and sluggish. (Remember the words of our soap opera friend: "Nothing gives me joy—not the clothes, the raise, the car, the house.") Our ever bigger houses, our oil-based economy, our addictive accumulation of possessions—these are making our planet ill. With our lifestyle we are eating up the planetary capital that God has created over millions of years.

Jesus invites us to downsize our lifestyle—to "power down," as Richard Heinberg describes the way of life required for a post-carbon world. Give back to the poor and to the earth what we have taken by fraud, before it is too late. Inherit instead the promise. Inherit eternal life.

As we gather here, the examining table in the doctor's office becomes the Communion table. Here Doctor Jesus gave you the only pill you will ever need. Take, eat—his body, given for you, in communion with God and with one another and with all creation. Given for life and for healing. This communion is eternal life!

This story can underscore both the urgency of our unsustainable way of life and the depth of Jesus' love for us. The rich man asks for an inheritance of "eternal life," yet he fundamentally misunderstands eternal life as something individualistic that he can own or inherit. He fails to see that eternal life is life in communion with God and with one another.

After the rich man departs, the story shifts to the final scene, in which the disciples ask, "Then who can be saved?" The Greek word *sozo* in verse 26 is another word that makes me think that this story may actually be a healing story. This same word can mean "save" or "heal," as in the story of Jairus's daughter, when Jairus asks, "Come lay hands on her so that she might be made well" (5:23); as in the story of the hemorrhaging woman, when she says, "If I but touch his clothes I will be made well" (5:28; compare 6:56 and 10:26); and as in the story of the blind man Bartimaeus, when Jesus tells him, "Go; your faith has made you well" (10:52).

"Who then can be healed?" the incredulous disciples ask. Their question points out the difficulty of lifestyle change, especially for the rich. "For mortals it is impossible," Jesus says, "but not for God; for God all things are possible."

That is the promise, the message of hope and healing for us, in the gospel: With God all things are possible. Even in the face of sobering ecological statistics such as the doubling of carbon dioxide in the atmosphere by mid-century, rising sea levels, the shrinking polar ice cap, accelerating extinctions, and the growing gap between rich and poor, what gives hope for our planet and for each one of us is the amazing restorative power of God's healing love for the world.

Our planet is very ill with the fever of global warming, and it is crying out to us. We are ill, and our world is ill; it is an urgent epidemic, but it does not have to be a sickness unto death. Jesus looks at us and loves us. With Jesus, all things are possible, even the healing of our affluenza. Doctor Jesus offers the cure to our deepest wounds: Let go of your possessions, your lifestyle of "more" that is making both you and the planet ill. Come, follow me, and find true treasure, in communion with your sisters and brothers and all creation. Come and be healed; come, inherit eternal life!

Barbara Rossing is professor of New Testament at the Lutheran School of Theology at Chicago where her research interests focus on the book of Revelation, ecology, and liberation. The author of numerous articles on biblical resources for environmental theology, her books include *The Choice between Two Cities: Whore, Bride, and Empire in the Apocalypse* and *The Rapture Exposed: The Message of Hope in the Book of Revelation.*

THE BIBLICAL VISION
OF ECO-JUSTICE

ROSEMARY RADFORD RUETHER

THIS SERMON WAS PREACHED ON EARTH DAY at the Pacific School
of Religion in April 2005.

> The earth dries up and withers,
>> the world languishes and withers;
>> the heavens languish together with the earth.
> The earth lies polluted
>> under its inhabitants;
> for they have transgressed laws,
>> violated the statutes,
>> broken the everlasting covenant.
> Therefore a curse devours the earth,
>> and its inhabitants suffer for their guilt. **(Isa 24:4–6)**

◈

> They will not hurt or destroy
>> on all my holy mountain;
> for the earth will be full of the knowledge of the LORD. **(Isa 11:9)**

◈

Since the 1970s there has been an increasing recognition that the Western industrial style of development is unsustainable, although this has yet to be acknowledged by corporate leaders. This system of development, based on an affluent minority using a disproportionate share of the world's natural resources, is fast depleting the base upon which it rests. Expanding this type of industrialization will accelerate the coming debacle. We need an entirely new way of organizing human production and consumption in relation to natural resources, one that both distributes the means of life more justly among all earth's people and also uses resources in a way that renews them from generation to generation.

As the seriousness of the ecological crisis of modern industrial development has become more and more evident, there has been an effort among theological or religious thinkers to respond to this crisis. To what extent have the different religious systems contributed to a destructive relation to the earth? To what extent do world religions have positive resources that can teach us to be more caring of the earth? Christianity in particular, as the dominant religion of Western industrial countries, has been challenged in this regard.

In 1967, Lynn White, a historian of science, wrote an article entitled "The Historical Roots of Our Ecological Crisis" in which he claimed that the biblical doctrine of human dominion over creation has been the key cause of the destructive relationship of Western Christians with nature. This article has been widely read and has caused much soul searching among both Christian theologians and Christian biblical scholars.

There have been two main responses by Western religious thinkers to this challenge. One response, dominant among scholars of the Hebrew Bible, has been to protest that Genesis 1:28—which mandates that humanity "fill the earth and subdue it; and have dominion over the fish of the sea and over the birds of the air and over every living thing that moves upon the earth"—has been misread as allowing humanity a destructive domination of creation. Read in the context of the view of humanity in relation to God and nature generally, the Hebrew Bible teaches that God remains Lord of creation. We humans are mandated to be caretakers of the earth under God, not autonomous owners who can do whatever we wish with the earth. Our relation to the earth should be that of stewards responsible to God, not destructive exploiters.

Other religious thinkers have rejected this stewardship model. They see this as still handing all creation over to humans as rulers. These thinkers see Scripture as much less recoverable for an ecological spirituality and ethic. They agree with White that the main impact of biblical thought has been to locate humanity outside of nature and over nature, rather than as a part of nature. They stress that we humans need to recognize that we are latecomers to the planet. Humans have existed on earth for only half a million years— a mere blip on the timetable of earth history that goes back four and a half billion years—most of that time as a nondominant species. Fish, birds, and land animals have been here far longer than we, and they got along quite well and indeed better before we assumed power over them.

These writers argue that we need a more animist view of the natural world that sees the whole of nature as sacred, as permeated by the spirit of the divine. We need to recover a sense of reverence for the earth and a recognition of our own place in it as one species among others. We need to learn how to enter into mutuality and fellowship with nature, rather than separating ourselves from nature and imagining ourselves as having been given a divine mandate to rule over it. Since, in the view of these thinkers, such views cannot be found in Scripture, we need to leave aside biblical thought and look to the religious worldviews of indigenous peoples, such as Native Americans, or to Asian religions, such as Hinduism or Daoism.

I have no objection to people exploring the ecological potential of other religions, especially if they enter into deep and responsible dialogue with other traditions and do not just seek to use them without real relationship to them. But I believe that the biblical traditions have precious resources for an ecological spirituality and ethic—for what I would call an eco-justice ethic—that should not be neglected. Moreover, it is evident that the almost two billion Christians, close to a third of humanity, are not going to be moved to concern about ecology by a message that claims their religion is a part of the problem but no part of the solution, and that it therefore should be discarded. If we wish for Christians to care about the ecological crisis, we must speak about it in language that appeals to the Bible. This is not simply a matter of strategy. It is also a matter of truth. In fact, the Bible has deep resources of ecology that we can and must recover.

Those who dismiss the Bible as hostile to nature have mistakenly confused the biblical worldview with its nineteenth-century German interpreters. In German thought, we find a view that sets nature against history and sees God as the Lord of history against nature. Nature is decried as static and stifling to the spirit, while history is seen as emancipatory, allowing us to transcend nature. This split between nature and history, however, is foreign to the Bible. In the Bible we have an understanding of God as the creator of the whole world, of the stars and planets, animals and plants, as well as humans. The same steadfast love of God is present when God "spread out the earth on the waters, . . . made the great lights," made "the sun to rule over the day, . . . the moon and stars to rule over the night," and also when God "brought Israel out from among [the Egyptians] . . . with a strong hand and an outstretched arm, . . . divided the Red Sea in two, . . . and made Israel pass through the midst of it . . . but overthrew Pharaoh and his army in the Red Sea" (Ps 136: 6–15).

The view of nature that triumphed in Western science from the seventeenth century onward sees nonhuman nature as dead matter without animating spirit. This shift in attitude toward nature is what historian of science Carolyn Merchant calls "the death of nature." But this view is totally foreign to the Bible and, indeed, to Christian thought generally until modern times. The Hebrew worldview, and that of Christianity until the scientific revolution, assumes that nature is alive, filled with soul or spirit. We interact with this animate spirit in nature. Nature is responsive to God as a community of living creatures who relate to God in their own right.

God is seen as taking profound pleasure in his work of creation, and creation in turn responds to God with praise. God rejoices in the world that God creates, and the planets, mountains, brooks, animals, and plants return this rejoicing in their relation to God. God visits the earth in rain showers, watering its furrows abundantly, blessing its growth. The earth responds with overflowing abundance and joy. "The hills gird themselves with joy, the meadows clothe themselves with flocks, the valleys deck themselves with grain, they shout and sing together for joy" (Ps 65:12–13).

The world of the Hebrew Scriptures, as well as that of Jesus in his hometown of Nazareth, was a world of small, mostly subsistence farmers. They were keen observers of nature, dependent on nurturing its growth in a stony and water-scarce environment. Hebrew religion also constructed an ethic of care for nature through practices of letting fields lie fallow periodically and regular land reform that sought to prevent overexploitation of the land. These agricultural laws were embodied in the Levitical codes about the cycles of the week, the sabbatical year, and the Jubilee.

In this reflection on the biblical vision of eco-justice, I would like to focus particularly on what I see as a key prophetic pattern of thought. This thought knits together the injustice of humans toward one another and the devastation of the earth. It also lays out a vision of redemptive hope in which a human conversion to justice renews the earth and restores harmony between humans, nature, and God. This view rests on an understanding of the covenant between humanity, the earth, and God—which is holistic. The land is itself an integral part of the covenantal relation between humanity and God. In this covenantal view, nature's response to human use and abuse itself becomes an ethical sign. The erosion of the soil, drought, the drying up of the springs of water, and the pollution of the earth are themselves judgments of God upon unjust ways of living on the part of humans with each other and with nature. Thus,

Psalm 107 declares, "He turns rivers into a desert, springs of waters into thirsty ground, a fruitful land into a salty waste, because of the wickedness of its inhabitants" (Ps 107:33–34). This text is a religious interpretation of the reality of the ecological disasters in the ancient Middle East, caused by abuse of the land in which deforestation and overirrigation were causing desertification and salinization of the land.

From the biblical point of view, when humans break their covenant with God and with one another by social injustice and war, the covenant between God, humanity, and nature is broken. War and violence in society and the polluted, barren, hostile face of nature are both expressions of this violation of the covenant. They are linked together as expressions of one reality. Isaiah 24 vividly portrays this link between social and ecological violation and violence:

The earth shall be utterly laid waste and utterly despoiled;

The earth dries up and withers,
 the world languishes and withers;
 the heavens languish together with the earth.
The earth lies polluted
 under its inhabitants;
for they have transgressed laws,
 violated the statutes,
 broken the everlasting covenant.
Therefore a curse devours the earth,
 and its inhabitants suffer for their guilt;

The city of chaos is broken down,
 every house is shut up so that no one can enter.

Desolation is left in the city,
 the gates are battered into ruins. (Isa 24:3–6, 10, 12)

But this divine judgment expressed in desolation in society and nature is not the end of the prophetic vision. When humanity mends its ways with God, the covenant of creation is restored and renewed. Restoration of just relations between peoples restores peace to society and also heals nature's enmity. Just, peaceful societies, where people are not enslaved and where violence has been overcome also blossom forth in a peaceful, harmonious, and fruitful land.

The biblical dream of redemption is one of a flourishing nature in the peaceful kingdom of God's shalom. Springs of water return, and the land flourishes abundantly: "The wilderness and the dry land shall be glad, the desert shall rejoice and blossom; like the crocus it shall blossom abundantly, and rejoice with joy and singing" (Isa 35:1–2). This redemptive promise includes abundant harvests: "The tree bears its fruit, the fig tree and vine give their full yield. . . . Rejoice in the LORD your God; for he has given the early rain. . . . The threshing floors shall be full of grain, the vats shall overflow with wine and oil" (Joel 2:22–24). "The time is surely coming, says the LORD, when the one who plows shall overtake the one who reaps, and the treader of grapes the one who sows the seed; the mountains shall drip sweet wine, and all the hills shall flow with it" (Amos 9:13).

Justice in human affairs and harmony with nature together reflect a humanity made right with God, thereby filling the earth with peace and abundance. As Isaiah puts it in his vision of a redemptive future, "They will not hurt or destroy on all my holy mountain; for the earth will be full of the knowledge of the LORD" (Isa 11:9). This redemptive vision that knits together nature and society as one is expressed succinctly as Jesus prays for God's kingdom to come, for God's will to be done on earth. In that coming of God's kingdom upon the earth, we can hope for all people to be fed. The debts, which turn some into debt slaves to others, will be forgiven. The temptations to dreams of power over others are surrendered. "Give us this day our daily bread; forgive us our debts as we forgive our debtors, lead us not into temptation, but deliver us from evil." The biblical kingdom of God is eco-justice realized on earth, as it is in heaven.

Rosemary Radford Ruether is the Carpenter Professor of Feminist Theology Emeritus at the Graduate Theological Union in Berkeley, California, and a visiting scholar at the Claremont School of Theology and Claremont Graduate University in Claremont, California. She is the author or editor of forty-two books and numerous articles on issues of feminist theology, ecology, and social justice, including *Gaia and God: An Eco-Feminism Theology of Earth Healing*, *Women Healing Earth: Religious Feminism and the Future of the Planet*, and *Third World Women on Feminism, Religion, and Ecology*.

THE EARTH IS YOUR NEIGHBOR

H. PAUL SANTMIRE

THIS SERMON WAS FIRST PREACHED during the season of Easter 1998 at historic Trinity Lutheran Church, Akron, Ohio, as part of that congregation's Earth Celebration Festival.

Peace I leave with you; my peace I give to you. **(John 14:27)**

◈

I was jogging along the street the other day—actually, not on the street. To protect my aging knees, I was running just off the edge of the street on a neighbor's neatly mowed lawn. As I jogged along, I was having fond thoughts about how friendly the people in my neighborhood have been to me. I was remembering how, as I slowly, oh so slowly, jog by, I typically wave at my neighbors and they happily wave back—wondering, no doubt, as they contemplate my tortuous gait, whether they are going to have to call 911.

Just as I was savoring that pleasant thought about neighborliness, the front door to the house I was running by opened. A man stepped out and called to me, "Would you please not run on the grass?" So much for neighborliness.

Apparently the man behind the voice assumed that he *owned* that grass. The man apparently was unaware of the fact that "the earth is the Lord's and the fullness thereof" (Ps 24:1). Nor, apparently, did the man want to share any of what he considered *his* turf with anyone else, surely not with some old guy plodding along on worn-out knees.

Be that as it may, the Bible gives us a completely different perspective on such things. As you well know, the Bible very much wants us to be neighborly toward others. That, of course, is the second "great commandment," according to Jesus. But what you may not realize is that according to the Bible neighbor-love is the way the Lord wants us to be toward *all* creatures—dogs and cats, whales and bald eagles, fields and mountains. If some stray dog had run across that man's lawn, would he have yelled at the dog, too?

The point on this day, when we celebrate all the blessings of God's good earth, is this: *The earth is your neighbor.* This theme suggested itself to me in conversation with the Gospel reading appointed for this, the Sixth Sunday of Easter, in which Jesus says to his disciples, "Peace I leave with you; my peace I give to you." I want to show you now the relevance of this peace that passes all understanding for *all* of our relationships, including those with grass and flowers, dogs and cats, whales and bald eagles, fields and mountains, and all the rest. (I will not explore here the obviously important relevance of neighbor-love for the man who told me to get off his lawn, nor its relevance for me, who at that time felt a little bit miffed by the whole experience!) The God whom we know from the pages of the Bible is the God who calls us to be neighborly to the earth itself. That is the theme I want you to ponder now.

I

Christians in this respect, as in many others, have not always practiced what they have preached. Nor, in this respect, have Christians always even preached what they ought to have preached.

Enter the idea of dominion. This is what lots of Sunday school kids used to be taught, and doubtless in some places some still are being taught such things. Yes, the earth is the Lord's, but the Lord gives it to you and to me as our own so that we can be productive, right? You can even quote Scripture in favor of this view, and Christians often have. Does not the Lord give Adam and Eve the garden and tell them to "till it and keep it" (Gen 2:15)? And does not the Lord say to Adam and Eve, "Be fruitful and multiply, and fill the earth and *subdue* it; and have *dominion* over the fish of the sea and over the birds of the air and over every living thing that moves upon the earth" (Gen 1:28)?

Well, yes—and no. To "till the earth and keep it" is simply a mistranslation. The original Hebrew is much better translated, "to care for the earth and to protect it." The word "keep" here is actually the same Hebrew word we use, in translation, in our benediction every Sunday—"the Lord bless you and *keep* you"—which is to say, *protect* you. So you, earth creature, are placed by God on this beautiful garden planet to care for the earth and to protect it, not to use it and to exploit it for any self-serving purpose.

Likewise with that other dominion text from Genesis 1 about "subduing." Yes, sometimes, in order to find food and shelter for our families and larger communities and for the poor of the earth, it is necessary to *wrestle* productivity from the earth, to subdue the earth, in that sense. But *how* you do that subduing is another question. In a neighborly fashion? In a friendly way? With a spirit of humble caring? I want to address that question now in terms of the words Jesus speaks to us about peace.

II

I found *Seinfeld* to be a remarkable TV show in many ways. It was a great show about *nothing*, from the beginning, as its own cast has said on more than one occasion. It was a comedy of trivialities. It was not a show that was big on caring or commitment, certainly not for the poor, nor for any other creature for that matter.

In the final episode, strikingly, Jerry and his friends, end up *in jail*—after all their trivialities have been paraded in front of them. The charge: failure to come to the aid of a neighbor in distress. The four of them just stood by and made fun of a guy who was being robbed. Kramer even made a video of it! At the end, the four of them sit there in jail—*appropriately* in jail, some might say—mouthing still more trivialities to keep them preoccupied.

The logic of the Bible is entirely different. It is the logic of a profound neighborliness, of a deep commitment to those in need. Take the story of the Good Samaritan, for example. In this parable, Jesus praises the Samaritan for going out of his way to reach out to a man who had been mugged. In contrast, a priest and a Levite passed by on the other side. They paid no attention to the man in need.

But this is only part of the biblical story. That logic of deep commitment to those in need, according to the Bible, begins with God. God is the one who constantly gives of himself, who constantly comes to the aid of those in need. And the greatest of the gifts God gives us, according to the Bible, is *himself* in Christ Jesus. God, who is a shepherding God, becomes our Good Shepherd in the person of God's only Son.

Watch this biblical logic of true neighborliness unfold. Saved by Christ, according to Scripture, Christ himself becomes your model and mine for the godly life. So Paul writes to the early Christian congregation at Philippi:

> Let each of you look not to your own interests, but to the interests of others. Let the same mind be in you that was in Christ Jesus,
>
> > who, though he was in the form of God,
> > > did not regard equality with God
> > > as something to be exploited,
> > but emptied himself,
> > > taking the form of a slave,
> > > being born in human likeness.
> > And being found in human form,
> > > he humbled himself

and became obedient to the point of death—
even death on a cross. (Phil 2:5–8)

God himself, in Christ, is the good neighbor of all good neighbors, the Good Samaritan of all Good Samaritans. In Christ, you and I are called to go and do likewise, to have the mind that was in Christ Jesus, the mind of true neighborliness, the mind of true friendship.

III

Here is where the idea of peace comes in, according to the Bible. Peace for the Bible involves putting an end to war, but not just the warring between humans that has so darkened our history. Peace for the Bible also means the cessation of what we might call the rape of nature. A case in point is the war that huge economic interests are currently waging on native peoples in the Amazon rain forests, by default if not by publicly announced intention, and the concomitant war against those forests themselves. The clear word of the Bible for this kind of situation is this: You shall make war no more.

But the biblical vision of peace does not just mean the end of war, however broadly that theme may rightly be understood. The biblical vision of peace discloses not just a world where a sinful humanity does not make war anymore. It shows us a world where many communities of people are actively engaged in the struggle for peace. Peace for the Bible means *making peace*. Peace means seeking out the lost and the weak and caring for them so that they can be restored to the rightful niche where God wants them to be. Peace means many peoples working together to create a world where every creature can flourish in its own way and to its fullest. This much is conveyed powerfully by the testimony of Genesis 1, where the Creator is depicted as seeing all things as a harmonious whole, which is to say, as "very good" (Gen 1:31). In this sense, for the Bible, the Creator wants the creation, right from the start, to be his peaceable kingdom.

More particularly, for the Bible, Jesus, in whom God so loved the world, blesses us with his peace. Jesus reaches out to us as our

Good Shepherd, as the best and truest friend we will ever have, and calls us to go and do likewise: to be peacemakers, to seek to restore the abused, to forgive the fallen, to heal the sick, and to care for the earth.

I saw a photo the other day of two women in parkas kneeling down on rocky soil, making little indentations with their fingers. They were high above the tree line in the White Mountains of New Hampshire. They were gently planting tiny shoots of Robbins' cinquefoil as part of a small but to this point highly successful volunteer project to keep that wildflower from going extinct, in a world where one of every eight plant species is endangered. They were being peacemakers, in the biblical sense of that expression.

God calls everyone, especially those of us who know we have been saved by Christ, to go and do likewise: to get down on our knees and to care for the little ones of this earth. God gives us Christians this holy vocation: to care for the garden planet on which God has placed us, and to protect it, not to exploit it or to do with it what we please.

What about animals? What, in particular, about animals whom we humans kill for meat? In twenty-five words or less, this is the Gospel truth: *You have no right to your Big Mac.* God created Adam and Eve to be at peace with the animals, not to kill them, not to eat them. It was only later, by grace alone, that God allowed us humans to eat meat, after the time of Noah. Some scholars have suggested that the historical realities behind the divine permission to eat meat were times of threatened famine, when eating meat was the only way humans could survive. So God permitted it, for survival's sake. But not because we have any right to eat "our" Big Mac.

Perhaps the most striking biblical role model in this respect is Noah himself. The whole point of the Noah story is not the divine concession that allows humans to eat meat, should that be necessary. On the contrary, the story far more urgently wants to announce to us God's glorious rainbow covenant of peace with all creatures and to show us Noah's righteous example, how he cared for all the animals and protected them from destruction.

It was no accident, then, that the movement to protect animals, rather than to exploit them and kill them without so much as a thought, emerged with great power in Western history among Christians who took the witness of the Bible and the example of Noah, in particular, with utmost seriousness. Consider, for example, Saint Francis, who felt called upon to love all the vulnerable creatures of this earth, tiny birds as well as little children, awesome wolves as well as fearful and banished lepers. It was Francis who created the Christmas crèche scene, with all the animals. This was his way of announcing the arrival of the peaceable kingdom of God in the Christ child. Francis fervently believed that the salvation and love brought into the world by that holy child of God was intended for all God's creatures.

Historically speaking, the political movement for humane treatment of animals first blossomed in Methodist churches in England, when hundreds of simple believers simply assumed that the life of self-giving love to which they had been called was precisely that, with no exceptions. Like Francis, those early Methodists took it for granted that as creatures who had been saved by Christ, the self-giving Shepherd of God, the faithful Friend from God, they themselves had been called to go and do likewise, to make peace with the whole world, to be neighbors of all creatures, to claim the universal rainbow promise of peace as their own.

IV

This all comes together in the Bible in the book of Revelation. The lesson appointed to be read with our Gospel lesson from John tells some of the story, but not the whole story. The reading from Revelation 21 begins with verse 10, where John the Seer proclaims: "And in the spirit [God] carried me away to a great, high mountain and showed me the holy city Jerusalem coming down out of heaven from God." Then the lectionary reading skips to verse 22, which is of course what we humans, for perhaps understandable reasons, most want to hear, because it is about *us* and *our* salvation.

But you cannot understand the fullness of God's love for the world, announced in the classic words of John 3:16, if you read only that much of Revelation 21. You have to begin at the beginning, verse 1, where John the Seer proclaims from the same mountain vantage point, "Then I saw a new heaven and a new earth; for the first heaven and the first earth had passed away" (Rev 21:1).

To understand that proclamation by John you have to be conversant with the proclamations of the ancient prophets, of visionaries like Isaiah, whose words we typically read at Christmas time when we contemplate, with Francis, the animals gathered around the newborn Christ, the Prince of Peace:

> A shoot shall come out from the stump of Jesse,
>> and a branch shall grow out of his roots.
> The spirit of the LORD shall rest on him.
>
> He shall not judge by what his eyes see,
>> or decide by what his ears hear;
> but with righteousness he shall judge the poor,
>> and decide with equity for the meek of the earth.
>
> The wolf shall live with the lamb,
>> the leopard shall lie down with the kid,
> the calf and the lion and the fatling together,
>> and a little child shall lead them.
> The cow and the bear shall graze,
>> their young shall lie down together;
> and the lion shall eat straw like the ox.
> The nursing child shall play over the hole of the asp,
>> and the weaned child shall put its hand on the adder's den.
> They will not hurt or destroy
>> on all my holy mountain;
> for the earth will be full of the knowledge of the LORD
>> as the waters cover the sea. (Isa 11:1–9)

Paul, or a close disciple of his, gave testimony to the same conviction, drawing more on the wisdom tradition of the Hebrew Scriptures than on the visions of the prophets. We are told in the Letter to the Colossians that God sent Christ to the cross in order to establish a *cosmic peace*: "through him God was pleased to reconcile to himself *all things*, whether on earth or in heaven, by making peace through the blood of his cross" (Col 1:19).

This, in a word, is the biblical vision. God sent Jesus, the Prince of Peace, to bring peace on earth and goodwill to *every creature*, and to call a special people, an exemplary people, to go and do likewise: to be neighborly, in proper proportion, to every creature, to be peacemakers with every creature, whenever that is humanly possible, so that the whole creation can flourish and thereby glorify its Maker and Redeemer.

Good Christian friend, go and do likewise. Let your caring know no boundaries. Seek to make peace with every creature. Claimed by the peace of Christ himself, always consider the earth to be your neighbor.

H. Paul Santmire is a historian and pastoral scholar in the discipline of ecological theology and environmental ethics. Widely recognized for his contributions to this field for more than thirty years, he is the author of *Brother Earth: Nature, God, and Ecology in a Time of Crisis*, *The Travail of Nature: The Ambiguous Ecological Promise of Christian Theology*, and *Nature Reborn: The Ecological and Cosmic Promise of Christian Theology*.

THE CARE OF THE EARTH

JOSEPH SITTLER

THIS SERMON WAS FIRST INCLUDED in *Sermons to Intellectuals,* ed. Franklin H. Littell (Macmillan, 1963) and then reprinted in Sittler's book *The Care of the Earth and Other University Sermons* (Fortress, 1964). It offers the perspective that our delight in creation ought to serve as the fundamental basis for our right use of it.

In the year that King Uzziah died, I saw the Lord sitting on a throne, high and lofty; and the hem of his robe filled the temple. Seraphs were in attendance above him; each had six wings: with two they covered their faces, and with two they covered their feet, and with two they flew. And one called to another and said:

"Holy, holy, holy is the LORD of hosts;
the whole earth is full of his glory." **(Isa 6:1–3)**

◈

This is the day that the LORD has made; let us rejoice and be glad in it. **(Ps 118:24)**

◈

It is of the heart of sin that people use what they ought to enjoy, and enjoy what they ought to use. (**Thomas Aquinas**)

◈

A sermon may move from idea to fulfillment in various and sometimes strange ways. It may be useful as an introduction to the theme of this sermon to say how that happened in the writing of it.

In April of last year I read a poem in the *New Yorker* magazine by Richard Wilbur. What the poet was saying struck me and stuck with me for several obvious reasons. Beneath the quite clear apprehensions that float about just under the surface of our minds there is a root apprehension that churns deep down at the center. It is vague, but it is also relentless and undismissable. And the poet's words interest this inarticulate anxiety, stop it cold, give it a "local habitation and a name." The substance of this anxiety is common to us all, and it is heavy. It is the peculiar function of the poet sometimes to say out loud and with resonant clarity what we all would wish to say had we the dark music and the language.

The substance is this: Annihilating power is in nervous and passionate hands. The stuff is really there to incinerate the earth—and the certainty that it will not be used is not there.

Nor have we anodyne to hush it up or power to run away from it. We can go skiing with it, trot off to Bermuda with it, push it down under accelerated occupation with the daily round, pour bourbon over it, or say our prayers—each according to his or her tactic and disposition. But it goes along, survives, talks back.

Not in abstract proposition or dramatic warnings but in powerful, earthy images the poet makes his point. The point is single, simple, and absolute: Human selfhood hangs upon the persistence of the earth; her dear known and remembered factualness is the matrix of the self.

When you come, as you soon must, to the streets of our city,
Mad-eyed from stating the obvious,
Not proclaiming our fall but begging us

In God's name to have self-pity,
    Spare us all word of the weapons, their force and range,
The long numbers that rocket the mind;
Our slow, unreckoning hearts will be left behind,
Unable to fear what is too strange.
    Nor shall you scare us with talk of the death of the race.
How should we dream of this place without us—
The sun mere fire, the leaves untroubled about us,
A stone look on the stone's face?
    Speak of the world's own change. Though we cannot conceive
Of an undreamt thing, we know to our cost
How the dreamt cloud crumbles, the vines are blackened by frost,
How the view alters. We could believe,
    If you told us so, that the white-tailed deer will slip
Into perfect shade, grown perfectly shy,
The lark avoid the reaches of our eye,
The jack-pine loose its knuckled grip
    On the cold ledge, and every torrent burn
As Xanthus once, its gliding trout
Stunned in a twinkling. What should we be without
The dolphin's arc, the dove's return,
    These things in which we have seen ourselves and spoken?
Ask us, prophet, how we shall call
Our natures forth when that live tongue is all
Dispelled, that glass obscured or broken,
    In which we have said the rose of our love and the clean
Horse of our courage, in which beheld
The singing locust of the soul unshelled,
And all we mean or wish to mean.
    Ask us, ask us whether with the wordless rose
Our hearts shall fail us; come demanding
Whether there shall be lofty or long standing
When the bronze annals of the oak-tree close.[1]

By sheer force of these lines my mind was pushed back against the wall and forced to ask: Is there anything in our Western religious tradition as diagnostically penetrating as that problem, as salvatory as that predicament?

Out of these back-to-wall reflections I therefore ask your attention to two statements that seem to me alone deep and strong enough to make adequate sense. These two statements have in common this: They deal with the *enjoyment* of things and the *uses* of things. Together they add up to a proposition: Delight is the basis of right use.

The first statement is the celebrated answer to the first question in the Westminster Catechism. No one will question the velocity with which this answer gets to the point, or that the point is worth getting at! The question is: "What is the chief end of humanity?" The answer: "To glorify God and enjoy him forever!"

The first verb, "to glorify," is not primarily intellectual. It does not concern itself with the establishment of the existence of God, or with a description of God's nature. The verb is not aesthetic either. It is not concerned to declare that God is good or beautiful, or propose that it is a fair thing to worship God. Nor is it hortatory, that is, it does not beat us over the head with admonitions about our duty to God.

The verb "to glorify" is exclusively and utterly religious! The verb comes from the substantive "glory," and that term designates what God is and has and wills within God's self; it announces the priority, the ineffable majesty, the sovereign power and freedom of the holy. Glory, that is to say, is what God is and does out of God's self, and when we use the term for what we do in response, that response is given and engendered by God's glory.

The priority-in-God and the proper work of this verb may be illustrated by its function in the sixth chapter of the book of Isaiah. The young prophet, rich and eager in his expectations of the new king, Uzziah, is stunned when the king dies. He goes into the temple, and then comes the vision of the glory of whose ineffable power the face of the king is but the reflection.

The glory is the light the holy gives off. The earth is a theater of the glory; it is rich with the ineffable glory because God, the holy one, has made it.

The holy is a numinous and absolute concept. It is not contained within other categories; it is a category. The holy both evokes and demands thought, but it is a misunderstanding to assume that thoughts can contain the glory and the holy. The holy certainly has the effect that Rudolf Otto in his great work, *The Idea of the Holy*, calls *mysterium tremendum et fascinosum*, but there is an unseizable plus to the term that eludes even the image-making genius of the Jews.

The holy invites prayer but rejects such an understanding of prayer as would make prayer a tool for working upon the holy, a device for making the holy disposable by humans. The holy demands service, but no service adds up to a responding equivalent—just as in our human love one serves the beloved but never affirms human service to be the measure of love.

The chief end of humanity is, then, to glorify God, to let God be God, to understand and accept God's life in ways appropriate to the imperial, holy singularity of God. The meaning of this has ethical, psychological, even political implications, to be sure. But the center is categorically religious.

But this statement about God and humanity, thus elevated, tough, and absolute, is conjoined in the catechism with a concluding phrase, "and enjoy God forever." The juxtaposition of commands to glorify and to enjoy is on several grounds startling to our generation. To enjoy is a strange thing to do about the holy God before whom even the seraphim hide their faces. This joining of the *holy*, which is what God is, with *joy*, which designates what humanity is to have and do in God—this juxtaposition, in that it is startling to us, says a good deal about the modern American understanding of the Christian faith. How it has come about that we are startled by what our ancestors joined together without batting an eye is a matter we cannot now go into but can only observe and ask after its significance. For we may have missed something. If the gravity of the glorification of the holy and the blithe humaneness of "enjoy God forever" seem strange, our churches in the very form of their buildings may be partly to blame. There is the clean, shadowless, and antiseptic colonial, the monumental melancholy of the Romanesque and Gothic adaptations—bereft of the color and ornament which in other lands are so devoutly joined in these forms. Our traditional churches affirm a heavy kind of solemnity that leaves us indeed with a lugubrious holy, but defenseless and aghast before the joy of, for instance, a Baroque church. Such a church is luxuriant, joy-breathing, positively Mozartean in its vivacity—replete with rosy angels tumbling in unabashed joy among impossibly fleecy clouds against an incredible blue heaven.

I shall not draw conclusions from that—only observe it and let it hang—that the gravity of a life determined by God, lived to the glory of God, is not necessarily incongruent with abounding joy. It is interesting to recall that the most rollicking music old periwig Bach ever wrote is not dedicated to the joy of tobacco (although he did that) or coffee (and he praised that) or the inventiveness among his fellow musicians, nor is it dedicated to the levity of the Count of Brandenburg, but is the choral prelude *In Dir ist Freude* ("In Thee is Joy")!

Thomas Aquinas, surely not the playful or superficial type, did not affirm Christianity as a consolatory escape hatch, or an unguent to the scratchy personality, or a morale builder to a threatened republic—all contemporary malformations. But he did say, "It is of the heart of sin that people use what they ought to enjoy, and enjoy what they ought to use." Apart from the claim that it is *sin* that people do that, and apart from the seriousness of the situation if that statement should turn out to be true, is the statement reportorially so?

It is so, for all of us, and in many ways. Thomas is simply condensing here the profound dialectic of use and enjoyment that distorts and impoverishes life when it is not acknowledged and obeyed. To use a thing is to make it instrumental to a purpose, and some things are to be so used. To enjoy a thing is to permit it to be what it is prior to and apart from any instrumental assessment of it, and some things are to be so enjoyed.

I adduce a small example; it may bloom in our minds into bigger ones. Wine is to be enjoyed; it is not to be used. Wine is old in human history. It is a symbol of nature in her smiling beneficence: "close bosom friend of the maturing sun." That is why it has virtually everywhere and always been the accompaniment of celebrative occasions, the sign of gladness of heart. It is to be enjoyed; it is not to be used to evoke illusions of magnificence, or stiffen timidity with the fleeting certainty that one is indeed a sterling lad. Where it is enjoyed it adds grace to a truth; where it is used it induces and anesthetizes a lie.

Observe in Psalms how the Old Testament man who sought to glorify God and enjoy him forever stood in the midst of nature. God gives "wine to gladden the human heart, oil to make the face shine" (Ps 104:15). "This is the day that the LORD has made," he exults, "let us rejoice and be glad in it" (Ps 118:24). Why? Not primarily for what we can turn the day's hours into, but rather on the primal ground that there are days—unaccountable in their gift-character— just there. And here we are, permeable by all we are sensitive to: texture, light, form, and movement, the cattle on a thousand hills. Thou sendest forth thy Spirit and they are! Let us rejoice and be glad in it!

It is of the heart of sin that humans use what they ought to enjoy. It is also, says Thomas, of the heart of sin that humans are content to enjoy what they ought to use. Take charity, for instance. Charity is the comprehensive term to designate how God regards humanity. That regard is to be used by humanity for humanity. That is why our Lord moves always in speech from the source of joy, that humanity is loved by the holy, to the theater of joy, that humanity must serve the need of the neighbor. "Lord, where did we behold thee? I was in prison, hungry, cold, naked"—you enjoyed a charity that God gives for use.

If the creation, including our fellow creatures, is impiously used apart from a gracious primeval joy in it, the very richness of the creation becomes a judgment. This has a cleansing and orderly meaning for everything in the world of nature, from the sewage we dump into our streams to the cosmic sewage we dump into the fallout.

Abuse is use without grace; it is always a failure in the counterpoint of use and enjoyment. When things are not used in ways determined by joy in the things themselves, this violated potentiality of joy (timid as all things holy, but relentless and blunt in its reprisals) withdraws and leaves us, not perhaps with immediate positive damnations but with something much worse—the wan, ghastly, negative damnations of use without joy, stuff without grace, a busy, fabricating world with the shine gone off, personal relations for the nature of which we have invented the eloquent term *contacts*, staring without beholding, even fornicating without finding.

God is useful—but not if God is sought for use. Ivan, in *The Brothers Karamazov*, saw that, and Dostoyevsky meant it as a witness to the holy and joy-begetting God whom he saw turned into an ecclesiastical club to frighten impoverished peasants with, when he had his character say, "I deny God for God's sake!"

All of this has, I think, something to say to us as teachers and students to whom this university is ever freshly available for enjoyment and use. Consider this: The basis of discovery is curiosity, and what is curiosity but the peculiar joy of the mind in its own given nature? Sheer curiosity, without immediate anticipation of ends and uses, has done most to envision new ends and fresh uses. But curiosity does this in virtue of a strange counterpoint of use and enjoyment. Bacon declared that "studies are for delight," the secular counterpart of "glorify God and enjoy God forever." The Creator who is the fountain of joy, and the creation which is the material of university study, are here brought together in an ultimate way. It is significant that the university, the institutional solidification of the fact that studies are for delight, is an idea and a creation of a culture that once affirmed that human beings should glorify God and enjoy God forever.

Use is blessed when enjoyment is honored. Piety is deepest practicality, for it properly relates use and enjoyment. And a world sacramentally received in joy is a world sanely used. There is an economics of use only; it moves toward the destruction of both use and joy. And there is an economics of joy; it moves toward the intelligence of use and the enhancement of joy. That this vision involves a radical new understanding of the clean and fruitful earth is certainly so. But this vision, deeply religious in its genesis, is not so very absurd now that natural damnation is in orbit, and humanity's befouling of its ancient home has spread its death and dirt among the stars.

Joseph Sittler (1904–1987) was a Lutheran clergyman who served as professor of theology at Maywood Theological Seminary and the University of Chicago and as Distinguished Professor in Residence at the Lutheran School of Theology at Chicago. He lectured widely and authored many books, including *The Ecology of Faith*, *Gravity and Grace*, and *The Care of the Earth*. For a collection of his environmental writings, see *Evocations of Grace*, edited by Peter Bakken.

Note

1. Richard Wilbur, "Advice to a Prophet," in *Advice to a Prophet and Other Poems* (New York: Harcourt, Brace and World, 1961): 12–13.

REST FOR THE LAND

Rogation Day

BARBARA BROWN TAYLOR

SEVERAL YEARS AGO I WAS INVITED back to Christ Episcopal Church in New Haven, where I was confirmed while a senior in seminary, to preach during the parish's sesquicentennial year. When I opened the prayer book to check the lections, I discovered that my Sunday was Rogation Sunday, an old harvest festival that remains on the church calendar. Since I had recently moved from the city to the country, where I was living closer to the land than ever before, I heard the Torah portion on agricultural Sabbath-keeping in an entirely new way. In this sermon, I was able to marry my love for God's word with my love for the land in a way that I hope is faithful to both.

> The LORD spoke to Moses on Mount Sinai, saying: Speak to the people of Israel and say to them: When you enter the land that I am giving you, the land shall observe a sabbath for the LORD. Six years you shall sow your field, and six years you shall prune your vineyard, and gather in their yield; but in the seventh year there shall be a

sabbath of complete rest for the land, a sabbath for the LORD: you shall not sow your field or prune your vineyard. You shall not reap the aftergrowth of your harvest or gather the grapes of your unpruned vine: it shall be a year of complete rest for the land. You may eat what the land yields during its sabbath—you, your male and female slaves, your hired and your bound laborers who live with you; for your livestock also, and for the wild animals in your land all its yield shall be for food.

You shall count off seven weeks of years, seven times seven years, so that the period of seven weeks of years gives forty-nine years. Then you shall have the trumpet sounded loud; on the tenth day of the seventh month—on the day of atonement—you shall have the trumpet sounded throughout all your land. And you shall hallow the fiftieth year and you shall proclaim liberty throughout the land to all its inhabitants. It shall be a jubilee for you: you shall return, every one of you, to your property and every one of you to your family. That fiftieth year shall be a jubilee for you: you shall not sow, or reap the aftergrowth, or harvest the unpruned vines. For it is a jubilee; it shall be holy to you: you shall eat only what the field itself produces.

In this year of jubilee you shall return, every one of you, to your property. When you make a sale to your neighbor or buy from your neighbor, you shall not cheat one another. When you buy from your neighbor, you shall pay only for the number of years since the jubilee; the seller shall charge you only for the remaining crop years. If the years are more, you shall increase the price, and if the years are fewer, you shall diminish the price; for it is a certain number of harvests that are being sold to you. You shall not cheat one another, but you shall fear your God; for I am the LORD your God. (Lev 25:1-17)

❖

There is no reason why any of you should know the word *rogation* or why it belongs in church. It is a word left over from the days when farmers were thought to be more essential to life on earth than attorneys, say, or graduate students. It is a word left over from those places where children grew up knowing that peanuts grow underground, not on trees, and that eggs start out warm, in nests, before they are ever collected in Styrofoam trays and chilled to stop the life in them from growing.

Back when village life was the norm and most parish churches looked out on fields of lush green and high gold, Rogation Days were the three days before Ascension Day when the faithful said special prayers for the fruitfulness of the earth—thanking God for it and begging God for it—because they knew how quickly a sudden storm could ruin a whole field of mown hay, or how thoroughly a cloud of grasshoppers could reduce a crop of new corn to stubble.

These dangers are not as apparent to those of us who live in cities and buy most of our produce in grocery stores. We will no doubt complain about the small, hard peaches this year, with no recollection of the late frost that killed most of the peach blossoms in Georgia and South Carolina last March. My husband Ed stayed up three nights in a row stoking fires in the orchard beside our house. On the third night, which was the coldest, I looked out and saw him fanning the warm wood smoke into the blooming tree boughs. He had every heat-producing device we owned out there, so that small flames flickered here and there in the dark grass. He had Coleman lanterns under the cherry tree, a kerosene heater under the plum tree, and under the peach tree, where he was standing, he kept a veritable bonfire of split poplar logs burning all through the night.

So these Rogation Days matter to me and to my neighbors. I live among farmers, or at least I used to. More and more of them have sold out and become real estate developers instead. They say they can no longer afford the taxes, now that city people like myself have arrived and driven up land prices. Nor can they compete with the huge farming conglomerates that control even local markets. So they either sell out to developers or become developers themselves, as the demand for second homes in our area rises.

Day by day, fields and pastures are paved and subdivided. Banks of rhododendron as tall as trees are bulldozed, and acres of old-growth forest come down so that cheap houses with vinyl siding can go up. With all the topsoil gone, the red dirt erodes and slides down into our creeks and rivers, where it piles up until the trout cannot live there anymore. I have a creek on my place that is all but filled in now. You can stand in the middle of it and shove a pointed stick three feet down through all the loose silt that has collected in it. When I came to this land five years ago, great blue herons fished for trout in that creek. Now both the trout and the herons are gone.

You already know the story, so I will not go through it all again. The bottom line is that the earth is in distress—a lot or a little, depending on your economic and political views. But whether you lean left or right, whether you are an unrepentant industrialist or a militant tree hugger, chances are that you still think of land as a resource—one to be protected or one to be profited from—but either way as something inert, with no rights or wishes beyond those of its owners.

In popular thought, land is clay in the hands of those who have gained possession of it. The owner says, "Let there be a subdivision," and behold, there is a subdivision. Or the owner says, "No trespassing—keep out," and lo, there is a private park. It is the will of the owner that determines the use of the land, and it is a rare owner whose thoughts never turn to the dollar value of the land.

That is why the twenty-fifth chapter of Leviticus is so interesting—a little snippet of the law of Moses that overturns all our notions about ownership of land. It is not yours and never was, God says to the people through Moses. You are all tenant farmers as far as I am concerned, and you have my permission to work the land for six years in a row. Whatever you make of it is yours to keep. You can put up a hundred jars of tomato pickles for your family if you want, or you can sell them at market for a shekel apiece, but on the seventh year, you shall hang it all up.

Park the tractor. Put the tools away. Oil your work boots and put them in the closet, because the seventh year shall be a Sabbath of complete rest for the land. There shall be no sowing, no pruning, no gathering into barns. There shall also be no shooing strangers off your property. If some wheat grows up from last year's seed, it is there for anyone who needs it. If some grapes still grow from the unpruned vines, they belong to anyone who is hungry for them—including the wild animals you used to shoot for stealing your fruit.

During the seventh year, they are all welcome to it. *You* are all welcome to it—landowner and servant, plow ox and wild jackal. You are all released from your roles. You are all excused from your work. You are all free to forage together in these wild, overgrown fields and vineyards that—if you will stop and think about it—may remind you of that time before time when you did not live by the sweat of your brow but walked with me in the garden in the cool of the evening.

Like the Sabbath itself, this sabbatical year was offered to humankind as a foretaste of heaven. It was meant to be a preview of the world to come, where there would be no more toil, no more striving, no more division between those who had and those who did not. It was a glimpse of the peaceable kingdom, where wild animals grazed side by side with formerly indentured ones who would never feel the sting of a whip again.

It was the vision of an earth in which forests, vineyards, and fields of dirt were as much creatures of God as the human creatures who exercised dominion over them, and it was a reminder to those same humans that they were only temporarily in charge—and never for more than six years at a time. On the seventh year, the land itself had a duty to God that they must stand back and allow it to fulfill. The land had a Sabbath commandment to follow, with which no human being was supposed to interfere.

We did interfere, of course. Some people grew rich on the black market fruit business during sabbatical years, while others slapped their heads and said they had lost all track of time. Was it really the seventh year again? Already? A little later on in Leviticus, Moses warns the people what will happen if they do not allow the land its rest. God will lay waste to it and scatter those who live upon it, he says. Then, while the people are in exile and the land lies desolate, it will enjoy the Sabbath years it missed (Lev 26:34).

This was not a scary enough threat, apparently. While the sabbatical year was briefly observed around the turn of the first millennium, it was largely ignored after that. According to one source I read, it still worries some extreme orthodox groups in Israel, but most of them get around it by arranging a fictitious sale of their land to a friendly Gentile every seven years, farming it as a sublessor, and then buying it back again after the sabbatical year is over.

You know why, do you not? Because there is hardly a human being alive who can sit and watch a field, a yard, or even a flower bed "go to waste" for a year. That is what we say about things that have been removed from our control, by the way. We say they are "going to waste," as if their worth depended on our involvement with them. And not only their worth but also our own. In our world, there is not much payoff for sitting back and letting things go. A field full of weeds will not earn anyone's respect. If you want to succeed in this life (whatever your "field" of endeavor), you must spray, you must plow, you must fertilize, you must plant. You must never turn your back. Each year's harvest must be bigger than the last. That is what land and people are for.

According to Moses, God sees things differently. When the fields are lying fallow, when purple morning glories cover last year's corn-stalks and the white-tailed deer help themselves to the wild muscadines that have overcome the vineyard—when the people who belong to this land walk through it with straw hats in their hands instead of hoes and discover that the three peaches that survived the frost are sweeter than the thirty they might have saved with their fires—God does not call this "going to waste." God calls this "observing the Sabbath" and wonders why human beings are so resistant to it.

What do we think will happen if we rest for a while? Whatever it is, we have been afraid of it for a long time, and what our fear has done is to separate us—from God, from one another, and from this patient, forgiving earth whose Sabbaths we have stolen. This land that gives us our food and our water, these trees that clean the air for us to breathe, all these green and growing things that bless our bodies with their beauty—these are not *resources*. They are fellow *creatures*, with their own rights and responsibilities before God. They have their own sacred duties to perform, if only we will let them.

I do not suppose it will ever happen. It never did, except for a couple of hundred years, but it is still the word of the Lord, as much as "Thou shalt not kill" or "Remember the Sabbath day, to keep it holy." Sometimes I think God did not say such things with any real expectation that we could or would keep them. I think maybe God said them for the record instead—so we would know who God is and how the world works, whether or not we ever choose to live according to that knowledge.

At the very least, the knowledge we are offered is that the earth does not belong to us. It has its own dignity, its own holiness, its own life in God. When the Sabbath comes, it comes for all God's creatures, stopping them right where they are to recognize their kinship under the dominion of one Lord. Each of us was meant to rest in that knowledge on a regular basis and to let the resting itself prick our dearest beliefs about who we are and what we are supposed to be doing here.

My prayer for each of you during these Rogation Days is that you will run into some tree, some body of water, some raindrop or blade of grass that shouts your name out loud, and that you will have the good sense to go over and introduce yourself—in the name of God the Father, God the Son, and God the Holy Spirit.

Barbara Brown Taylor is an Episcopal priest who teaches religion at Piedmont College in rural northeast Georgia. Barbara has delivered the Hastings Lecture at the College of Preachers in Washington, DC, the Donald Macleod Lectures in Preaching at Princeton Seminary, and the Lyman Beecher Lectures in Preaching at Yale University. A columnist for the *Christian Century* and sometime commentator on Georgia Public Radio, she is the author of ten books, including *When God Is Silent, Speaking of Sin: The Lost Language of Salvation*, and *Leaving Church: A Memoir of Faith*.

CREATION AS KIN

An American Indian View

GEORGE E. TINKER

THIS SERMON OFFERS US AN OPPORTUNITY to reflect on how diverse worldviews and cultural experiences shape the ways in which people relate to creation. The insights offered here present understandings held by many American Indians that may challenge and/or enhance Christian perceptions of how humans are to relate to the rest of creation.

> God saw everything that he had made, and indeed, it was very good. (Gen 1:31)

◈

Heavily dressed for the half-meter of snow covering the hillside, a small group of people stood quietly around what looked like a perfect, if rather large, Christmas tree. Mostly American Indians from a variety of tribes and all members of a predominantly Indian congregation, the people were speaking prayers on behalf of the tree. It could have been most any congregation's annual outing to harvest a Christmas tree for their church, except that these prayers were a thorough mixture of Christian prayers and traditional Indian tribal prayers. The two pastors held tobacco in their hands, ready to offer it back to the Creator, to offer it for the life of this tree, to offer it to the four directions, above and below, to offer it in order to maintain the harmony and balance of creation even in the perpetration of an act of violence. Someone wrapped a string of colorful tobacco tie offerings around the trunk. As four men sang traditional prayer songs around a drum, the people came one by one up to the tree to touch it and say their prayers, some actually speaking to the tree consoling words of apology, gratitude, purpose, and promise.

A real sense of cultural value was exposed in this gathering. This attitude toward creation and toward all the "createds" sets American Indians apart from most other Americans and most Europeans. Yet it is characteristic of many of the world's indigenous peoples and represents a set of cultural values that perseveres even in those indigenous communities that have been converted to Christianity. Perhaps an outsider would describe the attitude of these Indians as one of awe or wonderment. We American Indians think of it as neither, but would prefer to call it *respect*, the appropriate attitude necessary to fulfill our responsibility as part of the created whole, necessary to help maintain the harmony and balance, the interdependence and interrelationship of all things in our world.

The key word then, for the American Indian cultural context, is *respect*—in this case, respect for a tree. Even more important is the underlying notion of reciprocity. The prayers and the offering of tobacco are reciprocal acts of giving something back to the earth and to all of creation in order to maintain balance even as we disrupt the balance by cutting down this tree. The question Indian cultures pose for Christian people, especially those of Europe and North America, is this: How can respect for a tree, a rock, animals, or eventually other human beings find any place in the industrial-commercial world that has emerged out of modernity and now threatens all of creation with extinction? And what sort of reciprocity do we or will we engage in; what do we return to the earth when we clear-cut a forest or strip mine land, leaving miles of earth totally bare?

THE CIRCLE

American Indians and other indigenous peoples have a long-standing confidence that they have much to teach Europeans and North Americans about the world and human relationships in the world. They are confident in the spiritual foundations of their insights, confident that those foundations can become a source of healing and reconciliation for all creation. Let me use a couple of simple examples from an Indian perspective.

My Indian ancestors had a relationship with God as Creator that was healthy and responsible long before they knew of or confessed the gospel of Jesus Christ. They had a relationship with the Creator that was solidified in the stories they told around the campfires in each of our tribes, in their prayers, and especially in their ceremonies. This relationship began with the recognition of the Other as Creator, the creative force behind all things that exist, and long predated the coming of the missionaries. In that relationship, the people saw themselves as participants within creation as a whole, and they celebrated the balance and harmony of the whole of the universe in everything they did together.

In all that they did, our Indian ancestors acknowledged the goodness of the Creator and of all creation, including themselves. That was the point of the stories, the focus of their prayers, and the purpose of the ceremonies. They recognized the balance and harmony that characterized all of the created universe: Winter and summer were held in balance with one another. So also were hunting and planting, sky and earth, hot and cold, sun and moon, female and male, women and men. Our ancestors recognized all this as good, just as God did at the end of the sixth day (Gen 1:31).

If all American Indian spiritual insights and hence Indian theology must begin with creation, this is reflected already in the basic liturgical posture of Indians in many North American tribes. Our prayers are most often said with the community assembled in some form of circle. In fact, the circle is a key symbol for self-understanding in these tribes, representing the whole of the universe and our part in it. We see ourselves as coequal participants in the circle, standing neither above nor below anything else in God's creation. There is no hierarchy in our cultural context, even of species, because the circle has no beginning or ending. Hence, all the createds participate together, each in their own way, to preserve the wholeness of the circle. So when a group of Indians forms a circle to pray, all know that the prayers have already begun with the representation of a circle. No words have yet been spoken and in some ceremonies no words need be spoken, but the intentional physicality of our formation has already expressed our prayer and deep concern for the wholeness of all of God's creation. In this context Indians do not hold hands when they pray thus, unless they have been tainted by the piety of a white missionary. There is no need to hold hands because we know it is enough to stand in the circle already joined together, inextricably bound, through the earth that lies firm beneath our feet, the earth that is, after all, the true mother of each of us and of all creation.[1]

MITAKUYE OYASIN

The Lakota and Dakota peoples use a phrase in all their prayers that aptly illustrates the Native American sense of the centrality of creation. The phrase, *mitakuye oyasin*, functions somewhat like the word *amen* in Christianity. As such, it is used to end every prayer, and often it is in itself a whole prayer, being the only phrase spoken. The usual translation offered is "For all my relations." Yet like most Native symbols, *mitakuye oyasin* is polyvalent in its meaning. Certainly, one is praying for one's close kin, such as aunts, cousins, children, and grandparents. And "relations" can be understood as fellow tribal members or even all Indian people. At the same time, the phrase includes all human beings, all "two-leggeds" as relatives of one another, and the ever expanding circle does not stop there. Every Lakota who prays this prayer knows that our relatives necessarily include the "four-leggeds," the "wingeds," and all the living, moving things on Mother Earth. One Lakota teacher has suggested that a better translation of *mitakuye oyasin* would read, "For all the above me and below me and around me things"—that is, "for all my relations." With such a phrase, one can perhaps begin to understand the extensive image of interrelatedness and interdependence symbolized by the circle and the importance of reciprocity and respect for one another for maintaining the wholeness of the circle.

The American Indian concern for starting theology with creation is a need to acknowledge the goodness and inherent worth of all of God's creatures. We experience evil or sin as disruptions in that delicate balance, disruptions that negate the intrinsic worth of our relatives.[2]

George Tinker is a member of the Osage Nation and an activist in many American Indian causes. Since 1985, he has been professor of American Indian Cultures and Religious Traditions at Iliff School of Theology. He is the author of *Missionary Conquest: The Gospel and Native American Cultural Genocide* and coauthor of *Native American Theology*. Tinker is an ordained member of the Evangelical Lutheran Church in America and a participant in many academic organizations and movements dedicated to the liberation of Native Americans.

Adapted and reprinted by permission from *After Nature's Revolt: Eco-Justice and Theology*, ed. Dieter Hessel (Minneapolis: Fortress, 1992), 144–53.

Notes

1. To explore further some Native American perspectives on land, see John A. Grim, ed., *Indigenous Traditions and Ecology: The Interbeing of Cosmology and Community* (Cambridge, MA: Harvard University Press, 2001), and Winona LaDuke, *All Our Relations: Native Struggles for Land and Life* (Cambridge, MA: South End Press, 1999).

2. To read more about ecology from diverse cultural perspectives, see *Earth and Faith: A Book of Reflection for Action* (New York: Interfaith Partnership for the Environment, United Nations Environment Programme, 2001); Roger Gottlieb, ed., *This Sacred Earth: Religion, Nature, Environment* (New York: Routledge,

1996); David R. Kinsley, *Ecology and Religion: Ecological Spirituality in Cross-Cultural Perspective* (Englewood Cliffs, NJ: Prentice Hall, 1994); Mary Evelyn Tucker and John A. Grim, eds., *Worldviews and Ecology: Religion, Philosophy, and the Environment* (Maryknoll, NY: Orbis, 1994); Clara Sue Kidwell, Homer Noely, and George E. Tinker, *A Native American Theology* (Maryknoll, NY: Orbis, 2001); and Jace Weaver and Russell Means, eds., *Defending Mother Earth: Native American Perspectives on Environmental Justice* (Maryknoll, NY: Orbis, 1996).

GOD'S EARTH IS SACRED

An Open Letter to Church and Society
in the United States

GOD'S CREATION DELIVERS UNSETTLING NEWS. Earth's climate is warming to dangerous levels; 90 percent of the world's fisheries have been depleted; coastal development and pollution are causing a sharp decline in ocean health; shrinking habitat threatens to extinguish thousands of species; over 95 percent of the contiguous United States' forests have been lost; and almost half of the population in the United States lives in areas that do not meet national air quality standards. In recent years, the profound danger has grown, requiring us as theologians, pastors, and religious leaders to speak out and act with new urgency.

We are obliged to relate to Earth as God's creation "in ways that sustain life on the planet, provide for the [basic] needs of all humankind, and increase justice."[1] Over the past several decades, slowly but faithfully, the religious community in the United States has attempted to address issues of ecology and justice. Our faith groups have offered rich theological perspectives, considered moral issues through the lens of longstanding social teaching, and passed numerous policies within our own church bodies. While we honor the efforts in our churches, we have clearly failed to communicate the full measure and magnitude of Earth's environmental crisis—religiously, morally, or politically. It is painfully clear from the verifiable testimony of the world's scientists that our response has been inadequate to the scale and pace of Earth's degradation.

To continue to walk the current path of ecological destruction is not only folly; it is sin. As voiced by Ecumenical Patriarch Bartholomew, who has taken the lead among senior religious leaders in his concern for creation: "To commit a crime against the natural world is a sin. For humans to cause species to become extinct and to destroy the biological diversity of God's creation . . . for humans to degrade the integrity of Earth by causing changes in its climate, by stripping the Earth of its natural forests, or destroying its wetlands . . . for humans to injure other humans with disease . . . for humans to contaminate the Earth's waters, its land, its air, and its life, with poisonous substances . . . these are sins."[2] We have become un-Creators. Earth is in jeopardy at our hands.

This means that ours is a theological crisis as well. We have listened to a false gospel that we continue to live out in our daily habits—a gospel that proclaims that God cares for the salvation of humans only and that our human calling is to exploit Earth for our own ends alone. This false gospel still finds its proud preachers and continues to capture its adherents among emboldened political leaders and policy makers.

The secular counterpart of this gospel rests in the conviction that humans can master the Earth. Our modern way of life assumes this mastery. However, the sobering truth is that we hardly have knowledge of, much less control over, the deep and long-term consequences of our human impacts upon the Earth. We have already sown the seeds for many of those consequences. The fruit of those seeds will be reaped by future generations of human beings, together with others in the community of life.

The imperative first step is to repent of our sins, in the presence of God and one another. This repentance of our social and ecological sins will acknowledge the special responsibility that falls to those of us who are citizens of the United States. Though only five percent of the planet's human population, we produce one quarter of the world's carbon emissions, consume a quarter of its natural riches, and perpetuate scandalous inequities at home and abroad. We are a precious part of Earth's web of life, but we do not own the planet and we cannot transcend its requirements for regeneration on its own terms. We have not listened well to the Maker of Heaven and Earth.

The second step is to pursue a new journey together, with courage and joy. By God's grace, all things are made new. We can share in that renewal by clinging to God's trustworthy promise to restore and fulfill all that God creates and by walking, with God's help, a path different from our present course. To that end, we affirm our faith, propose a set of guiding norms, and call on our churches to rededicate themselves to this mission. We firmly believe that addressing the degradation of God's sacred Earth is *the* moral assignment of our time comparable to the civil rights struggles of the 1960s, the worldwide movement to achieve equality for women, or ongoing efforts to control weapons of mass destruction in a post-Hiroshima world.

ECOLOGICAL AFFIRMATIONS OF FAITH

We stand with awe and gratitude as members of God's bountiful and good creation. We rejoice in the splendor and mystery of countless species, our common creaturehood, and the interdependence of all that God makes. We believe that the Earth is home for all and that it has been created intrinsically good (Genesis 1).

We lament that the human species is shattering the splendid gifts of this web of life, ignoring our responsibility for the well-being of all life, while destroying species and their habitats at a rate never before known in human history.

We believe that the Holy Spirit, who animates all of creation, breathes in us and can empower us to participate in working toward the flourishing of Earth's community of life. We believe that the people of God are called to forge ways of being human that enable socially just and ecologically sustainable communities to flourish for generations to come. And we believe in God's promise to fulfill all of creation, anticipating the reconciliation of all (Colossians 1:15), in accordance with God's promise (II Peter 3:13).

We lament that we have rejected this vocation, and have distorted our God-given abilities and knowledge in order to ransack and often destroy ecosystems and human communities rather than to protect, strengthen, and nourish them.

We believe that, in boundless love that hungers for justice, God in Jesus Christ acts to restore and redeem all creation (including human beings). God incarnate affirms all creation (John 1:14), which becomes a sacred window to eternity. In the cross and resurrection we know that God is drawn into life's most brutal and broken places and there brings forth healing and liberating power. That saving action restores right relationships among all members of "the whole creation" (Mark 16:15).

We confess that instead of living and proclaiming this salvation through our very lives and worship, we have abused and exploited the Earth and people on the margins of power and privilege, altering climates, extinguishing species, and jeopardizing Earth's capacity to sustain life as we know and love it.

We believe that the created world is sacred—a revelation of God's power and gracious presence filling all things. This sacred quality of creation demands moderation and sharing, urgent antidotes for our excess in consumption and waste, reminding us that economic justice is an essential condition of ecological integrity.

We cling to God's trustworthy promise to restore, renew, and fulfill all that God creates. We long for and work toward the day when churches, as embodiments of Christ on Earth, will respond to the "groaning of creation" (Romans 8:22) and to God's passionate desire to "renew the face of the Earth" (Psalm 104:30). We look forward to the day when the lamentations and groans of creation will be over, justice with peace will reign, humankind will nurture not betray the Earth, and all of creation will sing for joy.

GUIDING NORMS FOR CHURCH AND SOCIETY

These affirmations imply a challenge that is also a calling: to fulfill our vocation as moral images of God, reflections of divine love and justice charged to "serve and preserve" the Garden (Genesis 2:15). Given this charge and the urgent problems of our age—from species extinctions and mass poverty to climate change and health-crippling pollution—how shall we respond? What shall we be and do? What are the standards and practices of moral excellence that we ought to cultivate in our personal lives, our communities of faith, our social organizations, our businesses, and our political institutions? We affirm the following norms of social and environmental responsibility:

Justice—creating right relationships, both social and ecological, to ensure for all members of the Earth community the conditions required for their flourishing. Among human members, justice demands meeting the essential material needs and conditions for human dignity and social participation. In our global context, economic deprivation and ecological degradation are linked in a vicious cycle. We are compelled, therefore, to seek eco-justice, the integration of social justice and ecological integrity. The quest for eco-justice also implies the development of a set of human environmental rights, since one of the essential conditions of human well-being is ecological integrity. These moral entitlements include protection of soils, air, and water from diverse pollutants; the preservation of biodiversity; and governmental actions ensuring the fair and frugal use of creation's riches.

Sustainability—living within the bounds of planetary capacities indefinitely, in fairness to both present and future generations of life. God's covenant is with humanity and all other living creatures "for all future generations" (Genesis 9:8–17). The concern for sustainability forces us to be responsible for the truly long-term impacts of our lifestyles and policies.

Bioresponsibility—extending the covenant of justice to include all other life-forms as beloved creatures of God and as expressions of

God's presence, wisdom, power, and glory. We do not determine nor declare creation's value, and other creatures should not be treated merely as instruments for our needs and wants. Other species have their own integrity. They deserve a "fair share" of Earth's bounty—a share that allows a biodiversity of life to thrive along with human communities.

Humility—recognizing, as an antidote to arrogance, the limits of human knowledge, technological ingenuity, and moral character. We are not the masters of creation. Knowing human capacities for error and evil, humility keeps our own species in check for the good of the whole of Earth as God's creation.

Generosity—sharing Earth's riches to promote and defend the common good in recognition of God's purposes for the whole creation and Christ's gift of abundant life. Humans are not collections of isolated individuals, but rather communities of socially and ecologically interdependent beings. A measure of a good society is not whether it privileges those who already have much, but rather whether it privileges the most vulnerable members of creation. Essentially, these tasks require good government at all levels, from local to regional to national to international.

Frugality—restraining economic production and consumption for the sake of eco-justice. Living lives filled with God's Spirit liberates us from the illusion of finding wholeness in the accumulation of material things and brings us to the reality of God's just purposes. Frugality connotes moderation, sufficiency, and temperance. Many call it simplicity. It demands the careful conservation of Earth's riches, comprehensive recycling, minimal harm to other species, material efficiency and the elimination of waste, and product durability. Frugality is the corrective to a cardinal vice of the age: prodigality—excessively taking from and wasting God's creation. On a finite planet, frugality is an expression of love and an instrument for justice and sustainability: It enables all life to thrive together by sparing and sharing global goods.

Solidarity—acknowledging that we are increasingly bound together as a global community in which we bear responsibility for one another's well being. The social and environmental problems of the age must be addressed with cooperative action at all levels—local, regional, national, and international. Solidarity is a commitment to the global common good through international cooperation.

Compassion—sharing the joys and sufferings of all Earth's members and making them our own. Members of the body of Christ see the face of Christ in the vulnerable and excluded. From compassion flows inclusive caring and careful service to meet the needs of others.

A CALL TO ACTION: HEALING THE EARTH AND PROVIDING A JUST AND SUSTAINABLE SOCIETY

For too long, we, our Christian brothers and sisters, and many people of good will have relegated care and justice for the Earth to the periphery of our concerns. This is *not* a competing "program alternative," one "issue" among many. In this most critical moment in Earth's history, we are convinced that *the central moral imperative* of our time is the care for Earth as God's creation.

Churches, as communities of God's people in the world, are called to exist as representatives of the loving Creator, Sustainer, and Restorer of all creation. We are called to worship God with all our being and actions, and to treat creation as sacred. We must engage our political leaders in supporting the very future of this planet. We are called to cling to the true Gospel—for "God so loved the cosmos" (John 3:16)—rejecting the false gospels of our day.

We believe that caring for creation must undergird, and be entwined with, all other dimensions of our churches' ministries. We are convinced that it is no longer acceptable to claim to be "church" while continuing to perpetuate, or even permit, the abuse of Earth as God's creation. Nor is it acceptable for our corporate and political leaders to engage in "business as usual" as if the very future of life-support systems were not at stake.

Therefore, we urgently call on our brothers and sisters in Christ, and all people of good will, to join us in:

Understanding our responsibilities as those who live within the United States of America—the part of the human family that represents five percent of the world population and consumes 25 percent of Earth's riches. We believe that one of the surest ways to gain this understanding is by listening intently to the most vulnerable: those who most immediately suffer the consequences of our overconsumption, toxication, and hubris. The whole Earth is groaning, crying out for healing—let us awaken the "ears of our souls" to hear it, before it is too late.

Integrating this understanding into our core beliefs and practices surrounding what it means to be "church," to be "human," to be "children of God." Such integration will be readily apparent in congregational mission statements, lay and ordained ministries, the preaching of the Word, our hymns of praise, the confession of our sins, our financial stewardship and offerings to God, theological education, our evangelism, our daily work, sanctuary use, and compassionate service to all communities of life. With this integrated witness we look forward to a revitalization of our human vocation and our churches' lives that parallels the revitalization of God's thriving Earth.

Advocating boldly with all our leaders on behalf of creation's most vulnerable members (including human members). We must shed our complacency, denial, and fears and speak God's truth to power, on behalf of all who have been denied dignity and for the sake of all voiceless members of the community of life.

In Christ's name and for Christ's glory, we call out with broken yet hopeful hearts: Join us in restoring God's Earth—the greatest healing work and moral assignment of our time.

Signed,

DRAFTERS

The Rev. Neddy Astudillo, Latina Eco-Theologian, Presbyterian Church (USA)

Father John Chryssavgis, Greek Orthodox Archdiocese of America

Dr. Dieter Hessel, Director of the Ecumenical Program on Ecology, Justice, and Faith

Bishop Thomas L. Hoyt Jr., President, National Council of Churches and Bishop of Louisiana and Mississippi, Christian Methodist Episcopal Church

Dr. Carol Johnston, Associate Professor of Theology and Culture and Director of Lifelong Theological Education at Christian Theological Seminary

Tanya Marcova-Barnett, Earth Ministry, Program Director

Bill McKibben, author and scholar-in-residence, Middlebury College

Dr. Cynthia Moe-Lobeda, Assistant Professor of Theology and Religious Studies at Seattle University

Dr. James A. Nash, social and ecological ethicist, retired

Dr. Larry Rasmussen, Reinhold Niebuhr Professor Emeritus of Social Ethics, Union Theological Seminary, New York City

Rev. Dr. H. Paul Santmire, Author and Teaching Theologian, Evangelical Lutheran Church in America

CO-SIGNERS

Dr. Karen Baker-Fletcher, Associate Professor of Theology, Perkins School of Theology, Southern Methodist University

Dr. John B. Cobb Jr., Emeritus Professor, Claremont School of Theology and Claremont Graduate School

Dr. Jay McDaniel, Director of the Steel Center for the Study of Religion and Philosophy, Hendrix College

Dr. Sallie McFague, Carpenter Professor of Theology Emerita, Vanderbilt University Divinity School, Distinguished Theologian in Residence, Vancouver School of Theology, British Columbia

Dr. Donald E. Miller, Emeritus Professor of Christian Education and Ethics, Bethany Theological Seminary, Richmond, Indiana

Dr. Barbara R. Rossing, New Testament Professor, Lutheran School of Theology at Chicago.

This statement was a project of the National Council of Churches Eco-Justice Program office.

Notes

1. American Baptist Churches, "American Baptist Policy Statement on Ecology: An Ecological Situational Analysis," http://www.webofcreation.org/Denominational Statements/americanbaptist.htm, accessed February 20, 2007.

2. "Address of His All Holiness Patriarch Bartholomew at the Environmental Symposium, Saint Barbara Greek Orthodox Church, Santa Barbara, California, 8 November 1997," in *Cosmic Grace, Humble Prayer*, ed. John Chryssavgis (Grand Rapids: Eerdmans, 2003), 220–21.